Do Guns Make Us Free?

Do Guns Make Us Free?

Democracy and the Armed Society

FIRMIN DeBRABANDER

Yale

UNIVERSITY PRESS

New Haven and London

Published with assistance from the Louis Stern Memorial Fund.

Yale University Press books may be purchased in quantity for educational, business, or promotional use. For information, please e-mail sales.press@yale.edu (U.S. office) or sales@yaleup.co.uk (U.K. office).

Set in Janson and Monotype Van Dijck types by IDS Infotech, Ltd.
Printed in the United States of America.

Library of Congress Control Number: 2015930849
ISBN 978-0-300-20893-1 (cloth : alk. paper)

A catalogue record for this book is available from the British Library.

This paper meets the requirements of ANSI/NISO Z39.48–1992 (Permanence of Paper).

10 9 8 7 6 5 4 3 2 1

Contents

Preface
"This Time Is Different"

We thought Sandy Hook would change things.

In December 2012, a lone gunman named Adam Lanza killed twenty first-graders and six adults at the Sandy Hook Elementary School with a Bushmaster semiautomatic rifle. Among those killed were the principal, Dawn Hochsprung, who confronted him as he shot his way into the building, the school psychologist, and four teachers. Of the many mass shootings that have scarred the nation's consciousness in recent years, this one stood out as especially appalling.

Following the massacre, President Barack Obama made an emotional appeal for stronger gun control measures. "I know this is not the first time this country has debated how to reduce gun violence," he said in his 2013 State of the Union address. "But this time is different. Overwhelming majorities of Americans—Americans who believe in the Second Amendment—have come together around common-sense reform."[1] Polls taken after Sandy Hook indicated that indeed, most favored strengthening gun control legislation.[2] One of the reforms Obama had in mind was closing the "gun show loophole," the provision that allows gun show vendors to sell weapons to individuals without performing a background check. One study showed that fully 80 percent of Americans supported closing this loophole, and that the percentages were virtually the same among self-identified Democrats and Republicans.[3]

Yet the president's allies in Congress failed. No changes were made to federal gun laws. Even the gun show loophole remained intact. To great fanfare, some states succeeded in making changes where the federal government failed—New York, Maryland, Colorado. One year after Sandy Hook, however, the country had loosened more gun regulations than it tightened. The *New York Times* reported that seventy gun-related measures enacted by statehouses in the year after the massacre expanded gun rights, and only thirty-nine imposed stricter controls.[4]

This fits with a longer pattern of gun rights groups getting their way, despite the mass shootings that have punctuated our news cycle with alarming regularity. The routine response of the largest gun lobby, the National Rifle Association, to these shootings is that we need still more guns and gun-friendly laws. As a result, carrying a concealed gun is permitted in all fifty states, and carrying one openly in forty-four. The NRA's response to Sandy Hook was to claim we needed guns in every school in the nation, in the hands of armed guards or, barring that, teachers and staff. Several school systems have taken to doing just that.

Then there are the proliferating Stand Your Ground laws, enacted in thirty states as of this writing, where citizens may shoot to kill if they feel threatened by another and in danger of bodily harm. The nature of said "threat" is notoriously subjective and vague—shooters may characterize any number of incursions or advances as threatening, and promising bodily harm. The law urges individuals to opt for force as a first resort—indeed, to be something quite close to roving vigilantes, according to the verdict in the case of George Zimmerman, who in 2012 shot and killed unarmed teenager Trayvon Martin. We may, like Zimmerman, go out of our way to confront those constituting supposed threats and, when they react badly, "stand our ground" there. In a more recent case that garnered a lot of attention, a Tampa man indicated that he would invoke the Stand Your Ground defense after shooting another man in a movie theater, saying he felt faced with bodily harm; it turned out his victim had thrown popcorn at him.[5] Other states are preparing to enact similar legislation.[6]

Despite the trend toward gun-friendly legislation, the American public is hardly at one with the gun rights movement and is uncomfortable with its current trajectory. The percentage of households with a gun has fallen since the 1970s.[7] Journalist Dan Baum points out that the number of gun stores is also dwindling, and that hunting, once a popular sport for gun owners—and a primary reason for having a gun—is on the decline.[8]

What, then, explains the gun rights movement's policy gains? When the gun control proposals following Sandy Hook failed in Congress, many wondered what kind of massacre might finally persuade the nation to insist on stronger gun control, and what was standing in the way.

The short answer is the NRA. The NRA, which channels the passion of gun rights advocates, is renowned for its political and financial clout, and its ability to strong-arm politicians. Many politicians are unwilling to take on the organization even when their constituents indicate they are not on board with the lobby's demands. Even President Obama, sensing the political winds, was silent on gun control through his first campaign and first term. He threw his weight against the NRA only when he was compelled to do so by the atrocity at Sandy Hook.

Yet there is also a more complicated answer. Our gun culture's roots go far deeper than just one well-connected organization. Our entertainment media are utterly awash in gun violence—maiming, massacres, serial killers. Countless video games, disparaged by cultural critics and the NRA alike, revel in gore and mayhem. Even though most of us do not see guns in our daily lives, they are a fixture of our cultural imagination. We are, furthermore, a warring nation. The United States has enjoyed few windows of peace since World War II. Our defense industry is the largest in the world and one of the engines of our economy. "In the United States, we have been surrounded with violence," philosopher Judith Butler writes, "having perpetrated it and perpetrating it still, having suffered it, living in fear of it, planning more of it, if not an open future of infinite war in the name of a 'war on terrorism.'"[9]

Guns are engrained in our national identity and have a privileged place in the country's founding narrative. The War for Independence was sparked by the Minutemen, ordinary gun-owning citizens, intent on securing their liberty. Their actions were sanctioned by the Founding Fathers, who inscribed the right to bear arms in the Constitution. For Thomas Jefferson and his contemporaries, the Second Amendment was deemed a critical measure for protecting democratic freedoms and the sovereignty of the people going forward. Even the iconic hero of our national expansion—the cowboy—embodies the virtues of gun rights. He is independent and self-reliant, at least in theory; on the range, he metes out justice as a self-deputized agent of the law.

Perhaps it is our intimate relationship with guns—if not in our everyday lives, then in our cultural imagination and national identity—that inclines the voting public to delay action on gun control, or at least, not to object too strenuously to the positions of the gun rights movement.

But the fact remains: our gun culture is a poor fit for a twenty-first-century democracy. Most Americans sense this. They sense it when they drop their kids off to schools that increasingly resemble bunkers, with entry systems borrowed from prison technology. They sense it when they must fear whom they argue with, or irritate—or whether they simply appear threatening—on the streets of Florida where, thanks to Stand Your Ground, citizens can shoot to kill over minor disagreements. They sense it when they see gun-toting individuals at public protests, in diners and coffee shops, or at the grocery store—such as when a man with a semi-automatic rifle slung over his shoulder entered a Kroger grocery store in Charlottesville, Virginia, in early 2013, and casually strolled the aisles. Frenzy ensued: shoppers poured out of the store.[10] Our gun culture is an ill fit when we must live in fear of mass shootings in churches, shopping malls, and colleges.

There is a sense that our gun culture has grown to dangerous extremes, but there is also insufficient motivation to act on the situation—a lack of clarity on why we should act on it, a lack of appreciation for its urgency, and in turn, a lack of passion to take on the very passionate gun rights movement. Political commentator Sean Trende says gun control is a low priority for the voters who support it.[11] His assessment was inspired by events in Colorado, which saw a recall in 2013 of two Democratic state senators who had supported the state's tighter gun control legislation, passed in the wake of the shooting in a movie theater in Aurora, outside Denver, in which twelve were killed and seventy wounded. This recall was deemed a stinging loss for the gun control movement because it had poured so much money into the race, and because both state senators were recalled in districts that were majority Democrat, and replaced with Republicans. It was revealed afterward, however, that Democratic voters were not inspired to come out and save the day for their gun control champions; gun rights voters, on the other hand, came out in full force.

Gun control fails to galvanize public opinion. I believe this has something to do with the case traditionally made for gun control, which the American public has not found sufficiently convincing or alarming. Something else is needed; something else must be added to the debate to highlight what is at stake—and what is at risk.

Eminent historians and legal scholars have critiqued the NRA's reading of the Second Amendment. They claim that it was not written to enshrine an individual right to gun ownership—and certainly not an absolute right. For most of our nation's history, the Supreme Court was unpersuaded by arguments that the Founding Fathers intended an individual right to bear arms, but in recent years, as the court leaned conservative, it has reversed this longstanding position and upheld the NRA's increasingly absolute interpretation.

Public health experts and criminologists, for their part, offer up statistics testifying to the dangers of widespread gun ownership and loose regulations. They point to other nations in the developed world, where low rates of gun ownership correlate with low numbers of gun-related deaths and crime. They offer abundant facts that reveal the folly of expansive gun rights. And yet their claims are often ignored.

I will take a different approach in this book. Scholars Joshua Horwitz and Casey Anderson point out that gun control advocates have put themselves in the unenviable position of proposing to achieve greater gun safety by curtailing personal freedom.[12] This has been a critical weakness of all gun control arguments. Policy opponents pounce on it, such as when Wayne LaPierre, executive vice president of the NRA, declared in a speech delivered one month after Sandy Hook, "We're told that to stop insane killers, we must accept less freedom . . . that accepting less freedom and protection for ourselves is the only 'principled' way to live."[13] This has proven a powerful argument. Americans intuitively reject the prospect of being less free, and given the choice will almost always opt for more freedom over less.

For the gun rights movement, the right to bear arms is the mark of liberty. It is no mistake that the NRA's magazine for its members is titled *America's First Freedom*, the premise being that gun rights underlie and protect all our other freedoms. The damage guns do is the price we must pay for the abundant freedom Americans enjoy, which guns symbolize and secure. One prominent gun rights proponent tells Baum, "You on the left look at the problem like gun violence and say 'We have to do something.' . . . We on the right are more inclined to say 'We're a big, messy, polyglot nation with an extraordinary amount of freedom, and a certain number of bad things are bound to happen.' Where did you get the idea that you can limit gun violence without infringing on people's rights?"[14]

But what if guns in fact make us less free? I will argue that the armed society to which the gun rights movement hastens us—a society where gun-free zones are increasingly rare, and civility is enforced by the gun—is no longer recognizably free. Guns are not the condition of freedom at all, but the opposite. They may turn out to be compatible with liberty, but at a certain point, as they proliferate and dominate the public sphere, they chase our civil rights and freedom away.

Guns do not liberate us from fear. They are a symptom of fear's domination over society. The gun rights movement capitalizes on fear wherever it resides in our culture, and drums it up to amazing heights.

Gun ownership, as it is championed by the gun rights movement, is no deterrent to or protection against government tyranny. Instead, the NRA's agenda would produce a fragmented nation where increasingly alienated citizens are unable to assemble and credibly contest rulers with despotic designs.

Gun rights, in their current form, prove a useful diversion for those in power. They are an "opiate of the masses," to borrow Marx's famous phrase, that provides a false sense of security and vigilance, while powerful interests exert control elsewhere, away from the public eye.

Guns are not compatible with free speech and assembly. As the philosopher Hannah Arendt wrote, "violence is mute" and fundamentally antipolitical.[15] Violence and the threat of it—such as the open brandishing of guns in public places—chasten speech and discourage assembly. Add to this the fact that the gun rights movement is prone to issuing remarks hostile to peaceful transitions of power—including calls for violent uprising—and it becomes increasingly clear that an armed society threatens democracy as well.

I would like to make two things clear at the outset. First, this is a political analysis of the gun rights movement and our gun culture. I will appraise the arguments put forth by the gun rights movement, rebut them in turn, and demonstrate their political and social implications. In many respects those implications are already upon us. I will not propose specific gun control regulations. I am not a policy expert but a philosopher, and I will evaluate our gun culture from that perspective. My aim is to highlight the contradictions inherent in the gun rights movement, and its opposition to our democratic aspirations.

Second, I am not a gun owner. I do not visit shooting ranges, nor do I hunt—though I happily benefit from hunting. I am not averse to others owning guns, provided ownership is wisely regulated. Baum points out that gun rights advocates loudly object to criticisms from those who do not know guns intimately, or appreciate them and respect them. This conveniently limits the pool of those permitted to weigh in on the gun debate: you must know guns, or better, admire them—or better still, own one or several—to be qualified to offer advice on their use and regulation. Note that this logic, too, would nudge us further toward an armed society: you have to be part of it to critique it. But this rests on specious reasoning. I am perfectly justified in speaking out on the pervasiveness of guns because I know what guns do. I have seen it and I have to live with it, as will my children. Every American has this qualification. A proliferation of privately owned guns—especially when they are used irresponsibly or recklessly, as happens too often, or when they are brandished in public—affects us all, armed and unarmed alike. Anyone interested in the future and welfare of our democracy may speak on this issue. In fact, we are obligated to do so.

My hometown of Baltimore opened 2014 with a dubious distinction: a murder a day—most involving guns. Growing up there, I have always known guns in that peculiarly American way. We did not have handguns or rifles in the house, though my father owned a shotgun for a time. The streets I lived on were safe, but neighborhoods only a few miles away were rife with violence. Local news outlets eagerly reported the gruesome discoveries made on the city's street corners. Baltimore has all the elements that David Simon so frankly and sadly depicted in the HBO television series *The Wire*. Many people in my hometown feel they live in an armed society—and very much want to escape.

Acknowledgments

Naturally, this book could not have been possible without the contributions of others. This includes Simon Critchley and Peter Catapano, who direct the *New York Times* Philosophers' blog "The Stone." The article that inspired this book was first published in "The Stone" in December 2012 and generated so much commentary and thoughtful feedback that I was encouraged to develop and expand the argument. I applaud Simon and Peter, and the *New York Times*, for providing a forum like "The Stone," which recognizes the urgency of including philosophical insight in contemporary debates—and invites philosophers to speak beyond academia to the public at large.

Thanks also to my editor at Yale University Press, William Frucht, who provided much encouragement for this book and the projects affiliated with it. I must also thank his colleagues at Yale for their assistance and guidance along the way.

I am grateful to my colleagues and the administration at the Maryland Institute College of Art (MICA) for supporting this work and providing a fruitful intellectual environment where it might take root and develop. I must thank Joe Basile and Jan Stinchcomb for helping me rearrange my teaching schedule to complete this book. I owe my students at MICA many thanks as well. Through many classroom discussions with them, the ideas in this book were conceived and deliberated. Our conversations always took place against the backdrop of Baltimore, my hometown; the courage and resilience of its residents, who endure the perennial gun violence of the city, inspired and emboldened me to offer a needed challenge to the extreme wing of the gun rights movement.

Thanks to the many friends and experts who have put a lot of thought to the issue of guns in America, and who offered their insights for my work. This includes Justin McDaniel, Peter Dimitriades and David Hess, Deborah Azrael from the Harvard School of Public Health, and Stephen Teret from the Johns Hopkins Bloomberg School of Public Health. I owe special gratitude to Jeff McMahan, the White's Chair of Moral Philosophy at the University of Oxford, for being such an enthusiastic and helpful supporter of this project from the start. And thanks to my "legal team," Jennifer Curry and Erin Cheikh, who helped answer important questions pertaining to gun rights legislation.

I was buoyed in my efforts by Issam and Margaret Cheikh, as well as by the larger Cheikh clan and the Soueids: thank you for the meals, conversation, and spiritual sustenance throughout the project. I am very grateful to my parents, René and Chris DeBrabander; they planted in me a love of philosophy as well as the initial questions about the nature of guns in America and the role they play in a free society.

ACKNOWLEDGMENTS

Thanks to my children, René, Malek, Mairead, and Hugh. Their futures are always in my mind as I deliberate about our democracy and an armed society. And thanks to my wife, Yara, my most invaluable editor. Her incisive comments are a consistently reliable guide, and her political acumen and activism are inspirations for the mission of this book.

Do Guns Make Us Free?

CHAPTER ONE

The Culture of Fear

OR a week after the shootings at Sandy Hook, the National Rifle Association was silent. Everyone was waiting to hear how the organization would react to this unprecedented slaughter of twenty Connecticut schoolchildren at the hands of a deranged shooter. Liberal pundits were sure that remorse and retreat were finally in order, and sure to come; the NRA would amend its ways and endorse, or at least accept, tighter gun control measures. At last, the NRA summoned the press for a statement, delivered by Wayne LaPierre. Instead of modifying his organization's position, he pushed it even more aggressively. Guns are—still—not the problem, he insisted. The Sandy Hook incident revealed that the problem is the mentally ill. *They* must be marked, monitored, or marginalized. In addition, he declared, "here's another dirty little truth that the media try their best to conceal: There exists in this

country a callous, corrupt and corrupting shadow industry that sells, and sows, violence against its own people."[1] LaPierre proceeded to cite a variety of violent video games, and then took aim at the film industry, singling out gory movies such as *American Psycho* and *Natural Born Killers*. Hollywood, he snarled, has

> the nerve to call it "entertainment." But is that what it really is? Isn't fantasizing about killing people as a way to get your kicks really the filthiest form of pornography? In a race to the bottom, media conglomerates compete with one another to shock, violate and offend every standard of civilized society by bringing an ever more toxic mix of reckless behavior and criminal cruelty into our homes—every minute of every day of every month of every year. A child growing up in America witnesses 16,000 murders and 200,000 acts of violence by the time he or she reaches the ripe old age of 18.[2]

The message was that the media inspires killers by supplying source material for their perverse imaginations. The media makes murderers out of those who would otherwise not be.

In the weeks that followed, LaPierre's claims were disputed back and forth. Gun rights advocates pointed out that the Sandy Hook shooter, Adam Lanza, had a fondness for violent video games, including the particularly bloody *Call of Duty 4*. But as one scholar pointed out, Lanza was one of millions playing *Call of Duty 4*, and "of those millions of players, few commit an act of violence, certainly not enough to say that, statistically, video game play is a principal cause—or even a significant cause—of real-world violent behavior."[3] The same can be said of television and movie violence, which is even more broadly consumed.

This has not deterred gun control advocates from endorsing serious measures against violent entertainment media. Representative Frank Wolf of Virginia is a staunch gun rights supporter who has consistently voted for measures to ease access to guns, but he has called for placing warning labels on violent video games stating that "violent media has been linked to aggressive behavior."[4] Psychiatrist Liza Gold writes of Wolf's efforts that "data supporting a causal relationship between video game violence and non-firearm violence is equivocal and unconvincing, as noted by a 2011 Supreme Court ruling when it decided a case against government regulation of violent video games. In short . . . curtailing First Amendment rights to protect inadequate regulation of Second Amendment rights is a legal non-starter."[5] Wolf's proposal would restrict free speech in favor of absolutist gun rights—a position in line with LaPierre's accusation that the entertainment media purvey "the filthiest form of pornography." The media must be constrained in what they are allowed to offer, when and to whom. This is preferable to limiting people's access to guns.

Following the shooting at the Navy Yard in Washington, D.C., in September 2013, where twelve were killed and three wounded, it was revealed that the assailant in this incident, too, was an ardent fan of violent video games. This prompted Elisabeth Hasselbeck, a host on Fox News channel's *Fox and Friends*, to complain that liberals were making the incident about gun control when the real issue was video game control. She explained her proposed regulations as follows: "What about frequency testing? I mean, how often has this [violent video] game been played? . . . If this indeed is a strong link . . .

to mass killings, then why aren't we looking at frequency or purchases per person, and also how often they're playing."[6]

Hasselbeck seems to endorse a serious intrusion on our personal liberties even while leaving expansive gun rights intact. She would have us institute a registry of violent video game buyers. The NRA, however, rejects similar efforts for gun buyers, on the basis that it is an invasion of privacy and places too much power in government hands. In order to maintain an absolute right to own guns, it seems that gun rights advocates are all too prepared to curtail our liberties in other areas. This is ironic since, as I will discuss in greater detail shortly, gun rights advocates like to argue that the Second Amendment is the single most important condition and guarantee of our freedom—including free speech and free expression. It is that one freedom without which all the others are lost.

Gun rights advocates would have us strain to see how the media inspires and incites violent behavior. I contend that it is far more important to consider how the media does a spectacular job filling us with extreme and unreasonable levels of *fear*—fear, moreover, of what is least likely to befall most of us, and certainly the prime gun-owning population. Our media makes guns appealing to those for whom violence is least pressing in their daily existence. Our media transforms violence, re-creates it, and makes it at once remote and very present, but in unexpected ways, so that it's like a specter looming over society. Our relation to violence is increasingly distant and artificial. In turn, our relationship to guns is increasingly disingenuous, our need for them frivolous.

* * *

Consider the following facts and figures, and what the\
say about Americans' deep love affair with guns—or rather,\
I should say, the love affair of *some* with guns. For despite the
dominance of gun culture in America, and in particular the
profusion of guns and gun-friendly laws, this love affair is
progressively limited to a smaller slice of the nation.

There are between 270 and 310 million privately owned
firearms in the United States.[7] Conservative calculations put
the rate of gun ownership in America at 88 guns per 100 people, easily the highest rate in the world; the second most
armed nation is Yemen, which lags quite far behind, at 55 per
100 people.[8] The U.S. has the highest number of gun-related
deaths among twenty-seven developed nations, according to
a 2013 study, at 10 per 100,000.[9] In Switzerland, which is
the next best armed among the developed nations, there are
45.7 guns per 100 residents, and 3.84 firearm-related deaths
per 100,000 people.[10] Japan has the lowest gun ownership
rate in the developed world, with 0.6 guns per 100 residents,
and 0.06 gun-related deaths per 100,000 residents.[11] Most
firearm-related deaths in America are suicides. The Centers
for Disease Control reports that in 2010, there were 6.3
firearm-related suicides per 100,000 people, and 3.6 firearm-
related homicides per 100,000.[12]

The profusion of guns in America has a lot to do with
lenient laws regarding their purchase, of course—and, critics
complain, the high number of gun-related deaths and injuries
has to do with lenient laws regarding safety training and
storage, as well as inadequate or faulty efforts to keep guns
out of the hands of criminals and the mentally ill. Anyone
who wishes to purchase a gun from a licensed dealer must

undergo a background check through the federally adminis-
tered National Instant Criminal Background Check System
(NICS), which can be completed in a matter of minutes. As
one licensed firearm dealer from Maryland explained, prospective buyers are not even required to provide their Social
Security number to run a background check—and information about illegal drug use derives from whatever answers
they may volunteer.[13] After receiving rudimentary information about the buyer, the FBI runs a background check. The
Maryland dealer says: "They give me a 'yay' or 'nay,' and out
the door you go. . . . It's quick and easy. And we take credit
cards."[14] The NICS is supposed to prevent the mentally ill
from purchasing guns, yet it often fails to do so. The NICS
relies on states to provide it with mental health records, but
most states do not supply this data.[15]

Numerous gun transactions in America occur without
background checks. For one thing, the FBI has a three-day
window in which to perform the background check; if it cannot do so, the prospective buyer may return to the licensed
dealer and purchase the weapon in question.[16] And then there
are the many private transactions where no background check
is required whatsoever—most notably at gun shows. It is
difficult to determine how many guns in America exchange
hands this way. Corinne Jones, reporting for CNN, states
that 20 percent of firearm transactions in America are private;[17] former New York City mayor Michael Bloomberg put
the figure at 40 percent.[18] Criminals have easy access to guns
through what law enforcement calls "straw purchasers." As
reporter Frank Main describes them, writing on the flood of
illegal guns in Chicago, these are "men whose full time job

in the underground economy is to buy guns from suburban stores and illegally sell them to criminals."[19] The result is that "most of the guns recovered in crimes in Chicago were bought in suburban gun stores."[20] Because police often seize these weapons and gang members quickly discard them after a crime, Main points out, there is constant high demand for guns in Chicago—as in other cities with high crime rates and a bustling drug trade—which suppliers are eager and happy to meet. Guns easily flow in this manner from jurisdictions with lax gun laws to those with stricter ones.

Other developed nations have made it much more difficult for individuals to purchase—and keep—guns. Australia has a rate of 15 firearms per 100 people, and 1.04 firearm-related deaths per 100,000.[21] If an Australian citizen wishes to buy a gun, he must take a safety course beforehand and prove "genuine reason" for owning a gun, beyond self-defense.[22] Furthermore, he must apply for a permit for each firearm he wants to purchase, and undergo a twenty-eight-day waiting period before approval is given.[23] Australia forbids the private, unregulated sale of firearms and restricts the amount of ammunition individuals may buy in a given period.[24] In addition, Australians are required "to comply with storage requirements" for their guns and submit to "an inspection by licensing authorities of the licensee's storage facilities."[25]

Canada has a relatively high rate of private gun ownership at 30 per 100 people, but only 2.44 gun-related deaths per 100,000 citizens.[26] Canadians who wish to purchase a gun must pass a firearms safety course and seek out a third-party reference as part of a process of applying for a firearms license—a license that must be renewed every five years.[27] Canada requires that guns be unloaded when stored, and secured with a locking device or locked in a cabinet.[28]

In the United States, by comparison, only eleven states require residents to obtain a permit or license in order to buy a gun.[29] Of these, eight require safety training.[30] Only three states impose any restrictions on the number of guns residents can buy in a given time period: California, Maryland, and New Jersey, as well as the District of Columbia, limit purchases to one handgun per month.[31] Eleven states have laws concerning the safe storage of guns—but these mostly require "locking devices to accompany certain guns manufactured, sold, or transferred."[32] Massachusetts alone stipulates that residents store their guns with a lock—and this is not subject to inspection or enforcement.[33]

Standing in stark contrast to the massive number of guns in the U.S. and the lax regulations sustaining our gun culture, however, the percentage of homes with a gun has fallen considerably since the 1970s. Four decades ago, half of American households had a gun; today it is just over a third.[34] Gun sales spiked after President Barack Obama's electoral victories in 2008 and 2012, and they surge with every whisper of new gun control legislation. We are a society flooded with guns, but they are concentrated in fewer hands than a generation ago. The households that are armed apparently have fearsome arsenals. Gun ownership is increasingly the domain of select portions of the U.S. population. And the demographics are telling.

Shortly after the Sandy Hook shootings, *New York Times* blogger Nate Silver analyzed some data on gun ownership rates in America. Unsurprisingly, he noted, Republicans are two times as likely as Democrats to own a gun, prompting him to state that "almost all of the decrease [in national gun ownership rates] has come from Democrats."[35] More interesting, though, is that exit polls from 2008 indicate that whites have by far the highest rate of gun ownership, as do those in rural America. Suburban residents have nearly a 50 percent higher gun ownership rate than city dwellers. And households with an income of $50,000–$100,000 also scored at the top, by a considerable margin. Substantiating and complementing much of Silver's findings, researcher Richard Legault observes that "race remains a significant predictor of HGO (Household Gun Ownership), as those in the non-white category have a 52 percent reduced odds of reporting" that they own a gun, and "living in the suburbs at [age] 16, living in a small town at 16, and living in a rural area at 16 consecutively increase the odds of reporting HGO."[36] Taken together, this suggests that gun ownership is primarily the interest of those Americans *most* removed from violence—rural and suburban middle-class whites. In a 2010 Pew Research Center study on public opinion concerning gun control, whites favored expansive gun rights at a far higher rate than their black counterparts, and conversely, blacks favored stronger gun control by a wide margin, even though their communities are disproportionately afflicted by violent crime.[37]

While the rates of gun ownership are falling, the gun rights movement has made great advances in legislation and policy. Across the nation, the movement is working aggressively to relax gun laws so that gun owners may bring their weapons to a wider array of public spaces. The goal, it would seem, is to make guns an omnipresent, normal feature of everyday life. Gun rights advocates use the occasion of mass shootings to justify this development: after Sandy Hook, for example, they claimed we needed *more* guns in public spaces, not fewer. The NRA proposed placing armed guards in every school in America, or alternatively, arming teachers and staff. Even as fewer Americans own guns, gun rights advocates steadily march us to that day when armed individuals will be a common sight, in settings where we might least expect—or welcome—them.

In November 2012, a new gun law went into effect in Oklahoma, which allowed residents with a concealed carry license to also carry guns openly in public. On the eve of the new legislation, the *New York Times* ran a story on those residents eager for the new law's arrival—and their comments tell us a great deal about the nature of gun ownership, how gun owners see themselves, and the significance of their choice to carry a gun. The reporter followed a group of men, guns on their hips, preparing to celebrate the new law by convening at a diner on the outskirts of Oklahoma City for a late-night meal. Anticipating the reaction that might greet his group of open carry revelers, even in such a conservative state, one of the men declared—with a hint of indignation—"It's just a peaceful assembly. We're all licensed by the state to carry. We've all been trained and vetted. Why wouldn't somebody want to have that kind of a group do business with them in their establishment?"[38] Apparently, many businesses were not enthused about the prospect of armed customers. But they are precisely the kind of people businesses should welcome, this open carry apologist insists, since they are a particularly honorable lot. The Oklahoma politician who sponsored the expansion of his state's open carry law stated: "I think the evidence is clear that gun owners are some of the most responsible people."[39] They understand their weapons, the reasoning goes: they practice with their guns, take care of them, and know how to handle them safely and accurately. Such responsibility reflects their character as model customers and citizens. Above all, as their exposed weapons should make clear, they have nothing to hide—*they* are not criminals. Criminals hide their weapons; it turns out this is a major argument offered in favor of open carry. In an editorial in *U.S. News and World Report*, open carry supporter John Pierce cited an FBI study that "revealed that criminals carefully conceal their firearms, and . . . eschew the use of holsters."[40] Of course, if the open carry movement gets its way and it becomes common to see armed people in public spaces—at the grocery store, in the mall, at the bank—criminals can stop hiding their weapons.

The *Times* reporter visited gun shops in Oklahoma that were eager for the business the new open carry law would bring. For one thing, it meant changes in the size and nature of the weapons people would buy. One gun retailer reported that he had seen a wave of customers "buying larger weapons, with longer barrels and with magazines that hold additional rounds, as they prepare to wear their guns unconcealed."[41] Why would open carry prompt someone to trade up to a larger weapon? Surely a small firearm will serve ordinary customers just as well—if, say, they are accosted at a neighborhood diner or mugged on the street. Apparently not, according to the shop owner. "The old saying within the community," he explained, "is 'It's better to have it and not need it than need it and not have it.'"[42] In other words, you can never be too prepared. A small handgun that fits under your blazer or in a purse might be sufficient to ward off—or kill—an attacker, but surely a larger weapon with a larger magazine would serve the purpose better. The sight of something truly massive and intimidating might cause a mugger to turn and run, thereby preempting any confrontation. A favored motto of the open carry movement is "Guns save lives."[43]

One Oklahoma towing company manager, also interviewed for the *Times* article, credited his holstered pistol with deterring criminals, citing a recent incident in which a group of prospective robbers came to fetch their impounded car—presumably to steal it. The group fled, the manager said, at the sight of his weapon. "I never saw a weapon," he explained, "I never drew my weapon. There was no need to. My openly carried firearm deterred whatever it was they had in mind, and I'm sure it wasn't to bring me a thank-you card."[44] How did he know they were criminals? How did he know they were up to no good? He doesn't say. Why did he presume their intentions were malevolent? Were his assumptions somehow symptomatic of the weapon on his hip? Proponents of open carry assure us, after all, that "bad people" circulate freely and often, which is why you need to be visibly armed in the first place. How did the world get so much more dangerous for open carry proponents than for everyone else? When open carry advocates make it through the day in one piece, they may give their weapons credit for ensuring their safety by deescalating situations that might otherwise turn violent. But how do they know?

Even state senators who work in an eminently safe place like the Texas State Capitol building, it seems, are party to this view. Texas is a gun-friendly state, and this spirit extends to its lawmakers, many of whom regularly carry guns. A *New York Times* report on these armed legislators revealed that "when Gov. Rick Perry gave his State of the State speech in February 2011 in the House chamber, he stood a short distance from Representative Chuck Hopson, who paid close attention with a .22 caliber five-shot revolver in his right boot and a .357 Magnum within arm's reach in a drawer of his desk."[45] What is Mr. Hopson ready for? Perhaps an armed attack on the governor mid-speech? There have been no such attacks in the State Capitol's history, and the account suggests that Texas' armed lawmakers might be a distinctly paranoid bunch. Rebutting such a notion, the legislators "described carrying weapons in the Capitol as a personal security habit, doing what they did elsewhere in the state, whether shopping, dining, praying or driving. They also wear their weapons, they said, for the same reason they kept jacks in their vehicles and fresh batteries in their smoke detectors at home."[46] One state senator commented: "The reason you carry a gun on you is like the reason you carry insurance. You don't expect a tornado to blow down your house."[47] He admits the gun is for the rare and unthinkable—but a gun carrier is just someone who opts to think about the unthinkable more than the rest of us. Alternatively, I might suggest, his gun inspires him to imagine the unthinkable more than the rest—it breeds wariness.

In one respect, this is a bizarre, almost preposterous notion—the lawmaker doubly armed, five-shooter in his boot during the governor's speech. It's as if he were awaiting an assassination attempt. But isn't that what security personnel are for? This legislator, however, is ready for anything. It's not paranoia but exceptional responsibility. That licensed gun owners may bypass metal detectors in the Texas State Capitol stems from and fortifies this pretense. What if they should require a security pat-down for other reasons, for example, in case they might be carrying a bomb? What if they should suddenly harbor ill intentions? It seems the license to carry a gun has become, in this setting, a badge of integrity. This is not to say we should think otherwise. But it is remarkable how many gun owners presume they are evidently and manifestly the most responsible and well-intentioned among us—and furthermore that they can pick out those with bad intentions, and possess the moral clarity and unique resolve to dispense with these individuals if necessary. A gun signals uprightness, by this account—or it brings about a person's moral and cognitive transformation.

Gun enthusiast and blogger Robert Farago explains, "Once you put a gun on, you gain situational awareness. . . . I felt grown up. It was like a coming-of-age thing. I felt like an adult."[48] By "situational awareness," Farago means he became more perceptive of his environment and the dangers that lurk there—or the avenues by which they might approach him. At lunch with his friend David Kenik, another avid gun owner, he sits facing the entrance, as does Kenik. "Look at the way Robert and I are facing," Kenik says. "Crime happens everywhere. There is no place to feel safe."[49] He admits he seldom sees criminal incidents; the rural corner of Rhode Island where he lives has little crime—though he points out there was an armed robbery at a store near his home some years ago. As he sees it, Kenik says, citing an oft-used gun rights metaphor, "We have sheep and we have sheepdogs. Robert and I are sheepdogs. . . . Getting rid of the sheepdogs will not get rid of the wolves."[50]

If sheepdogs are highly responsible, conscientious, and morally upright—if they are our defenders from criminal activity—then perhaps it makes sense to arm young men in our most dangerous and crime-ridden neighborhoods, and hope for a similar character transformation. In his book *Gun Guys*, which chronicles conversations with ardent gun apologists across the nation, Dan Baum comments on this remarkable view. He quotes from Farago's blog: "If young black urban men liked guns so much . . . train more of them to shoot."[51] Baum explains Farago's logic this way: "By holding out the prospect of getting a permit to carry legally if they stayed straight and passed their gun-handling classes, training young men to get their concealed carry licenses might actually make better citizens of them."[52] As in Farago's own case, concealed carry might cause them to "grow up" and behave responsibly and conscientiously. Baum seems sympathetic to this view. It has merit, as he states elsewhere, because "it's been shown that when you let people carry guns, they behave well with them."[53] Legal carry, concealed or open, urges people to treat their weapons carefully and respect the awesome power at their disposal. They will not use, or treat, or view their weapons lightly. And of course, if visible to all in the neighborhood, especially the "bad guys," the guns carried by our morally corrected youth will deter crime.

This view, Baum tells us, explains the special ire emanating from gun owners in response to calls for increased regulation. Gun owners feel disrespected by regulation and its underlying assumptions. They are a proud bunch, Baum explains, who cherish "their personal mastery of death-dealing objects" and as a result feel that "they are somehow more responsible than the non-carrying public."[54] Further, they are indignant that "people who don't understand guns want to ban them," meaning the intrinsically irresponsible, who in turn ascribe moral shortcomings to all, indiscriminately.[55] As one gun store owner says to Baum, "Why do liberals hate guns? ... They don't believe in personal responsibility, that's why, and think the government should take care of everything!"[56]

A recurring theme in these comments—a theme seen throughout the gun rights movement—is that guns are celebrated by those who hardly require them, all things considered. The open carry proponents in Oklahoma live in areas where, outside of imagined threats, violence is rare. They are a privileged lot who have this added element of personal insurance. They are uniquely and specially empowered individuals who stand out in, or above, society. I contend that they would not be so brash if faced with the real threat of violence on a daily basis. Guns are not so liberating or empowering in inner-city communities plagued with real and pervasive bloodshed. For the urban shop owner who carries a gun to open and close his business, his weapon is not some added sign of freedom and power. It represents a deficiency of these things. He carries a gun because he feels compelled by the daily threat of robbery or assault.

Carrying a gun is "liberating" or "empowering" for those who don't need to use them—like the diners in suburban Oklahoma City, or state senators safely ensconced in the Texas State Capitol. This cannot be said of inner-city residents. For them, gun rhetoric falls flat, and open carry is an absurd proposition.

For most Americans, society in the early twenty-first century is becoming remarkably safer. The Harvard psychologist Steven Pinker has claimed that we are enjoying one of the most peaceful periods in recent U.S. history.[57] Sociologists scramble to come up with explanations for our plummeting crime rate, which has been steadily falling since the early 1990s. New York City's murders have fallen from over 2,000 in 1990 to 400 in 2012.[58] Washington D.C., once known as the "Murder Capital," has seen a similarly amazing drop, from more than 400 murders per year between 1989 and 1993, at the height of the crack epidemic, to just 88 in 2012.[59] According to FBI figures, the violent crime rate for the nation as a whole fell 49 percent between 1992 and 2011.[60] FBI data show declines in all major crime categories, including rape, robbery, aggravated assault, and property crime. "Violent victimizations by strangers"—the sort of thing we are urged to be armed for—have declined 77 percent since 1993, according to the Bureau of Justice Statistics.[61]

Further underscoring most Americans' relative safety, violent crime is highly concentrated, not only in certain areas but among certain populations. In Baltimore, this was neatly summarized in a controversial *New York Times* article from 2013 on the city's violent crime. After falling from one a day in the early 1990s, Baltimore's murder rate has stubbornly resisted following the sharp downward trend of neighboring Washington. Baltimore's mayor at the time of the report, Martin O'Malley, had ridden into office on a reputation as a crime-fighter, and boldly promised to cut the city's murder rate in half. While he never attained his goal, his administration still found reason to tout a safer city. The city's Health Commissioner declared that "Baltimore is actually a very safe city if you are not involved in the drug trade."[62] Police officials pointed out that 90 percent of the city's murder victims in 2005 had criminal records, a majority of them for violent crime. This prompted the deputy police commissioner to quip that "our victims have identical records as our suspects."[63] Locally, the article proved controversial because it seemed like city officials were sweeping the violence under the rug, as if to say that murderers and victims alike were already lowlifes, so we don't need to get too worked up over their fates. The violence is incestuous—and marginalized. This trend, noted back in 2005, continues today. Baltimore's safest neighborhoods get safer, while some unfortunate areas remain violent.

Chicago has also faced an intractable murder rate, even while its peers—New York and Los Angeles most prominently—have reduced theirs to record lows. Defying national trends, Chicago's murder rate actually rose in 2012. But again, in the midst of this spike, the *Chicago Tribune* noted that the violence was highly concentrated. In a report from July 2012, the paper pointed out that through six months of that year, "201 of the 259 homicide victims . . . were African Americans. While blacks make up about 33 percent of the city's population, they accounted for 78% of the homicide victims."[64] This, the article explains, followed the disparate racial trends among the city's murder victims over the past two decades. Further, regarding the 2012 death toll, "143 of the homicide victims . . . were listed as being at least affiliated with a street gang," and of the African American murder victims, "133 of those 145 . . . had arrest histories."[65] Criminologist David Kennedy has argued that Chicago's murders are carried out by select "groups of extremely active street offenders."[66] In studying the city's crime figures, Kennedy further narrowed down the violence to one particularly besieged neighborhood—Garfield Park—where a colleague had "identified a network of just a few thousand street offenders" involved in "most of the homicides that have taken place in that neighborhood" over the past five years.[67]

Violent crime is on the decline in America. Those who continue to suffer from it are an increasingly restricted—and ignored—lot. Even so, the American public has hardly recognized that it is appreciably safer. Gallup polls released in 2010 and 2011 reveal that most people believe crime is on the rise and getting worse.[68] Gun rights advocates are not ones to disabuse us of this notion.

The perception that crime is rampant is a fundamental element of gun culture. Gun rights advocates argue that more of us should be armed because of the pervasive threat of violence in this society. They share our mortal fear of crime—or sense it particularly—but they are determined to do something about it. John Pierce, the open carry advocate, offers a dramatic form of this argument on his organization's website.

Under the heading "Why would the average citizen need to carry a gun?" Pierce answers with stories plucked from the day's news, with links to television news clips: "You might be robbed, have your throat slashed, and be beaten with a hammer," as happened to a store clerk in Dallas; "you might be robbed and thrown onto subway tracks," like a woman in Philadelphia; "you might be stabbed while shopping at Bed, Bath and Beyond with your baby," like the woman randomly attacked in New Jersey; "you might be beaten with tire irons and baseball bats after getting pizza," like an unsuspecting patron outside a New York restaurant.[69] Pierce concludes this litany of horrors with the warning, "the wolves walk among us . . . one day the predator's eyes will flick towards you . . . and you better be ready."[70]

Social critics have long complained about media influences that distort Americans' perception of crime and incline us to excessive and irrational fear. Television news, which provides Pierce's chilling examples, is especially guilty, it seems. A study from the late 1990s on crime coverage by the major news outlets in Baltimore found that "the typical television news broadcast devotes 38 percent of its 'news hole'—which excludes weather, sports, promotions and ads—to crime coverage, and 9 percent . . . to accidents and natural disasters. Education coverage accounts for about 4.3 percent (37 seconds of a nightly half-hour show) and politics for 4.4 percent (38 seconds)."[71] Summarizing more recent reports, sociologist Valerie Callanan states that "roughly one-third of all television news is comprised of crime-related content, which is overwhelmingly violent and focused on the most *atypical* crime events."[72] In a sense, this is unsurprising when you consider the kind of competition the news—especially the local late-night news—is up against. It must lure viewers gorged on the sensational, the gruesome, and the sexually titillating. Accordingly, local news outlets interrupt their ads with breathless reports of a body found on a street corner, a bullying incident gone horribly wrong, or the next crime trend (or health scare) viewers should be aware of, mimicking the suspense of the competition. In an egregious case, a Baltimore station, promoting coverage of an incident in which a fourteen-year-old girl and her boyfriend conspired to murder the girl's father, ominously asked, "Why do some kids kill?" followed by a clip of an expert stating earnestly, "They will strike at the most vulnerable moment!"[73]

National stories of gore and grief also attract a news audience—the Boston marathon bombings in April 2013 were a boon to news programs, which offered near-continuous coverage of the hunt for the perpetrators—but they are not nearly as effective as dispatches on local mayhem. Local news stations are liable to make viewers believe their hometown is besieged by random violence. As Callanan points out, "the reporting is apt to be relatively thin, essentially devoid of context, details, and explanation, but instead graphic and sensational. Thus, viewers of television news are receiving the message that crime is 'out of control' and likely to strike anyone at any time."[74] News outlets are less likely to reveal the incestuous nature of murders in Baltimore, for example; they won't mention the crime records of victim and assailant, if these are known at the time. This information would be detailed in later reports, but these seldom emerge publicly, and never on the eleven o'clock news. They would be the natural subject for newspaper reporting, which provides a fuller picture of crime in a given region. But newspaper readership has plummeted in the digital age, and papers, most of which are owned by national chains, have been cutting local reporting for years to save money. Detailed background coverage of local crime has been a casualty. In any case, most people get their crime information from television news, which is more entertaining.[75]

Entertainment and news media sow the impression that murderers live in our midst, strangers stalk our children, and even loved ones secretly scheme to do us in. No one is to be trusted. This is the overarching message of the popular "newsmagazine" programs that air on the major networks on weekend nights—*20/20*, *Dateline*, *48 Hours*. These shows bill themselves as investigative journalism. *Dateline*'s website declares that the show is "dedicated to . . . social justice."[76] And yet these shows are largely devoted to lurid murder mysteries, often involving unsuspecting victims targeted by spouses, family, friends. *Dateline* and company are what Callanan calls "crime-based reality shows,"[77] but they draw on their fiction-based competition and emulate their methods to build and keep an audience. Regular news outlets are guilty of the same thing, but the newsmagazines add a different element; they provide a narrative that is largely absent from the eleven o'clock news. The dramas that *20/20* and *48 Hours* favor involve people who could be drawn from their mostly suburban, middle-class audience, meeting unthinkable ends. They strengthen the message that these crimes could happen to someone just like you.

The most popular television entertainment also works hard to suggest that society is thick with serial killers and that gruesome, ritualized murders are everyday events. Forensic specialists on *Bones* flirt and spar over the maimed, desiccated corpses on their examination tables. In 2012, it was reported, the vast majority of "primetime drama pilots commissioned by the networks are some form of crime, cop or conspiracy caper."[78] A major staple in this vein has been NBC's *Law and Order*, which has spawned six spin-offs, often airing concurrently, over the past twenty years. The same network has also hosted the *NCIS* franchise ("Naval Criminal Investigation Service"), and CBS counters with a bevy of *CSI* shows ("Crime Scene Investigation"). Explaining the proliferation of this programming, which has crowded out medical and legal dramas, one media critic summed it up as "television comfort food. . . . Audiences like to see justice served."[79] In most shows it is served in a bloody, often gory context.

But this is far from the real thing. Gruesome Hollywood depictions spark deep, irrational fear of crime, but they do not communicate or reflect its real face, which is readily seen—if we care to look—in our inner cities and countless poor communities across America. While Americans eagerly devour spectacular bloodshed as entertainment—and use that to justify their need for a gun, indeed, *many* guns—hundreds of people meet an unglorious, unremarked death on the streets of cities like Baltimore every year. The television viewing public does not come to know the mean conditions of their demise, the quick, blunt ends of desperate lives. The fates of Baltimore's murdered poor are hardly celebrated or studied by the media, and are instead belittled or swept under the rug by police and politicians. Suburbanites commute to work every day amidst the violence that afflicts Baltimore's most desperate neighborhoods on either side of the highway; they flock to football and baseball games downtown, oblivious to the misery that rules the city's roughest streets and how they are so surely insulated from it.

For poor blacks—who are disproportionately affected by violent crime—the America they know can be a veritable war zone. According to a Bureau of Justice Statistics report, between the years 1976 and 2005, the homicide rate for white Americans was 4.8 per 100,000, but an astounding 36.9 for blacks.[80] The United States Conference of Mayors, one of the loudest voices calling for gun control, noted in 2012 that "homicide is the leading cause of death for African American males between the ages of 15 and 24."[81] African Americans comprise just 15 percent of the nation's child population, but "made up 45 percent of child gun deaths in 2008 and 2009," the Children's Defense Fund reports.[82]

Many of our nation's mayors, as well as many African Americans, complained following the Sandy Hook shootings, when the American public seemed newly aware of gun violence, that the constant flood of gun deaths in our inner cities is neglected and ignored. The *Washington Post* ran an article on residents of the most dangerous neighborhood in the District, noting their frustration that the killings "in mostly white, middle class Newtown, Connecticut" spurred political concern. "Twenty-six people died in Sandy Hook Elementary. In the District's Sixth Police District, an area of fewer than 10 square miles . . . 19 lives were lost to gun violence last year and 55 people were wounded in shootings. The year before that, 22 people were killed and 35 were wounded. Eighty-eight lives were lost in the city last year."[83] A quarter of

Washington's murders took place in one small part of the city, a neighborhood subjected to a merciless onslaught of violence. It is no surprise that inner-city residents tend to find the notion of "gun rights" a bit offensive. Of the homicide epidemic that afflicts the African American community at large, the Centers for Disease Control points out, "more than 90 percent of the violence is from other blacks, mostly from guns."[84] As one Washington resident put it, "[guns] are for wars, and we have a war in the inner city."[85] It is hardly conceivable that the rest of America would tolerate all the talk equating gun rights and freedom if middle-class whites were killing one another at similar rates.

While NRA official Wayne LaPierre complains that the media inspires violent behavior, its most pernicious effect is something else. It drums up fear in those most removed from the real violence in our society—even while we are urged to ignore the reality and instead focus on the fanciful, the imagined, the dramatized. The media spreads the fear that is so prevalent in our gun culture, giving rise to the irrational claims of gun owners and gun rights proponents regarding crime and the need for a gun. Our cultural relation to violence is hardly intimate, as many tend to think; to the contrary, it is highly abstract.

Consider that, while our entertainment and news media serve up heady doses of fake violence on a daily basis, the American public is largely shielded from candid or live depictions of bloodshed. A notable case in point was the coverage of the people who jumped from the twin towers on 9/11. Photographs of the jumpers were arguably the most disturbing images coming out of the tragic events that day, so much so that they were quickly banished from the press. "Most newspapers and magazines ran only one or two photos [of the jumpers], then published no more," *USA Today* reported; that paper printed only one such image.[86] It turns out there was video footage of the jumpers, in which one can even hear them landing on the pavement, but this footage was not widely circulated and never made it onto the network news. People seen videotaping the jumpers were scolded for doing so. One fire official at the scene reportedly yelled at a cameraman, "Don't you have any human decency?"[87]

This is a remarkable statement when you consider that the American public harbors no similar squeamishness or moral uncertainty about fictional (or fictionalized) violence. Media critic Mikita Brottman writes that when CBS aired a two-hour documentary about 9/11 six months after the attacks—a special that the network billed as "brutal," "dramatic," and "sickening"—it provided "no graphic footage of injuries, no falling bodies, no images of death. . . . Incredibly, the CBS documentary *9/11* contains blood in only one single scene, when a firefighter . . . is shown to have a small cut on his upper cheek."[88] Of course, Brottman points out, if you had changed the channel while the show was airing, "you would have had little trouble finding the kind of graphic footage of human death so conspicuously absent from the CBS documentary."[89]

The American audience is fed a steady diet of embellished, staged violence, yet it hardly knows the real thing. Violent death has become unrecognizable. One witness on 9/11 described a female jumper falling: "It was slow motion.

After she hit the ground, there was nothing left."[90] In another report, a fireman stated that he saw a pile of jumpers on the street—"But it didn't look like bodies to me," he said.[91] This does not sound like death as the average television viewer knows it—there has to be a body to dissect, a recognizable human form to identify—or alternatively, a blanched skeleton that is suitably familiar and academic, like something out of a museum display. Our news media deemed footage of the actual deaths of 9/11 jumpers too traumatic.

The killings of private security contractors during the second Iraq War received the same treatment. In some of the most graphic footage of that war, charred, mangled corpses of American contractors from the Blackwater Corporation are seen hanging from a bridge in Fallujah in 2004. Though those images circulated freely in the international press, they were hard to find in the domestic media. Presumably they were considered too disturbing for American audiences. This fit with the broader media coverage of U.S. war dead in the Iraq War. In a controversial decision, the Defense Department refused to release even pictures of American coffins arriving at Dover Air Force base.

What's the point in protecting viewers from such imagery but readily supplying Quentin Tarantino's *Kill Bill* films, in which upward of eighty-eight bodies—and their parts—litter the screen in just the first volume?[92] Tarantino effectively mocks American audiences for their allegiance to fictionalized gore: the heroine, played by Uma Thurman, lops off heads with her samurai sword, and gushers of blood erupt; headless bodies become fire hydrants of blood, dousing Thurman, the other corpses, and the entire set. Or consider *Saving*

Private Ryan, Steven Spielberg's Oscar-winning epic, which opens with a searing re-creation of the Allied troop landing at Normandy in 1944. In one shot, a young GI lies on the beach eviscerated by enemy fire, holding in his entrails, calling out for his mother. In another, a dazed GI searches for his severed arm, picks it up, and stumbles to the barricades with the other soldiers. Tom Hanks's character grabs a wounded soldier on the beach to drag him to safety; a German shell explodes nearby, deafening Hanks and sending him flying. He staggers to his feet and resumes dragging his colleague, only to notice the load is lighter—the soldier has been ripped in half, and only a bloody stump remains. The media refrains from showing the real wages of war, but has no similar compunction when it comes to detailed Hollywood renderings. Ironically, *Saving Private Ryan* was praised for the accuracy of its portrayal of warfare—authenticity that might teach us the awful truths of war.

Ours is a bloodless bloodlust, if you will, a prime example of what philosopher Slavoj Žižek scorns as the "typically postmodern logic of a chocolate laxative . . . [where] we get the desired result without having to suffer unpleasant side effects."[93] Our taste for violence is sated, but we have no blood on our hands. In our suburban pods, at safe remove from the real thing, we understand violence less, and respect it less— and in turn respect less the weapons that mete it out. This is the context that makes the brandishing of deadly force a "liberating" thing, whose real power and gravity elude us.

We also know war less and less as well. This is shocking given that we are by far the most martial nation on earth, with a defense budget that in 2012 exceeded those of the next eight nations combined, and a defense industry that supplies much of the planet with instruments of war.[94] Despite supposedly serious concerns about our national debt, we found the cash to engage in two protracted wars following 9/11—and to wage a new type of war with no clear front line, or enemy, or end: the War on Terror.

Yet never has the American public been so untouched by war. Our youth has hardly felt the impact, unlike the 1960s, when antiwar demonstrations raged on college campuses and draft cards were burned. We have no draft today, and our volunteers are drawn heavily from minority populations and the poor, and lured by the professional and educational benefits that the U.S. military offers. Our wars in Iraq and Afghanistan were also marked by the significant role played by private contractors, either supporting the military or providing additional security. These facts conspired to make the American public profoundly insulated from the human costs of war.

The striking feature of the way we wage war in the twenty-first century is how relatively bloodless it is—for us. American soldiers are solemnly memorialized in our newspapers and on the nightly news, giving the impression that we are paying and acknowledging a high price for our battle with terror. We are persistently reminded that "freedom is not free." And yet, our death toll hardly compares to that of our opponents. Indeed, the disparity is huge, though it is little discussed and largely unnoticed on our shores. As of May 2013, the official death toll for U.S. military personnel in Afghanistan stood at 2,085—360 of whom were nonhostile casualties (such as victims of friendly fire).[95] For a decade-long war, 1,725 deaths is an astonishingly low figure. While no official figures have been released for the number of Taliban dead, there is a somewhat clearer picture of civilian deaths in Afghanistan: from 2007 through 2011, the United Nations estimates that almost 12,000 Afghan civilians were killed.[96] As for Iraq, the Department of Defense stated in 2013 that upward of 4,400 U.S. military personnel died during that incursion.[97] The numbers of Iraqis who perished in that war, and the civil strife that followed, have varied according to different reports, but the World Health Organization put the figure at 150,000 between 2003 and 2006. Another source put the number at 600,000 over the same period.[98]

We have hardly felt at war over here, though we constantly speak of it; we invoke the vigilance and suspicion that is part of this new War on Terror and remind ourselves of the sacrifices we must make. But it has been business as usual at home for the most part, while we visit destruction upon populations thousands of miles away.

Drones fit perfectly with our new designs for war. More than half of new Air Force recruits are in the drone program, and it is easy to see why: they can fight from the safety of our own shores or behind the protective walls of overseas bases. They never see or touch a battle zone that might place them in danger, and inspire the uncomfortable questions that typically plague wartime presidents. Drone pilots on domestic bases can commute to work, sow mayhem thousands of miles away, and be home in time for dinner with the kids. This feature has brought unexpected stresses and caused high levels of burnout among drone pilots. From half a world away, they come to intimately know their targets—and their targets' families and daily routines—before obliterating them, with the hope that the families and innocent victims are away at the time. Controversy in the drone program surrounds the supposed guilt of those targeted. One Air Force official stated that drone pilots watch a suspect "do bad things" and then follow him through his daily routine for weeks before pulling the trigger.[99] It is reasonable to wonder how one may reach an accurate judgment of character and virtue from thousands of miles away. Another military official said the government "assumes 'military-aged' males in proximity of a drone strike are combatants unless it finds out otherwise."[100] In hearings for the new CIA chief in 2013, Senator Diane Feinstein claimed that civilian casualties from the US drone strikes were in the "single digits" each year, but an independent study estimated the death toll from drones between 2004 and 2013 to be "471 to 881 civilians, including children."[101]

Drone warfare is troubling on several counts. One is the fact that our president wages drone warfare in nations against whom we have not declared war. The American public has largely accepted this new and terrifying presidential power. When Senator Rand Paul conducted a day-long filibuster in 2013 aimed at drawing attention to the president's secretive drone program, one Republican senator, reflecting the opinion of many of his colleagues, said he didn't object to the program per se; he deemed it necessary—he just wanted the president to be more open about it with Congress.[102] Drones are an essential tool in the War on Terror, where a shadowy enemy hides across many nations, and in often lawless terrain. The changed nature of war demands new methods of fighting. This is the prevailing opinion. Politically, however, drones pose an impressive danger in the ease with which government can now wage war. And without end, because it's difficult to say when or if drone warfare has achieved victory.

The emergence of drones is troubling from a cultural point of view, too. They accustom us to a kind of brutality we hardly imagine or understand—a brutality amplified by the ease with which we engage it and tolerate it. Drones promise to remove even our soldiers from the deep acquaintance with bloodshed that has traditionally marked their vocation. Drone warfare is evidence of our increasingly tenuous relationship with violence and the lack of caution and respect we accord the weapons at our disposal. It is another element that makes violence so very banal, such that we hardly know or appreciate the power in our hands.

Gun culture feeds off our increasingly bizarre and tenuous relationship to violence. It is, I have argued, simultaneously nourished by a growing removal from blood and mayhem, carried out by our various media, also in the machinery of war we so blithely endorse.

A prominent feature of our gun culture and the irrational fear it cultivates is the tendency, indeed eagerness, to see the world neatly divided between forces of good and evil. In a now famous phrase uttered after Sandy Hook, LaPierre defiantly declared that "the only thing that stops a bad guy with a gun is a good guy with a gun."[103] In the same speech, he suggested that a significant portion of "bad guys" are mentally ill and argued that addressing gun violence must therefore involve enforced treatment and monitoring of the mentally ill. Politicians, he maintained, must focus on getting the names of the mentally ill into a national database. He introduced his call for new awareness of the mentally ill with these stark words: "The truth is that our society is populated by an unknown number of genuine monsters—people so deranged, so evil, so possessed by voices and driven by demons that no sane person can *ever* comprehend them. They walk among us every day."[104] This portrayal of the mentally ill is alarming: we hardly know them, and normal, law-abiding citizens cannot be counted on to understand or detect the evil in our midst. Furthermore, LaPierre declared, there is a "much larger and more lethal criminal class" stalking the streets: "killers, robbers, rapists and drug gang members who have spread like a cancer in every community in this country."[105] So, we are besieged by professional killers on one side and the mentally deranged on the other. The former are a danger external to our families and daily routines, the latter a danger lurking within, largely unrecognized except when it erupts in vicious bouts of violence.

LaPierre invokes a particular notion of crime and criminals: they are a cancer we cannot control; they are resistant to treatment; they have their hearts and minds set on malfeasance. In a subsequent speech, he scorned the gun control crowd's call for universal background checks: "There is nothing 'universal' nor 'reasonable' about [universal background checks]. They ought to stop calling it what it will never be. Criminals will never be a part of it. And . . . neither will those adjudicated mentally incompetent and dangerous by a court of law."[106] There is no stopping these people, in other words—they are devoted to a life of crime, bent on the cause of destruction and theft. They are part of a "criminal class." To be sure, LaPierre's account captures some criminals, but not the many—or most—who lapse into crime, even just one crime, unwittingly and not according to any great plan in life but due to misfortune, mistakes, or a lack of better options. As LaPierre has it—outrageously—criminals make up their minds in advance that crime is their vocation, and they will strenuously avoid background checks as a result. This is far from a realistic account of human nature. But it is satisfyingly simplistic.

The gun rights movement has long done battle in this manner, characterizing the world in Manichean fashion. Drawing on the heresy that Augustine and the early church disputed centuries ago, it depicts a world populated by forces of good and evil, engaged in a cosmic, never-ending battle; they are clearly delineated, unadulterated, and unequivocal. Evil is intractable and unrepentant. LaPierre's "mentally deranged" are wholly other, completely different from normal, sane people—and utterly unresponsive to reason. They are an ideal manifestation of an evil that cannot be mediated or negotiated. The proper response to this evil is violence—the more arms and the more powerful, the better.

At first blush, it might seem strange to some that the gun rights movement has become so deeply intertwined with the Christian right. How does the call to be at the ready to blow people away fit with Jesus' message of love, charity, and forgiveness? The Manichean language of the gun rights movement indicates how this odd alliance can occur. It is only a small step from LaPierre's worldview to a theological account of the human condition wherein we are locked in an epic battle with evil, and God has given righteous souls license—even a mission—to eradicate evil on earth. This account leans heavily on Old Testament references and undergirds the notion of the "Christian soldier"—the name, not so coincidentally, of a prominent gun shop in Baltimore.

In laying out the Christian case for guns, Larry Pratt, executive director of Gun Owners of America and former director of Patrick Buchanan's presidential campaign in the mid-1990s, cites a passage in the book of Exodus which says that one is justified in killing a thief who has invaded his home—though only in the dark of night (Exodus 22–23). Commenting on the latter condition, *National Review* blogger David French sees evidence of God's grace—for the shooter—since it excuses "the citizen in the midst of the fear and ambiguity of a nighttime invasion."[107] Pratt also offers a quote from Proverbs 25:25: "A righteous man who falters before the wicked is like a murky spring and a polluted well." Meaning, Pratt tells us, he lacks moral clarity and resolve: it is our task and obligation to exact a penalty on the wicked. "We would be faltering before the wicked if we chose to be unarmed and unable to resist an assailant who might be threatening our life," Pratt explains. "[We] have no right to hand over our life, which is a gift from God, to the unrighteous. It is a serious mistake to equate civilized society with one in which the decent people are doormats for the evil to trample on."[108] Again, the "unrighteous" are definitively and patently so, and they merit the penalty a responsible gun owner might carry out. Pratt gives us a particular vision of what it means to be Christian: it is to be ready to meet the "unrighteous" with "lethal force"; it is to be a foot soldier in God's battle with sin manifest on earth, and the evil that grips men's souls and won't release them save through the grace of God. This is a theology that puts little emphasis on the ability of people to be converted by charity, love, or forgiveness. It sees lost souls who are God's charge principally, if not exclusively, while He sanctions us good citizens in fending them off as need be and burnishing our moral credentials in the process. As another Christian gun apologist put it, Scripture's stories "illustrate the defense of life, liberty, and property in the midst of a fallen world (and fallen governments)."[109]

In this distinctly apocalyptic vision of the world, governments, too, conspire to crush well-intentioned individuals. Like the "monsters" who stalk our streets, government can be handled with force only by good (Christian) citizens—citizens, Pratt points out, who abide by Psalm 144 and praise the God "who trains my hands for war and my fingers for battle."[110] Remarkably the Bible even provides support for those opposed to government regulation of firearms. With the first recorded murder of Abel by Cain, Pratt argues, "God's response was not to register rocks or impose a background check on those getting a plough, or whatever it was that Cain used to kill his brother. Instead, God dealt with the criminal. Ever since Noah, the penalty for murder has been death."[111] What is the lesson here? Taken together, it seems to be that we emulate God in exacting judgment on evildoers, independently of the law or of government sanction, motivated by moral intuition and personal conviction of God's will. God effectively sanctions a righteous vigilantism; He urges us to impose His will on earth, as individuals first and only secondarily through government. Pratt is not alone in this view. As reported by the British political scientist Martin

Durham, a 1992 conference of Christian gun apologists concluded that "there was ... Biblical precedent for what had
been termed 'vigilante action' and clear guidance as to how
Christians should deal with oppressive government."[112] One
committee at the conference, Durham writes, "had discussed
leaderless resistance ... defined as "a concept wherein Yah-
weh gives each man his inspiration for defensive action."[113]

Another passage from the Gospel—Matthew 15—depicts
Jesus criticizing the Pharisees for, in Pratt's view, "opposing
the execution of those deserving death—rebellious teenagers."[114] Jesus must be referencing teenagers, Pratt surmises,
because he is talking about people who have dishonored their
mother and father—who else could they be? According to
Mosaic law, Jesus reminds the Pharisees, such an offense is
deserving of death, but they willfully ignore it, and upbraid
him instead for eating with gentiles. It's likely Jesus sought to
expose the Pharisees' hypocrisy in their partial and self-serving
application of Mosaic law, or better yet, their ambivalence regarding the law and their recognition that certain precepts are
unacceptable—like the requirement to execute disrespectful
teenagers. As Jesus repeatedly teaches, it is better to abide by
the spirit than the word of the law. This is not how Pratt sees
it. In this episode, he argues, Jesus condemns those who ignore God's commandments and affirms that righteous individuals, when faced with governing officials unwilling or unable to prosecute wrongdoers, must take the law into their
own hands. His Jesus emerges as a staunch libertarian who
sanctions vigilantism: forceful and resolute, a stern, demanding, unyielding—and unforgiving—moral teacher and judge.
Ostensibly motivated by the shootings at Columbine High

School in Colorado in 1999, where two students killed twelve people and injured twenty-one, and which occurred shortly before he wrote these words, Pratt concludes that "man's wisdom today has been to declare gun-free school zones which are invaded by gun-toting teenage terrorists whom we refuse to execute. We have learned little from Christ's rebuke of the Pharisees."[115]

It is God's will that righteous individuals be armed, and armed well, and regulated as little as possible in the use of arms. In a similar vein, echoing the theological arguments surrounding the gun rights position, David French invokes philosopher John Locke's claim that "the right of self-defense is a fundamental law of nature."[116] I will say more about the Lockean argument for gun rights in the next chapter, but for now, it is sufficient to acknowledge the significance, for the gun rights movement, of Locke's appeal to the divine. He was a prominent inspiration for our Founding Fathers, who in turn drafted what some consider a quasi-divine document: in Lockean fashion, the narrative goes, the founders sought to channel God's will and articulate the law of nature He imparted to us—namely, the U.S. Constitution. Thus the gun rights movement aligns itself with the "originalists," that camp of legal interpreters who hold our Constitution to be rigid and unchanging—something we must accept word for word, in the way that literalists accept the Bible. As a rebuke to those who claim that God's message changes over the course of the Bible, Pratt cites Hebrews 13:8: "Jesus Christ is the same yesterday, today and forever." There is no deviation in God's word. If it seems so, that is an error, and the burden is on us to read the prescriptions of Christianity correctly.

One prominent evangelical leader demonstrated this view in a provocative interview soon after the Sandy Hook shootings. When asked about the "New Testament justification for owning firearms," Dr. Richard Land of the Southern Baptist Convention, the largest Baptist organization in the world and the largest Protestant body in the United States, replied: "Do unto others as you would have them do unto you."[117] Though this dictum is typically invoked to urge peaceful coexistence, Land cites it to justify lethal force. He explains, "if you see your neighbor being attacked, if you see your neighbor in danger, you have an obligation and a responsibility to do what you can to protect them."[118] You can carry out this responsibility in superior fashion with a weapon in hand. When the host asked if he recognized "an obligation to turn the other cheek," Land replied, "I think I do, personally. But the difference between personal [defense] and defending others, you know, it's the justification that's used for soldiers and others and police officers, and I think for private citizens as well."[119] He concluded the interview by saying that he would aim as far as possible to opt for peace, but reserves the right to employ violence—as a mark of Christian responsibility—in order to "love his neighbor as himself."

Tellingly, Land prefaces his arguments by reminding the host that "we live in an age of worldwide terror."[120] It is no ordinary fear that motivates gun rights proponents but a nearly existential one. This is also, of course, highly irrational. Someone might point out to Land, for example, that relatively few Americans have perished in the War on Terror; others bear the brunt of it. It has long been noted that the War on Terror betrays strong theological overtones. Sometimes these are overt, such as when the war in Afghanistan was initially dubbed Operation Infinite Justice—a title that was quickly scrapped. The War on Terror is analogous to the war on evil in one prominent respect: terror and evil are both shadowy, primal, intractable forces that resist negotiation. Terror, and terrorists, can only be handled with resolute force.

LaPierre lapses into apocalyptic visions that would be familiar to Christian gun apologists. Consider the fearsome declarations he issued in early 2013, as he sought to stoke opposition to congressional gun control initiatives:

> President Obama is leading this country to financial ruin, borrowing over a trillion dollars a year for phony "stimulus" spending and other payoffs for his political cronies. Nobody knows if or when the fiscal collapse will come, but if the country is broke, there likely won't be enough money to pay for police protection. And the American people know it. Hurricanes. Tornadoes. Riots. Terrorists. Gangs. Lone criminals. These are the perils we are sure to face—not just maybe. It's not paranoia to buy a gun. It's survival. It's responsible behavior, and it's time we encourage law-abiding Americans to do just that.[121]

This is an impressive, almost desperate call for fear. LaPierre cites dangers where few loom. I am, for example, unsure what "riots" he has in mind—perhaps this is a veiled racist reference to the many urban riots of the 1960s that followed the assassination of Martin Luther King, or the race riots that consumed Los Angeles in 1991 after the Rodney King beating. The implicit racism might also explain his mention of Mexican drug cartels earlier in the same letter, and the porous southern border, responsible for the spread of Latin American criminal elements in American cities—which, LaPierre declares, have made Phoenix "one of the kidnapping capitals of the world."[122] LaPierre also describes the aftermath of hurricane Sandy as offering a glimpse of the "hellish world" that "gun prohibitionists" would deliver, where "looters ran wild in south Brooklyn."[123] This is simply not true. The few instances of looting after the hurricane were sporadic and short-lived; in fact, most people remarked how quickly New York returned to law and order despite the widespread power outages and strained public services.

It is tempting to dismiss LaPierre as inventing the facts to manufacture fear. But it seems he does not have to work so hard. We grow more fearful as a society even while major crime indicators should give us cheer. It seems our fear becomes amplified as the danger becomes less obvious, less tangible, less present and pervasive; it grows as threats are more alien, or as philosopher Judith Butler might say, "spectral." For example, the defining feature of the War on Terror, which Reverend Land invokes in support of gun rights, is how it justifies itself endlessly in relation to the "spectral infinity of its enemy," as Butler would say.[124] A War on Terror has no foreseeable or imaginable end. Its enemy is faceless and impossible to define—an enemy that by its nature regenerates itself.

The War on Terror, Butler explains, delivers a prime example of a "derealized" opponent, a devastating blow—most of all to ourselves. She writes in her 2003 essay "Violence, Mourning, Politics,"

If violence is done against those who are unreal, then . . . it fails to injure or negate those lives since those lives are already negated. But they have a strange way of remaining animated and so must be negated again (and again). . . . Violence renews itself in the face of the apparent inexhaustibility of its object. The derealization of the "Other" means that it is neither alive nor dead, but interminably spectral.[125]

The names, faces, and histories of our opponents, and even of our Afghan and Iraqi allies and the civilian casualties in the War on Terror, remain hidden, unremarked and unchronicled. The numbers of their dead are wholly ignored. By contrast, the 9/11 victims were eulogized impressively and extensively, but Butler argues that our mourning is incomplete and ineffective, also inhumane, so long as in mourning we remain oblivious to others. Writing at a time when the invasions of Afghanistan and Iraq were being promoted by the Bush Administration as quick, clean operations, she predicted that our manufacture of the enemy would land us in a "chain of violence."[126] An unreal, spectral enemy who is not liable to extinction or death incites us to recognize ever more opponents and terrorists in unanticipated frontiers.

Later, Butler laments how the War on Terror inaugurated a new designation of the enemy. Detainees at Guantanamo Bay, for example, were deemed "dangerous people," to quote one Department of Defense official, captured while "seeking to harm U.S. soldiers or allies."[127] If released, it was said, they might pose an even greater danger. In this case, given the prisoners' treatment, "dangerous" becomes a self-fulfilling prophecy. This War on Terror, Butler maintains, is foolhardy and reckless, prone to identifying manifold targets the world over and creating many new enemies in the process. Such are the fruits of a hostile and suspicious foreign policy.

The War on Terror shares a psychology with the gun rights movement. The manufacture of enemies, and of fear, can be an endless production. We are liable to see and create dangers to the extent that we characterize them partially, naively, and irresponsibly. The very designations "evil," or "insane," or "terrorist" absolve us of any duty to try to understand or respect such people. Further, this outlook leads us to see them everywhere. LaPierre wants us to see Phoenix as a den of kidnappers, and Brooklyn as a place whose residents are one power outage away from barbarism. There are always dangers out there; there is always something we might fear—provided we decide to fear it.

As the ancient Stoic philosophers were wont to argue—Seneca, Epictetus, Marcus Aurelius, among others—fear, like all the harmful passions, is a matter of choice. I choose to fear something, though it is not deserving of such. As Seneca liked to say, Nature is not coy in her plan for us; she does not conceal her designs. Any rational person who is frank about his or her fate and situation will clearly recognize the threats that abound, any of which will strike sooner or later. Thus, Seneca claimed, we should not be surprised or indignant when fate deals a harsh blow—did you think, he asks, that you would be spared? The cure for fear is understanding; I must understand first of all that the world and its many threats are beyond my control. The more I understand myself, my surroundings, and the world, the more fear will diminish, and so will the harmful, irrational acts that tend to follow from the passions. Fear is fundamentally irrational, and a font of subsidiary passions, the Stoics wish to say. It can achieve nothing productive—you cannot absolve or disperse all threats—but only make yourself more miserable, more paranoid, and liable to act out desperately, erratically, and harshly. LaPierre, remarkably, is casting about for new things to fear. He is searching for things to get worked up about—and to get us worked up, too. Ardent gun owners fancy themselves supremely responsible, alert, and practical; they are disillusioned and clear eyed—the "sheepdogs among us." For Seneca, however, they are far too busy manufacturing threats to be counted rational.

Butler might say that if we should look at our opponents in this War on Terror and recognize them for what they are—people with personal tragedies and fears, motivated by anger, nourished on prejudiced and incomplete accounts of America, also on immense poverty, and injustices domestic and global—this would erode our paralyzing fear and the violent tendencies it inspires and excuses. We must see them as more than mere black holes of unwavering malice.[128] An abstracted enemy balloons into an indomitable specter and elicits unmanageable levels of fear, with irrationalities that ripple through society.

Gun rights advocates suggest we are freer to the extent that we recognize the threats around us, even those unforeseen, and remain perpetually on the alert for them. Real freedom, the Stoics counter, lies elsewhere: it is the resolve to coexist with pervasive threats and not be overly influenced or coerced by them. Freedom is a state of mental resolve, not armed resolve. Coexisting with pervasive threats, Seneca would say, is the human condition. The person who lives with no proximate dangers is the exception. And it's no sign of freedom to live always at the ready, worried and trigger-happy, against potential threats; this is the opposite of freedom. It is, according to the Stoics, a form of servitude. It is to be at the mercy of passions and to give them tyrannical power over us. Freedom resides in the ability to live and thrive in spite of the dangers that attend our necessarily tenuous social and political existence—dangers that are less fearsome and debilitating to the extent that we understand and acknowledge them.

Gun rights advocates tend to claim they are the realists in this debate, and their policy opponents are hopeless, naïve idealists. That's what the gun shop owner indicates to Baum: "Liberals think everybody can be perfected, everybody is good!"[129] The gun shop owner disagrees: you can never eradicate violence. Reverend Land calls gun-free zones a fantasy because guns will invariably show up there, sometime, somehow. Well yes, in a society of 300 million guns, this is likely true. Moreover, they are right to point out that if you strenuously diminished the number of privately held guns to levels seen in Japan or England, you would still have shootings and other violent incidents—"bad guys" will just use knives like, for example, like the attacker in China who stabbed twenty-two school-children in December 2012.[130] You can never get rid of dangers, gun rights advocates tell us, and that is why we need to be armed. But "liberals," or at least gun control advocates, have not suggested they aim to make danger vanish from the earth.

We are back to the point where gun rights advocates are just those people who decide they will live under the influence of fear. They will recognize the dangers that surround us, even while criminologists say those dangers are diminishing. No life, no individual, is ever absolutely free from danger. But here is the problem: this "armed resolve" of gun rights advocates creates dangers where few existed before. Gun owners are a disproportionately suspicious lot—as if their weapons infected them with extreme doses of mistrust. Perhaps it's because owning, and certainly bearing, a gun serves as a mark of suspicion—a threat—that makes others suspicious and hostile in turn. Gun owners see a hostile world—and guns are bound to make it so.

The gun rights movement sees itself already in pitched battle, whether with the forces of evil, terror, the criminal element, or cultural forces that can hardly be clearly outlined. This was the path of former NRA leader Charlton Heston, whose rallying cry was that the nation is embroiled in "cultural warfare," with gun owners on the front lines. Liberty is challenged, he maintained, by an assortment of threats: political correctness, minority rights claims gone wild, individual freedoms transformed into moral license. Social and cultural trends that are destroying liberty, Heston argued, mean that someone will soon come for our guns, too. In a speech at Harvard in 1999, Heston declared, "I believe that we are again engaged in a great civil war, a cultural war that's about to hijack your birthright to think and say what resides in your heart. I fear you no longer trust the pulsing lifeblood of liberty inside you . . . the stuff that made this country rise from wilderness into the miracle that it is!"[131] LaPierre has built on Heston's argument and themes, but upped the ante. Now gun owners are the front line of defense in a society falling into chaos. In the heat of battle, we cannot afford the luxury of skepticism, doubt, humility; we can't afford charity in our judgment of others, especially those who might pose a threat. War demands that we see the world definitively. It requires us to paint with broad brushstrokes, consign some to rough treatment, and make human rights sacrifices.

Many complained that the NRA suggested such a view when, following the Sandy Hook shootings, it claimed that our government's refusal to acknowledge and properly handle the mentally ill—not guns—was the heart of the problem. In making this case, LaPierre offered up a shockingly simplistic characterization of the mentally ill. He said that because our government refuses "to create an active national database of the mentally ill," we have no idea how many "copycats are waiting in the wings for their moment of fame from a national media machine that rewards them with wall-to-wall attention and a sense of identity that they crave."[132] The idea that copycat killers come principally from the ranks of the mentally ill has no basis in any research; in fact, many experts contend quite the opposite.[133] And still, it is the mentally ill—a category that has been muddled with "insane killers" and "evil monsters"—whom we must guard against and whose rights must be restricted for the common good. On *Meet the Press*, LaPierre went further, declaring that "we have a mental health system in this country that has completely and totally collapsed. We have no national database of these lunatics. . . . So when they go through the National Instant Check System and they go to try to screen out one of those lunatics, their records are not even in the system."[134] Aside from his liberal use of the antiquated term "lunatic," what's striking here is LaPierre's reference to the National Instant Criminal Background Check system. It is the NRA's position, he claims, that "anyone adjudicated mentally incompetent" should be added to that registry, which is normally reserved for criminals.[135] That LaPierre is eager to lump the mentally ill together with criminals is not surprising given his familiarly apocalyptic assessment of mental health care: "They're not serious about fixing the mental health system. They've emptied the institutions and every police officer knows dangerous people out there on the streets right now. They shouldn't be on the streets, they've stopped taking their medicine and yet they're out there walking around!"[136]

Predictably, the nation's psychiatrists and mental health advocates objected to this rhetoric. The CEO of the American Psychiatric Association complained that LaPierre's statements underscore the unfortunate association of mental illness with evil—a "relic of the past" that serves "only to increase the stigma around mental illness and further the misconception that those with mental disorders are likely to be dangerous."[137] The head of the National Alliance on Mental Illness, Michael Fitzpatrick, was even more stinging. He complained that the NRA's depictions of the mentally ill were negligently vague and foreboding, and effectively called for expanding the ranks of those deemed mentally incompetent to include "teachers who take prescriptions for anxiety or depression, police, fire fighters and veterans returning home from Afghanistan."[138] Referring to the NRA's call to place "anyone adjudicated mentally incompetent" on the NICS registry, Fitzpatrick said he was worried about "confusion surrounding the highly stigmatizing term 'mentally defective' and the uncertain meaning of 'adjudicated.' "[139] Who would do the adjudicating, and on what basis? Who is to be deemed mentally defective, and to what end? What implications are to follow for such people? Fitzpatrick argued that the NRA's approach is self-defeating; it offers no genuine concern for the mentally ill, no constructive approach to their predicament, and no additional safety from deranged shooters. "The NRA's proposal to create a bigger 'active' national database will only discourage people reaching out for help," he stated. "Stigma will be imposed. Stigma will be internalized. Stigma will turn into prejudice and discrimination."[140]

The boundaries defining mental illness are hardly clear and fixed. As Fitzpatrick points out, the mentally ill include many respectable and otherwise law-abiding, sensible, and well-meaning folk, hardly "monsters" by any account. As one APA official explained, "about one quarter of Americans have a mental disorder in any given year, and only a small percentage of them will ever commit violent crimes."[141] It is ironic that the NRA, supposedly a defender of individual liberty, advocates increasing the ranks of those who are monitored, even forcibly medicated and institutionalized—all to ensure the absolute freedom of some. LaPierre's imagined solution for the mentally ill is needlessly coercive, and violent in itself. Of course, it's hardly LaPierre's concern whether his proposals benefit the interests of the mentally ill. It's his job to argue, at whatever cost, for the interests of gun owners. Such is the charge of a political lobby, and there are few more single-minded and shameless—or effective—than the NRA. That said, its irresponsible approach on this account provides evidence of the gun rights movement's tendency to stigmatize, and it reveals the harsh consequences to which this tendency would lead. To that extent, the NRA's approach is incompatible with the intentions and standards of a democracy.

The moral outlook of the gun rights movement is harsh and intolerably cruel. It creates a self-fulfilling prophecy: in treating persons harshly and viewing the world with suspicion and hostility, it reaps hostility in return. Gun rights advocates offer a simplistic, ultimately false way of appraising humanity. Evil does not exist as LaPierre suggests it; criminals are not born such, and don't behave as gun rights advocates, in their black-and-white universe, imagine they do. Human behavior is unpredictable and often morally unclear. It is not always susceptible to clear moral judgment—at least by us, fallible humans that we are. Amidst all this imperfection, where judgments of character often err and fear is often unfounded, guns are a poor solution. They escalate simple conflicts and too frequently transform our imperfection into tragedy.

CHAPTER TWO

Guns, Government, and Autonomy

T the heart of debates over gun rights are competing visions of the meaning and intent of the Second Amendment of the U.S. Constitution. The controversy is exacerbated by the amendment's ambiguous wording: "A well-regulated Militia, being necessary to the security of a free State, the right of the people to keep and bear Arms, shall not be infringed." Many have wondered why, for example, the provision starts by mentioning militias, and especially what that might mean in a day when militias—at least as our forebears knew them—do not exist. Did the Founding Fathers have in mind a collective right to bear arms, or an individual right? Did they intend to convey the right of gun ownership only to active participants in state militias, like the famed Minutemen of Concord, Massachusetts, the organized and well-trained volunteer force whose confrontation with the British army sparked the

Revolutionary War? Or did the founders wish to ensure that gun ownership is a right for all citizens, unconnected to membership in a militia—or to any other limit?

Whether the Second Amendment sanctions a collective or individual right to own guns depends on the larger political purpose the Founding Fathers envisioned. Gun rights advocates insist that this purpose was to provide a last-ditch protection against government tyranny when political measures have failed. It is thus meant as a backup to the constitutionally sanctioned checks and balances internal to our government. The Second Amendment is a constant reminder, say gun rights advocates, that our politicians must work to resolve their differences and pursue their agendas within the political rules of the game. If they do not—if they step outside those rules and look to amass personal power over that of the people—they will pay a stiff penalty at the hands of an armed citizenry jealous of its freedom.

In upholding this interpretation of the Second Amendment, gun rights advocates maintain that they are unswervingly, even uniquely, faithful to the will of the Founders. Former NRA leader Warren Cassidy once said of his organization: "You would get a far better understanding if you approached us as if you were approaching one of the great religions of the world."[1] Gun rights groups are famous for an adulation of the Founding Fathers that smacks of religious devotion. They see themselves as the loyal and true heirs of Revolutionary America, and emphasize their singular piety by adorning themselves in the trappings of patriotism. Consider the iconic image of Charlton Heston, leader of the NRA, with a Revolutionary era flintlock rifle held high.

Author and journalist Osha Gray Davidson offers an instructive description of his visit to an NRA convention in San Antonio in 1991 shortly after the first Gulf War. On the night the main speakers were to address members in a huge ballroom, the proceedings started with a stirring video of our victorious troops coming home from war, intercut with images of ordinary Americans grasping their guns, staring earnestly into the camera. This brought the crowd to its feet. Amid whoops and cheers, Wayne LaPierre marched onto the stage and barked, "What a night for Patriots!" Pointing to the giant American flag behind him, he declared, "These colors don't run!"[2] Gun ownership is patriotic and a sign of solidarity with those who risk the most for this nation. Davidson's account highlights a mixture of nationalism and militarism that seems curious, coming from people who are supposedly worried about government power—as if the armed forces are somehow wholly distinct from government and purified of the taint of its excesses.

In a forceful editorial in the *Washington Times*, conservative commentator Andrew Napolitano writes, "The historical reality of the Second Amendment's protection of the right to keep and bear arms is not that it protects the right to shoot deer. It protects the right to shoot tyrants, and it protects the right to shoot at them effectively."[3] The Second Amendment has a political heritage we must not forget or ignore. Gun control advocates like to assure hunters that they are not coming after their rifles—but Napolitano reminds us that that is beside the point: the right to own guns is not for hunting or self-defense primarily, though those purposes are certainly protected. No, the Founders' principal interest in arming the electorate was that it might serve as a threat to those in government. As one NRA representative put it, the Second Amendment is "literally a loaded gun in the hands of the people held to the heads of government."[4] Historian Larry Schweikart writes that "Modern governments are well aware of the fact that . . . the fundamental argument for gun ownership is that an armed population cannot be controlled or tyrannized as easily as an unarmed population. It's no surprise, then, that the government has relentlessly sought to demonize guns."[5]

Accordingly, gun rights advocates argue, any attempt by government officials to regulate, monitor, control, or limit privately owned arms puts us on the slippery slope to tyranny. Gun regulations show the government acting on its real, power-hungry designs. Such laws are an attempt to consolidate power over and against the citizenry, and literally take power out of its hands. When those in power get a taste for gun regulation, no matter how slight, they will inevitably move to confiscate all guns, often violently. Gun rights advocates often point to the sieges at Ruby Ridge, Idaho, in 1992 and Waco, Texas, a year later as prime examples of government overreach in the name of gun control—and the bloody shape such overreach can take. At Ruby Ridge, U.S. marshals and the FBI sought to arrest Randy Weaver at his home compound for firearms offenses, and were subsequently engaged in a gun battle that left three dead, including Weaver's son and wife. In the Waco incident, agents from the Bureau of Arms, Tobacco, and Firearms raided the compound of the Branch Davidian religious group, also for alleged firearms offenses. Again, a standoff ensued, as did a fifty-one-day siege that culminated in a botched FBI assault and a deadly fire that claimed the lives of seventy-six members of the Branch Davidian group. Violent showdowns do not occur when the government seeks to regulate food protection or worker safety. But when the FBI sought to impose gun control measures on the Branch Davidians, scores of people died. Why? For LaPierre, the answer is obvious: these incidents, he said at the time, showed that "we are clearly on the road to government oppression."[6] In gun control, a government that exerts power gets a taste for more; it becomes vicious and despotic.

The final bulwark against government amassing power and acting on oppressive designs, gun rights advocates maintain, is guns in the hands of the citizenry. Take guns away, and suddenly, government aggression will manifest itself—sometimes horrifically. Gun rights advocates often point out genocidal agendas perpetrated by governments on unarmed populations. In a letter to the Supreme Court contesting Chicago's handgun law in 2012, Daniel Schmutter of the group Jews for the Preservation of Firearms Ownership wrote that

> During the 20th Century, more than 70 million people, after first being disarmed, were slaughtered by their own governments. This pattern appeared in Ottoman Turkey (1915–1917), the Soviet Union (1929–1945), Nazi Germany and Occupied Europe (1933–1945), Nationalist China (1927–1949), Communist China (1949–1952, 1957–1960 and 1966–1970), Guatemala (1960–1981), Uganda (1971–1979), Cambodia (1975–1979) and Rwanda (1994) just to name a few.[7]

In the same vein, Napolitano remarks how the Holocaust might have looked different "if the Jews in the Warsaw ghetto had had the firepower and ammunition that the Nazis had."[8] These arguments put any government intent on gun regulation in the ignominious company of Stalin and Hitler; at the very least, gun regulation inadvertently facilitates what tyrants do.

Throughout the twentieth century, the Supreme Court favored a collective reading of rights protected by the Second Amendment and remained unswayed by arguments to the contrary. Then, in a landmark 2008 case, *District of Columbia v. Heller,* the Court reversed itself: in a split decision, the Supreme Court affirmed that the nation's founders intended gun ownership as an individual right. This was greatly satisfying to the gun rights movement, which has staunchly insisted upon an individual, and increasingly absolute, right to be armed. Gun rights advocates believe the political backdrop of the Second Amendment supports their position. But what should we make, then, of the mention of the militia, which, by virtue of its prominent place atop the Second Amendment, suggests a collective or at least qualified reading of the right to own guns? LaPierre quotes George Mason, the author of the Bill of Rights, who said during a debate over ratification of the Constitution in the Virginia Senate: "I ask sir what is a militia? It is the whole people, except for a few public officials."[9] LaPierre believes Mason made clear "his deep set belief that the individual armed citizen was the key to protection against government excesses and in defense of freedom."[10] If a militia can, as Mason suggests, comprise the whole population, this implies that all its component individuals may be armed. The principal distinction Mason draws here, gun rights advocates believe, is between "general" and "select" militia. The latter, as its name suggests, is a limited force of trained and armed citizens specially selected for the job. Our Founding Fathers could not have intended the Second Amendment to apply only to a select militia, Justice Antonin Scalia writes in his majority opinion in *Heller*, since they knew that "the Stuart Kings Charles II and James II succeeded in using select militias loyal to them to suppress political dissidents, in part by disarming their opponents."[11] Select militias can be corrupted and put in the service of the ruling powers; but it is precisely to oppose and threaten government corruption that the Second Amendment was conceived.

The Second Amendment was written to effect a twofold purpose, according to historian Joyce Lee Malcolm: first, to "guarantee the individual's right to bear arms for self-defense and self-preservation," as opposed to merely collective defense; second, to point out that a "militia necessitated an armed public"—a general militia, that is, since "a select militia was seen as little better than a standing army."[12] These were anathema to those wary of government tyranny, since it was at the hands of King George's standing army that the colonists had so recently suffered oppression. The nation's founders, Malcolm maintains, intended that the whole population might be armed, so that a militia (or militias) might be drawn at a moment's notice to oppose a central government drunk on power. She writes, "the clause concerning the militia was not intended to limit ownership of arms to militia members, or return control of the militia to the states, but rather to express the preference for a militia over a standing army."[13]

Legal scholar Saul Cornell argues, by contrast, that "the original meaning of the Second Amendment was neither an individual right of self-defense nor a collective right of the states, but rather a civic right of citizens to keep and bear the arms needed to meet their legal obligations to participate in a well-regulated militia."[14] Cornell aims to do justice to the full sense of the phrase "a well-regulated militia." The colonial militias that contemporary gun rights advocates so admire, he argues, were subject to numerous regulations the NRA would hardly suffer today. And, he points out, this made sense: if the militia was meant to be a credible fighting force, capable of taking on frontier threats as well as invading armies—and the U.S. government, too, on occasion—it needed regulations and rules to make it so. It could be no ramshackle unit, pulled together instantaneously. Apparently, Cornell reports, this had too often been George Washington's impression of colonial militias during the Revolutionary War, which is why Washington ultimately favored the creation of a standing army, over the opposition of many of his peers who felt that a standing army would tempt government corruption.

The English jurist William Blackstone, whose *Commentaries on the Laws of England* provided considerable inspiration to the framers of the U.S. Constitution, asserted "the right of subjects to have arms . . . as a public political function." "This right," Cornell explains, "was legally distinct from an individual right to personal self-defense."[15] Guns are not to be owned exclusively or even principally for self-defense, but that is a secondary function. The right of gun ownership is indelibly linked to a communal purpose first and foremost— the defense of the community. Cornell thus admits that individuals may have weapons, but by situating them in a communal definition and casting doubt on an absolute right to individual gun ownership, he seeks to lay the ground for government regulation of this right. "None of the early state constitutions," he notes, "adopted personal language protecting an individual right to keep and carry arms for personal defense."[16] The states conceived this right as necessarily linked to service in a militia, and thus linked to a larger public purpose and role. Thomas Jefferson, insofar as he sought to sever this link, was the forerunner of the modern NRA—but Cornell says he was an anomaly among his peers.

In his book *Living with Guns*, Craig Whitney argues that the U.S. Constitution and the state constitutions did not set out to articulate an individual right to bear arms because our Founders already presumed that this right was handed down from English common law. This, Whitney believes, helps make sense of the phrase "the right to bear arms shall not be infringed."[17] The individual right to gun ownership was deemed a preexisting right, already exercised in abundance on the frontier for purposes of hunting and self-defense. As such, it did not require articulation and protection. What did require articulation was the right to organize individual gun owners into militias that might oppose government and a standing army. Whitney agrees with Cornell that the Constitution is perfectly open to gun regulation.

Napolitano writes, "we also defeated the king's soldiers because they didn't know who among us was armed, because there was no requirement of a permission slip from the government in order to exercise the right to self-defense."[18] The Second Amendment's unique power to provide a credible threat against government oppression exists only if gun ownership is unlimited, unregulated, and unmonitored, Napolitano suggests. The government ought not know whence its citizen threat comes; it can't know whom to fear or even what kinds of weapons to fear. This is necessary to hold power in check as the Founding Fathers wanted it. "Today," according to Napolitano, "the limitations on the power and precision of the guns we can lawfully own not only violate our natural right to self-defense and our personal sovereignties, they assure that a tyrant can more easily disarm and overcome us."[19] If gun rights were written to oppose government—because they are precisely what those in power abhor, a check on the temptation to abuse—we must not, as a matter of democratic principle and prudence, tolerate infringement of those rights. Further, Napolitano makes clear, this same democratic principle justifies the legal ownership of all manner of weaponry. Citizens should not be prevented from having assault weapons with high capacity magazines because those are precisely the kind of weapons our government would, might—will?—use against us. This logic would doom the machine gun ban, which has been in place since the 1930s. Open Carry should follow, too: why shouldn't we be able to remind our rulers of the power we are prepared to employ if they overstep their bounds? It is important to note how the political argument put forth by the gun rights movement poses a significant obstacle to most gun control legislation. Public health researchers looking to stem gun violence, for example, would have us monitor the sale and ownership of guns in order to keep them out of the hands of registered offenders and the mentally ill. Yet gun rights advocates argue that we cannot tolerate a registry of gun owners because it would undermine the essential and urgent political purpose of the Second Amendment. As lawyer and author

David Kopel sums it up, "the tools of political dissent should be privately owned and unregistered."[20]

The gun rights position on the Second Amendment is noteworthy for its enduring suspicion of government. The Founding Fathers, goes the thinking, outfitted our Constitution with the means to resist government because they were highly aware that, on occasion, government must be resisted. The lesson drawn from the Revolutionary War and our painful separation from Britain was clear to the founders, according to gun rights advocates: power—and a standing army at its behest—corrupts. More precisely, centralized power corrupts. It was the Framers' task to create a central government at the heart of the states that would hold the nation together and perform several necessary tasks without infringing on the hard-fought freedoms of these states and their citizens. The Bill of Rights was a product of the long fight between the Federalists and Anti-Federalists in the creation and ratification of the Constitution, which laid out the powers of the national government and the rights of citizens. George Mason, in the Federalist camp, provided the Bill of Rights, Cornell explains, as a way to win over the Anti-Federalists, who were wary of an overly powerful central government and resistant to measures that would strengthen it. Mason aimed to assuage Anti-Federalist fears of a standing army by counterbalancing it with an armed populace and the militia they might form. Contemporary gun rights forces fashion themselves as heirs of the Anti-Federalists. At best, they say, central government is bumbling, slow, and aloof; at worst, it preys upon the citizenry and schemes to expand its sphere of control. Those in Washington ultimately wish for nothing less than total domination.

Napolitano puts it starkly: "The essence of humanity is freedom. Government—whether voted in peacefully or thrust upon us by force—is essentially the negation of freedom."[21] Stated thus, government is a reasonable target of suspicion and opposition. Napolitano somewhat qualifies his rhetoric in the dramatic conclusion to this piece, written to deride gun regulation efforts in the wake of the Sandy Hook massacre:

> Most people in government reject natural rights and personal sovereignty. Most people in government believe that the exercise of everyone's rights is subject to the will of those in government. Most people in government believe they can write any law and regulate any behavior, not subject to the natural law, not subject to the sovereignty of individuals, not cognizant of history's tyrants, but subject only to *what they can get away with*. Did you empower the government to impair the freedom of us all because of the mania and terror of a few?[22]

Napolitano considers the nanny state, which would limit gun ownership in the name of protecting us all—because it knows what is best for us—simply a cloak for oppression. Given a taste for control, government soon lapses into arbitrary power—it will do "what it can get away with" because that is what government does. It is not to be trusted, even—perhaps especially—when it supposedly has our interests in mind. By Napolitano's estimation, those who enter politics are inherently untrustworthy and power hungry. They get into this line of work because they lack faith in individual freedom and decision-making, and ultimately hope to override it. Politicians are by their nature tyrannical.

Napolitano repeatedly refers to the notion of personal or individual sovereignty in order to assert an unlimited right to bear arms. The latter, he declares, is an extension of "the natural right to self-defense" as sanctioned by "the ancient principles of the natural law," which teaches that "our freedoms are pre-political and come from our humanity and not from government."[23] Government is a secondary political feature, created as a necessary evil when we surrendered some of our natural freedoms so that we might protect the rest. "Each human being is sovereign," he writes, and "the government derives all its powers from the consent of the governed."[24] The government rules at our pleasure, and an armed populace is key to ensuring this.

Napolitano's language invokes the seventeenth- and eighteenth-century social contract theory that inspired the Founding Fathers. According to this theory, which was put forth in various incarnations by celebrated political thinkers like Thomas Hobbes, Benedict Spinoza, John Locke, and Jean-Jacques Rousseau, government is not a natural entity co-existent with our genesis but rather an artificial creation that emerged at some later stage in human history. This theory draws a strict line between a state of nature, which is pre-political, and a civil state, which is entered into and often borne grudgingly. Nevertheless, humans freely and deliberately leave the state of nature for the civil state, thereby making government a willful creation of the people—something that exists, as Napolitano puts it, only by our consent. Government is thus something that we also retain the right to dissolve. LaPierre believes he has enlisted just such an argument from the Founding Fathers when he quotes Thomas Jefferson: "Governments are instituted among Men deriving their just powers from the *consent of the governed.* That whenever any form of Government becomes destructive of these ends, it is the Right of the People to alter or abolish it."[25]

Social contract theory was intended to assert and preserve the natural rights and liberties of citizens as far as possible in civil society. As the name suggests, the basis of government is considered contractual: individuals surrender some of their rights and powers to the collective so that they might have the security to enjoy their remaining rights more fully. Hobbes offers the first, and most disturbing, account of this contract and the state of nature that necessitates it. As Hobbes has it, humans are equal by nature and have unbounded rights in nature. But this is not as pleasant as it sounds. We are equal, Hobbes argues, in that we all have the ability to overpower one another and take what we want: some may use brawn, others may use brains, but everyone is justified in looking over his shoulder worried for his demise. Further, the state of nature is an all-out contest for resources; this is our unbounded right. The upshot, according to Hobbes, is a state of "warre . . . of every man, against every man," and we are eager, indeed desperate, to leave it.[26] For Hobbes, the circumstances of this state of nature lead to a contract whereby individuals consign tremendous power to a sovereign who is outside the contract and, as it were, holds a sword over the citizens' heads to ensure that these abominable creatures abide by the contract's terms. Absolute government is a necessary and paradoxical result of Hobbes's vision. The state of nature, conjured against the backdrop of England's Civil War, is a solemn reminder of what awaits people should they choose to upend government.

John Locke provides a rather different account of the state of nature and the social contract it implies. His version proved especially influential to the Founding Fathers, and crucially, gun rights advocates maintain, Locke provides considerable philosophical support for the right to bear arms. They point to a passage in Locke's *Second Treatise on Government* where he worries that unarmed subjects may enable the ruling party to "make prey of them when he pleases."[27] Further, say gun rights advocates, Locke would be a staunch supporter of the right to bear arms because he is uniquely emphatic about our right to self-defense, which we have by nature and retain in civil society. As columnist Charles Cooke sums it up,

> John Locke, who was crucial to the Founders' thinking, held that we are possessed of the inalienable right to our own bodies. From this we get the "life, liberty and the pursuit of property" construction that was subtly changed in the Declaration to make more explicit the personal nature of property. And from the notion that one controls one's body and may defend it, we get the attendant right to bear arms; you can't defend yourself with parchment.[28]

Cooke refers here to a key element of Locke's *Second Treatise*, the basis of labor and property rights. Citizens in a free society own their bodies; this is what distinguishes them from slaves. By extension, they have a right to the fruits of their bodies' labor. Thus property rights are inalienable. If, as it seems, Locke was intent on asserting the individual's right to preserve, maintain, and protect the integrity of his own person and the property that extends from it, surely he knew this could be most effectively performed by the gun, not mere laws—"parchment," in Cooke's words.

Locke aimed to preserve the larger structure of Hobbes's contract while ensuring significant reforms. Specifically, he sought to edge away from the Hobbesian defense of absolutist government and lead us toward something more democratic. He lays the groundwork for this departure in his competing account of the state of nature. Where Hobbes describes us as intractably egoistic and voracious, Locke holds that we are motivated by moral intuition, planted in us ultimately by God. We recognize our fundamental equality, Hobbes argues, in our equal ability to kill and take what we desire. Locke, however, tells us that "the State of Nature has a Law of Nature: as we are all equal and independent, no one ought to harm another in his life, health, liberty or possessions."[29] To recognize this fundamental equality is to know that others are like me, with the same desires and needs, beset by similar limitations, suffering similar trials. As we would not wish our own agenda to be infringed, so we will not infringe upon others. Locke's man is thus guided by a self-preserving prudence that Hobbes denies.

Locke develops this basic prudence into a robust sense of justice. "In transgressing the Law of Nature," he writes, "the Offender declares himself to live by another Rule than that of reason and common Equity, and in this case, and upon this ground, every Man has a right to punish the Offender and be Executioner of the Law of Nature."[30] Everyone may seek reparations from the offender, according to the nature and gravity of the offense. It is rightful for humans in a state of nature to demand the life of a murderer, Locke argues, even to kill a thief.[31] My property is an extension of my body, for Locke, both as the product of my bodily labor and as the means of its preservation. In this respect, a thief who harms my property effectively makes war on me, also because he "allows not time to appeal to our common Judge," but demands a reaction from me immediately, at that moment.[32] In the state of nature, where there is no common judge to say what I should do, the law of nature permits that I kill him because, for all I know, that is his intent for me.

There is an essential parity, according to Locke, in the law of nature that we intuit and accept. We recognize a wrong when it is committed, and instinctively know what constitutes fair punishment. Locke admits it is a "strange doctrine" that "in the State of Nature every one has Executive Power of the Law of Nature" and is empowered to adjudicate fair punishment and reparations.[33]

Thus far, gun rights advocates can take cheer. Locke appears to sanction law enforcement at the level of the individual citizen, thanks to an inborn sense of justice each possesses. Hobbes's individuals cannot be armed because they instinctively cause mayhem; Locke's individuals instinctively demand justice, a demand that also extends to our relationship with government. Locke holds that contracting members of society, for whom and by whose consent government exists, retain the right to dissolve that government should it fail to serve them. This is justified when a magistrate alters the laws without consultation or consent of the people and "sets up his own Arbitrary Will in place of laws," or when he aims to destroy or lay claim to their property or persons.[34] In so doing, the magistrate effectively declares war on the people, and can be dealt with like any offender in the state of nature. "Whoever uses Force without Right, as everyone does in Society, who does it without Law, puts himself into a State of War with those against whom he so uses it," Locke writes, "and in that state all former ties are cancelled, all other Rights cease, and everyone has a Right to defend himself and resist the Aggressor."[35]

Locke seems in line with the gun rights movement in two ways: first, he appears to support the individual citizen acting as an enforcer of the law, employing an internal sense of justice to confront offenders, and necessarily armed to resist those who would make war on him. It is this natural right of self-defense, and our instinct to carry it out, that grounds civil society and undergirds the moral and legal order that defines it. Because Locke "described a right to self-defense as a 'fundamental law of nature,'" *National Review* columnist David French claims, "gun control represents not merely a limitation on a constitutional right, but a limitation on a God-given right of man that has existed throughout the history of civil society."[36] Further, French writes, "state action against the right of self-defense is by default a violation of the natural rights of man," which the social contract is intended to uphold and preserve.[37]

It is also a necessary feature of this social contract that the people retain the right and ability to enforce it, and to make sure that government honors it. Locke's language regarding this provision suggests that an armed populace is necessary, since a tyrannical government is one that has declared war on us. Taken together, Cooke writes, Locke's social contract theory and the Founding Fathers' commitment to it suggest that

> The progressive notion that the police and armed forces should hold a monopoly on the legal violence necessary to defend each individual thus betrays both foundational principles and the traditionally auxiliary role of law enforcement in American society. The police, as the Supreme Court has repeatedly held, are employees of the public, not the sole enforcers of public order. Americans who would leave the means of violence in the hands of the state and, inevitably, the criminals would remove the means of self-defense from the one group in American life for whom the social compact was constructed: the People. This will not do.[38]

This appears to be a powerful, and reasonable, contention: a free society cannot tolerate a monopoly of armed force in the hands of those who would govern us. This puts us at their mercy and compromises our natural and God-given freedom. Guns—in the hands of private citizens—are thus necessary to ensure that the people's consent to be governed is ongoing.

The adulation gun rights supporters accord Locke is mistaken on several accounts. Cooke suggests that Locke inspired the Founding Fathers to give the police and armed forces an "auxiliary role" in maintaining peace and order, so that government might not enjoy a "monopoly on legal violence." Auxiliary to whom? Whose work shall the police and armed forces complement? Apparently, Cooke means that armed individuals are to play a major—perhaps principal—role in enforcing the peace. This makes sense in one respect, since ordinary citizens, unsullied by government involvement, will perhaps be less greedy for power. As Locke suggests, each of us is gripped by an innate sense of justice and eager to be "executioners of the law of nature."

Yet, Cooke's suggestion is alarming. For one thing, it violates the principle of self-preservation if I, as an ordinary citizen, chip in with law enforcement efforts. It is a good way to get shot by police who don't discern my good intentions, and instead think I may be another armed criminal. Or, in a world of unmarked citizens assisting in law enforcement, some other similarly concerned and committed individual who doubts my intentions may shoot me down preemptively.

Furthermore—and this is what makes Cooke's suggestion preposterous—we have designated law enforcement officials for a reason: they are specially trained, organized and vetted whereas ordinary citizens are not. We allow some few to have a monopoly on force because, in an altercation, we cannot have bullets flying everywhere. That does nothing to restore peace and order but does quite the opposite. I realize many gun rights advocates consider themselves among the specially trained lot of armed individuals, on par with professional law enforcement. Their talk of responsibility suggests that they know and respect the powerful weapons in their hands. The NRA offers its members copious training; they scoff at gun critics for their lack of knowledge and understanding of arms. Cooke makes clear, however, how this notion of responsibility points toward vigilantism. Indeed, that is effectively what Cooke defends. Yet we prosecute vigilantism because, as Locke himself knew, it poses a dire threat to public order. I believe it goes without saying (or it should) that we cannot have armed individuals roving our streets looking to enforce the law by their own might. What if their sense of justice, and apprehension of injustice, is compromised? That is a recipe for disaster. We have enough problems with police who go astray and make errors in judgment.

Though Locke's state of nature is less foreboding than Hobbes's, it is important to realize that he urges us to leave it and enter civil society. Gun rights advocates must recognize this. Yes, according to Locke, we are animated by an inherent sense of right and wrong, and parity in punishment, but each individual is not sufficiently equipped to carry it out. In fact, Locke suggests, each individual is likely to *violate* his instinct for justice in a state of nature. Of his "strange doctrine" that man is executioner of the law of nature, Locke acknowledges that "it's unreasonable for Men to be Judges in their own cases, that self-love will make men partial to themselves and their friends—and that Ill Nature, Passion, Revenge will carry them too far in punishing others."[39] And what happens when an individual gets carried away in his "executive powers" and punishes an aggressor excessively? He turns himself into an offender and aggressor, justifiably subject to the wrath of the law and of other individuals who would prosecute it. Because of our emotion, our limited perspective and understanding, Locke believes, we cannot be trusted as individuals to prosecute the law. Rather, our sense of justice, in concert with our native limitations, may land us in a state of war. Such are the "Inconveniences of the State of Nature," Locke explains, for which "Civil Government is the proper Remedy."[40] In particular, civil society, and the social contract that grounds it, recognizes a common judge, an independent entity that carries out our instinct for justice and makes sure, to the best of its ability, that justice is done. In civil society, people seek as far as possible to rely on the rulings of this common judge—and not their own. This is the distinguishing mark of civil society.

A lingering sense of injustice is at the root of so much war. One group feels it suffers injustice at the hands of another, and acts out in righteous anger. In so doing, it inflicts perceived injustices on the other party, who in turn react with righteous anger. The cycle of violence thus sparked may smolder for years, decades, generations. In many cases, neither party is entirely wrong; their moral convictions are sound. But that is not the problem: the problem, for Locke, is how to exit this cycle, which, precisely through the ardent moral convictions of all involved, would continue indefinitely. He explains, "To avoid this State of War (wherein there is no appeal but to Heaven . . .) is one great reason of Men's putting themselves into Society and quitting the State of Nature, for where there is an Authority . . . from which relief can be had by appeal, there the continuance of the State of War is excluded and the Controversie is decided by that power."[41]

Gun rights advocates see the social contract as providing an unbounded right of self-defense and self-determination. As Napolitano would say, the individual is sovereign by nature, the gun is the mark of sovereignty, and a government that takes this gun away violates the individual's sacred sovereignty. But Locke seems intent on pointing out, rather, that when all are sovereign, the sovereignty of the individual is intolerably tenuous. It is precisely to secure individual sovereignty that we must enter civil society—and make certain sacrifices along the way, chief among which is the individual's role as executioner of the law of nature. In a state of nature one has unlimited right,

> yet the enjoyment of it is very uncertain, and constantly exposed to the invasion of others: for all being kings as much as he, every man his equal, and the greater part no strict observers of equity and justice, the enjoyment of the property he has in this state is very unsafe, very unsecure. This makes him willing to quit a condition, which, however, free, is full of fears and continual dangers; and it is not without reason, that he seeks out, and is willing to join in society with others, who are already united, or have a mind to unite, for the mutual preservation of their lives, liberties and estates, which I call by the general name, property.[42]

Gun rights activists often cite property rights as a prominent reason for opposing gun regulation: I must be able to defend my property effectively, and Locke is nothing if not a staunch supporter of individuals' property rights. But in the passage above, Locke invokes a different basis for property protection altogether: I require common assistance if I would effectively protect property rights. To the extent that individuals take it upon themselves to protect their property, the institution of property itself is endangered.

The NRA decrees that "guns are synonymous with freedom, the very basis of democracy," political commentator Paul Rosenberg writes, "but according to John Locke . . . this gets things exactly backwards: it's the inability of guns—or any other private means—to secure our freedom that establishes the foundation for our civil government, and the freedom it secures."[43] Individual gun owners armed with a sense of righteous justice risk plunging us back into the state of nature from which Locke wishes us released. Boastful language of self-defense, or as Cooke has it, *serving justice*, suggests that gun rights extremists almost yearn for the state of nature. For Locke, that is utter folly—and highly destructive for us all. Or perhaps it is more apt to say, as Rosenberg does, that gun rights extremists are already "*psychologically* living in the state of nature, strikingly oblivious to the fact that we as a country do not live in that state, but rather in a civil and political society *precisely* to curb those fears and dangers, in order to secure the most precious and fundamental of our rights."[44] This may explain LaPierre's apocalyptic words about kidnaping-prone Phoenix. It is because he senses society's imminent collapse and inherent frailty that he believes citizens are justified in arming themselves. For him, perhaps, the state of nature is already here. This is an unavoidable but also highly dangerous feature of civil society: the laws will fail some, or appear to—whereupon they will say the social contract is dissolved, with all that that entails. For Locke, we cannot have some in civil society operating as if they were in a state of nature. It risks returning us all there—it means, sooner or later, LaPierre's warnings will prove themselves true.

Like Hobbes, Locke is ultimately wary of rebellion in light of the tremendous risk it carries. Though we certainly have that right by logic of the consent of the governed, Locke favors the peaceful process of dissolution over the prospect of violence—or even the threat of it. Rebellion, he writes, is "an opposition, not to persons, but authority, which is founded only in the constitutions and laws of the government." Thus whoever defies those laws—whether ruler or citizen—is to be counted a rebel.[45] The distinguishing feature of civil society, Locke claims, is that people have "excluded force," while those who resort to force "bring back again the state of War, and are properly Rebels."[46] This may be necessary if law has vanished—but citizens who rebel had better be sure it has. Rebellion ought not be invoked lightly: you are threatening to usher in a state of nature, and all its attendant perils. In fact, it is rather treacherous and foolish for citizens even to invoke the threat of rebellion. For, those in power, says Locke, have the "temptation of force . . . and the flattery of those around them," and threats of rebellion might cause them genuine worry about their self-preservation—provoking an accordingly violent response.[47]

This discussion of Locke's social contract theory evokes the debate surrounding Stand Your Ground laws that gun rights groups so vocally support. As of 2014, and despite numerous highly publicized controversies stemming from the law—including the Trayvon Martin shooting in 2012, and the shooter's acquittal, which prompted widespread protests—twenty-two states have Stand Your Ground laws on the books.[48] The NRA backed the legislation with considerable financial support, contributing mightily to legislators who have sponsored and voted for the bills. Stand Your Ground laws are a bold new legal frontier, an expansion of "castle doctrine" laws, and a departure from the common-law requirement that persons faced with a threat—in public—have the duty to withdraw or avoid confrontation if possible, and use force only as a last resort. Castle doctrine is a common law doctrine that absolves an individual of the obligation to retreat if he is threatened in his home—his "castle"; at home, faced with a threat, he may employ force as a "first resort." Castle doctrine has been incorporated into law in forty-six states as of 2012, and in many states, expanded beyond the home to include, among other things, one's car, and one's workplace.[49] Stand Your Ground laws absolve an individual *anywhere* of the duty to retreat, if he or she detects an imminent threat to his or her person. Florida's Stand Your Ground statute says that one may meet force with force, "including deadly force if [the individual] reasonably believes it is necessary to do so to prevent death or great bodily harm to himself."[50] In the case of Trayvon Martin, the shooter pursued the teenager, went out to confront him—armed—and when he felt threatened, "stood his ground."[51]

The NRA praises such legislation for "turning focus from criminals' rights to those of the law-abiding who are forced to protect themselves."[52] Prior to Stand Your Ground, persons shooting would-be attackers bore the burden of proof that they were acting in self-defense. This effectively put law-abiding citizens on the defensive and raised the bar for convicting the would-be attacker of a serious crime, leading to lesser charges. In the eyes of gun rights advocates, this was a way of criminalizing the behavior of lawful gun owners and putting them on par with criminals. Just as law-abiding individuals must have the right to own whatever guns they will, and not feel ashamed to carry them in public, so they must be allowed to use them for their rightful purpose, especially if attacked. As the NRA has it, we must presume the innocence, intent, and acumen of lawful gun owners. Criminals must be put on the defensive; they, not law-abiding citizens, must be the ones at a legal disadvantage in these cases. As LaPierre puts it, the castle doctrine and Stand Your Ground laws mean that "if you're in your home, and your glass breaks in the middle of the night, there is a presumption that that person is there to cause you imminent fear of death or bodily harm. If you're in your car and someone assaults you and tries to pull you out there's a presumption that that person is there to cause you imminent fear of death or bodily harm."[53] In each case, the assailant may have only theft in mind; these laws urge us to presume worse—and act on that presumption.

Another argument offered in support of Stand Your Ground laws, predictably, is that they provide superior deterrence against criminal behavior. Gun rights advocates maintain that in states that have such legislation, criminals know they have less legal protection than those they would attack; victims are emboldened to fight back, making life harder for criminals. In addition to enhancing gun owners' moral and legal protections, Stand Your Ground also gives teeth to the concept of gun ownership: how can guns be a deterrent if citizens have the duty to run from threats? Besides, LaPierre might say, isn't fleeing a form of moral weakness?

Seen in a certain light, Stand Your Ground might look like a great victory for individual sovereignty. Individuals are empowered to defend themselves to the fullest, even against the mere suspicion of a threat. They do not have to run or seek police assistance; in the heat of the moment they can be their own "executioners of the Law of Nature." Who are we to judge the nature and degree of the danger an individual senses in a time of danger? Defending the law against its critics, LaPierre urges us to sympathize with victims in these incidents: "Have you ever been threatened? I mean you talk to crime victims in the country. . . . It's the most terrifying moment of their life. They really are in a state of overwhelming reactive panic, instinctively they'll do anything at that point to save themselves."[54] In other words, a threat is a highly personal experience. We can't hope to understand or appreciate the terror, or judge how people may react. To criticize it calmly afterward, and say, well, you could have run away at that moment, or defused the situation in this way, or screamed for police protection—or shot the assailant in the leg, incapacitating him—this is abstract, pompous, even insulting. It smacks of the elitism typical of gun critics. As LaPierre puts it, "this duty to retreat may sound fine at an Ivy League cocktail party, it doesn't work very well in the real world."[55]

Yet LaPierre's comments reveal the folly of the law from Locke's standpoint. The examples he cites sound eerily similar to behavior Locke envisioned in the state of nature— behavior that prompts our leaving it. In the state of nature, says Locke, individuals are justified in thinking that assailants mean to do them grave harm; they are permitted to presume the worst about offenders. But this is only because they lack a common judge who might—ought to—inform them otherwise. We must escape as far as possible the realm of such presumption, where individuals act on their own instincts, passions, and prejudices. It is precisely because individuals, when they feel threatened, might be inspired to do terrible things, with terrible recriminations in turn, that we must limit individual sovereignty in such situations. To put it otherwise: when people feel such strong passions, and are liable to act irrationally, that is precisely when we must prevent them from wielding deadly force, as far as possible. LaPierre, however, would do the opposite. He admits that crime victims are beset by "overwhelming . . . panic" and will "instinctively do anything . . . to save themselves." They are moved by emotions and sensibilities that are inherently untrustworthy—what *won't* people do to save their lives? Yet just when their judgment is least reliable, LaPierre would empower them to use deadly force. This runs directly counter to the point of civil society, which aims to make the law, and the ruling of a calm, informed, and objective third party, override our limited, self-serving emotions.

Critics contend that Stand Your Ground undermines law as such. In Florida, for example, Stand Your Ground cases are first dealt with by a judge who may singlehandedly wave off criminal prosecution if he believes the shooter felt a credible threat to his life. Then there is no criminal trial at all. The father of an unarmed man shot by a neighbor, who was subsequently granted Stand Your Ground immunity by a judge, complained that "somehow, we've reached the point where the shooter's word is the law. The victim doesn't even get his day in court."[56] It contributes to a sense of injustice when unarmed individuals are shot dead while the shooter not only faces no penalty, but is not even tried.

A similar outrage, of course, followed the acquittal of George Zimmerman, Trayvon Martin's killer. Defenders of the law were quick to point out that Zimmerman's lawyers had waived his pretrial Stand Your Ground hearing, which might have granted him immunity from criminal prosecution, and instead sought to defend him before a jury. But it turns out that "the issue of 'stand your ground' was in the jury instructions under the self-defense rubric in which justifiable use of force was to be considered."[57] Thus, as many commentators noted, the verdict was wholly unsurprising; the jury ruled as it felt compelled by Florida law. This prompted John Oliver on the *Daily Show* to exclaim: "That is what makes this so much worse—that we can get a verdict like this not because the system is broken down, but because the system works exactly as it was designed!"[58] In his capacity as neighborhood watchman, Zimmerman followed Martin, who was not engaged in any criminal activity; he ignored a police dispatcher's advice to leave Martin alone and wait for assistance; he left his car to confront Martin face to face, armed; and he admitted to shooting and killing the unarmed teenager. None of this was sufficient to convict him on any criminal charge. These details, Oliver suggests, outrage our sense of justice and throw the institution of the law into doubt. One prosecutor said of Stand Your Ground laws: "You lose faith in the legitimacy of the justice process if you feel cases are unresolved or resolved in a way that suggests a sort of unfair or biased result. At a very basic level [these laws] change how we view the sanctity of human life. If we're allowed to shoot somebody for reaching into your car to grab a purse, does it mean that we don't value human life the way we thought we did?"[59] Stand Your Ground laws now protect individuals who issue the ultimate penalty for even minor infractions—on the ground that they *thought* the offender meant to do worse. These laws sanction the escalation of violence in situations where escalation was not necessary. Locke clearly indicates that the whole point of civil society is to do the opposite: haul us back from the brink of chaos to more civil interactions.

Former Miami police chief John Timoney complains that Stand Your Ground laws blur the distinction between police and citizens. Previously, only sworn police officers had the right to face down criminals and meet force with force. But Stand Your Ground, Timoney argues, actually grants average citizens expanded powers in law enforcement, since citizens can seek immunity from trial through Stand Your Ground hearings. "A police officer," says Timoney, "is held to account for every single bullet he or she discharges, so why should a private citizen be given more rights when it came to using deadly force?"[60] Stand Your Ground permits the average citizen to use deadly force against perceived threats, but the average citizen, unlike a trained, experienced police officer, is at a disadvantage in *evaluating* threats. Timoney writes that "citizens feel threatened all the time, whether it's from the approach of an aggressive panhandler or squeegee pest or even just walking down a poorly lighted street at night. In tightly congested urban areas, public encounters can be threatening. . . . This is part of urban life. You learn to navigate threatening settings without resorting to force."[61] Stand Your Ground would instill the opposite tendencies. It allows us to opt for violence first. Timoney points out that homicides in Florida "categorized as justifiable have nearly tripled since the law went into effect."[62] Florida has effectively sanctioned killing as a permissible resolution to altercations between citizens.

Accounts of many of these incidents reveal that it is often questionable whether the offender meant to do harm to the shooter. So that we might understand people's intentions better, and defuse the cycle of violence before it starts, Locke advises that people remove themselves from potentially violent situations ahead of time, and seek the reference and refuge of a common judge. I realize this is not very satisfying to those yearning for vengeance, those yearning to correct insults to their self-esteem. But it is just this yearning that Locke finds so treacherous.

Two especially egregious cases that made headlines in 2014— both in Florida— further illustrate dangers with Stand Your Ground laws. In a Tampa movie theater, retired police officer Curtis Reeves pulled his gun on Iraq War veteran Chad Oulson after the two men argued and Oulson threw popcorn in Reeves's face. Reeves's lawyer, Stephen Romine, immediately announced his intention to invoke Stand Your Ground in his client's defense, telling reporters that his client felt faced with the threat of "great bodily harm," as the Florida Stand Your Ground law stipulates. At that moment, in the darkened movie theater, Reeves did not know what Oulson intended to do to him; he did not know the nature and magnitude of Oulson's threat—he did not know that Oulson had no weapon. Under Florida law, the lawyer argued, Reeves was permitted to presume the very worst of Oulson's intentions. The law is not concerned with the nature of the disagreement that ended in one man's death—it is not concerned with how petty the argument was, how trifling, or that it involved a profound, tragic misjudgment. Florida's Stand Your Ground statute, Romine argued, is merely concerned with whether "Reeves thought Chad Oulson would hurt him."[63] In that case, Reeves was indeed justified in using force—even "deadly force."

Ultimately, Reeves's lawyer decided not to request Stand Your Ground immunity. But as journalist Amel Ahmad points out, reporting on another controversial killing, Stand Your Ground laws "influence society long before they reach the courtroom."[64] The mere existence of these laws embolden, indeed, incite citizens to be armed and wield their weapons quickly and instinctively. And Stand Your Ground influences courtroom decisions even when the law is not invoked directly; it promises to change the legal culture of Florida, and of other states with such laws on their books.

Ahmad tells of the case of Michael Dunn, who sent a barrage of bullets into an SUV of black teenagers in the parking lot of a Jacksonville convenience store after he objected to the their loud music and an argument ensued. Seventeen-year-old Jordan Davis was killed, and Dunn was charged with murder. Dunn told the jury he felt threatened; he said he thought the teenagers had a gun. The police found no such gun, and Davis's friends said they were unarmed. Ahmad points out that, "'Stand Your Ground' was included as a consideration in jury instructions" and that "after more than thirty hours of deliberations over four days, the jurors couldn't agree on whether Dunn acted in self-defense in killing Davis."[65] He was found guilty of three counts of attempted second-degree murder, for shooting at Jordan Davis' three friends. The jury could not agree on whether he was guilty of murdering Jordan Davis, resulting in a mistrial.

Thomas Blomberg, professor of criminology at Florida State University, believes the state's Stand Your Ground law caused the mistrial: "The twelve-member jury may have genuinely thought Dunn was initially justified in firing the first several bullets to defend himself from Davis but then went too far by continuing to shoot as the fleeing teens drove off.

... They were trying to interpret the jury instructions, and clearly struggled with it, having deliberated for thirty hours. Normally, you don't shoot first and ask questions later. But the conduct promoted by 'Stand Your Ground' creates a different context, and that's what the jury struggled with."[66] As law professor Donald Jones told Ahmad, "In this case, Dunn could have moved his vehicle. He didn't have to subject himself to the loud music. But the law promotes the idea that you can use force whenever you feel threatened."[67]

Six months later, Michael Dunn was retried. With significant effort from the Florida state attorney's office, which was heavily criticized for the earlier mistrial, the new jury concluded that Dunn was in fact guilty of first degree murder. Where the first jury seemed open to the argument that Dunn acted in self-defense, the prosecution in the retrial worked hard to persuade the second jury otherwise. A major difference in the retrial was the testimony of Dunn's former fiancée, who had been with him the day of the shooting (she was in the convenience store when shots were fired). Dunn's fiancée stated that he never mentioned to her that he thought the teenagers had a gun. Her testimony proved crucial when coupled with the statements of the surviving teenagers that they had no weapons the day of the shooting. As Syreeta McFadden writes in the *Guardian*, "The 'stand your ground' defense withers when your victims are alive, and doubly fails when they serve as witnesses to a crime, living to tell the tale. The dead do not talk."[68] In that case, there is a good chance Curtis Reeves will not get off so easily, too, for the killing of Chad Oulson—Stand Your Ground will not save him. There were several witnesses in the movie theater the day of Oulson's death. At the time of this writing, Reeves's case has yet to be decided.

Some claimed Stand Your Ground legislation was somehow vindicated by Dunn's conviction: the law does not sanction or inspire wanton, instinctive killing in the streets. Many will likely say the same if Reeves is convicted. And yet McFadden reminds us that Stand Your Ground has a fatal flaw, made all the more glaring in the Dunn case: the law privileges the shooter. The jury must, and will, rely upon his or her word—especially if the victim is dead. Only witnesses can debunk a shooter's claim of self-defense. But what of all those private, isolated conflicts, on a lonely street corner or wooded lot late at night, and of course, the many domestic violence cases that take place behind closed doors? Stand Your Ground offers killers a reliable defense in those cases, as well as those where no reliable witnesses can be found.

Adding to the perversity of Stand Your Ground laws, Craig Whitney writes, "criminals can take advantage of these same laws and make it more difficult for police to prosecute them."[69] A robber, for example, only has to say—if there are no other witnesses—that the unarmed citizen he shot on the street had attacked *him*, and like George Zimmerman, he felt mortally threatened. His victim, if dead, cannot give testimony to the contrary. Stand Your Ground puts police at a disadvantage in bringing killers with criminal intent to justice. Thus, Whitney concludes, it makes all of us less safe. Affirming the advantage these laws offer criminals, one Florida prosecutor explains, "people who've been through the legal system are going to be more seasoned to using the law. And it doesn't take a master of fiction to turn a homicide into Stand Your Ground."[70]

Stand Your Ground makes sense in one respect: it is the necessary legal complement for expanded rights of gun ownership. Why have such weapons, and carry them in public, if we are not able to "defend ourselves" with them? Are they supposed to just sit in our purses, or on our hips? If assailants know we are barred from using guns liberally, won't they just become bolder? For a gun to serve its purpose and effectively ward off "bad guys," gun owners must be able to use them without fear of punishment.

Yet Stand Your Ground laws clearly allow for altercations to become needlessly escalated. Imagine how the absence of a gun, and a law sanctioning its use, might have changed the Zimmerman case. What if Zimmerman, in his capacity as neighborhood watchman, had not been armed? What if he felt sufficiently restrained by the law to leave the gun in his car? It is fair to presume that the exchange with Martin—if it happened at all— would have been very different. Zimmerman might have been less emboldened to ignore the police dispatcher's advice, exit his car, and follow and then confront the hooded stranger. Had he done so, when confronted with Trayvon Martin's anger he might have had to slink (or run) away, and wait for the police. He would have had egg on his face. I suspect it is that kind of embarrassment many gun owners refuse to tolerate; with a weapon in hand, they have a better chance of forcing punks to back down. But there is also a greater chance someone dies.

The castle doctrine suggests that the home is a legal oasis— perhaps "legal black hole" is more accurate—where the individual homeowner is his own law. Stand Your Ground moves this multiplicity of individual laws to the street. For Locke, the mark of civil society is that a single law holds sway universally. We must graduate from that state where multiple executioners prosecute justice as they see fit. Judging from LaPierre's ominous assessments, the NRA would likely say citizens need the castle doctrine and Stand Your Ground to defend themselves from the lawlessness that already exists. It is precisely because you cannot count on police presence in your home, or even nearby, that you must be armed to defend yourself. LaPierre asks, "would you rather have your 911 call bring a good guy with a gun from a mile away . . . or a minute away?"[71]

Locke would retort that to the extent that people fear for their lives in their homes or on the street, this reveals a larger failing in the institution of the law, and in our efforts to maintain lawful behavior. The solution is not to arm more people and empower violent, instinctual, unreflective reaction, as the castle doctrine and Stand Your Ground laws do. This is precisely what undermines lawfulness in the first place. Such laws allow citizens to make extralegal and extreme behavior their first option, when our guiding light and instinct in a society that would aim to be civil, according to Locke, is to avoid such behavior. Yes, Locke maintains a right of self-defense in civil society—but it is a last resort. Our primary duty in civil society is to retreat in threatening situations, to defuse the situation, not because we can always do so practically, but because that imposes on everyone the obligation to defer to law—instinctively—and insist on the supervision and peaceful maintenance of law. That is a message we ought to be giving criminals, too, though they might not heed it. Stand

Your Ground tells criminals that they can shoot first and plead later that they felt threatened. It is no deterrent. In a violent society that increasingly sanctions the violent resolution of altercations, everyone—including especially the criminal class—is inured to violence and hardly deterred by the presence of guns. If Florida homeowners are now permitted to shoot intruders on sight, would-be criminals will simply arm themselves better and be quicker on the draw. And the NRA makes it easier for everyone to be well armed.

Throughout the Stand Your Ground debates, gun rights advocates present a "bring it on" attitude: gun owners aren't afraid of criminals, criminals ought to know what's coming to them, and the law will back up the gun owners' courage. But guns carry this force only because of the broader civil order that already reigns. LaPierre eagerly disputes this assessment and declares that we already live in hell—so strap on your weapon. But if that were really true, guns would hardly inspire such bluster. In a society where peace is maintained by private firearms, all are insecure, and all must fear for their lives. The gun offers little real security, and certainly no *sense* of security in a society where all have arms and are ready to use them. It is the greater security instituted by law that allows individuals to swagger confidently with gun in hand in the first place. The gun rights movement betrays a shocking ignorance of the rule of law that already pertains in our society. This ignorance, and the agenda it proposes, undermine the very rule of law they claim to uphold.

Gun rights advocates also reach for Locke because he sanctions the citizens' right to dissolve government, and mentions the weakness and vulnerability of an unarmed populace. Because the consent of the governed lies at the heart of the U.S. Constitution, the governed must have the ability to keep their magistrates in line, threaten them effectively if need be, and physically oust them on occasion. Senator Tom Coburn remarked that "the Second Amendment wasn't written so you can go hunting, it was to create a force to balance tyrannical force here."[72] How, exactly, is this balance to be achieved? What does it consist of? Napolitano explains that "the principal reason the colonists won the American Revolution is that they possessed weapons *equivalent* in power and precision to those of the British government."[73] Accordingly, the Founding Fathers intended that the citizenry should have force equivalent to the governing powers. How else would you hold the latter in check? Napolitano believes we must have access to "the same instruments [tyrants] would use upon us."[74] Like other gun rights defenders, he cites examples of unarmed peoples mowed down by evil regimes. But he never says what would have been required for persecuted people to resist these regimes effectively. Napolitano bemoans the fact that the Jews did not have the same firepower the Nazis had— but what would this mean? Panzers? Aircraft? A navy? Surely rifles and machine guns would not have been enough to stop the Nazis, considering the arsenal at their disposal and the broad social support for their persecutions.

Osha Gray Davidson cites an ad that the NRA ran following the Tiananmen Square protests in 1989. Beneath an image of a battered student surrounded by troops, the copy read, "The students of Beijing did not have the 2nd Amendment right to defend themselves when the soldiers came. America's founding fathers understood that an armed people are a free people . . . free to rise up against tyranny. That's why the individual armed citizen remains one of democracy's strongest symbols."[75] In fact, the enduring image of Tiananmen Square suggests otherwise: the single protester, unarmed, holding a line of tanks in check, stepping side to side to halt their advance. How would a gun have enhanced the man's position in this situation? He is facing down a line of tanks—would a gun let him do so more effectively? To the contrary, the Chinese government would have welcomed this: a gun would have given it an excuse to blow him away immediately. It is precisely because the protester was unarmed that the tank drivers were unsure how to act. And it is precisely because of the power of this image that it is so assiduously censored in Chinese media: it suggests the amazing power of individuals— unarmed—to frustrate one of the most powerful regimes on the planet. If the protester had been armed and shooting at tanks, the regime might be less reluctant to transmit the image. A gun would have made it easier for the government to control and distort the narrative by depicting him as a terrorist or criminal. Tyrannical governments hardly fear rifles, handguns, even assault weapons in the hands of citizens. These weapons are an invitation to meet force with force— and do away with any lingering pretense of civility.

Besides—and this is where the argument on these shores becomes so very preposterous—the United States has the most sophisticated, fearsome military on the planet. In 2011, the government spent more on defense than the next thirteen nations combined, and outspent the number two military in the world (China) seven times over.[76] Would Napolitano and

Coburn advise outfitting ordinary citizens with military-grade weaponry and military capabilities in order to achieve "balance"? That is silly and also impossible, given that some of the weapons in the government's hands are immensely expensive. American citizens have empowered their government to arm itself too well to be matched even by other nations. The Second Amendment hardly gives citizens any hope of balancing government power. As Rosenberg explains, "Clearly, what was once a living possibility is no longer the case. The rationale dies, because the underlying facts do not support it."[77]

Some gun rights extremists apparently believe they can wage guerilla warfare against this historically well-armed government. A popular article making this argument, noting that the North Vietnamese held off the U.S. military by just such means, is daringly titled "Armed Revolution Possible and Not So Difficult."[78] I believe that the Vietnamese, who know intimately the devastation wrought by that war, would hardly call their experience "not so difficult." It is a preposterous claim that, to the extent that it proves anything, demonstrates only the amazing abstractness of violence in our society that permits some to invite insurrection and war in the streets as if it were a good idea. Stanley Fish, writing about an online article on the signs of imminent tyranny, reports that one of the commentators to the article declared "Secession is near. Can't wait."[79] How can the commenter say this seriously, unless he is oblivious to the real implications of civil war? Unless he is spoiled by the very rule of law and takes it for granted?

The journalist Dan Baum encounters this argument when he visits the Goldwater Institute in Phoenix. When he expresses doubt that "a bunch of guys with rifles in their closets" could topple the U.S. military, the institute's director eagerly declares that "Vietnam is the defining war of your lifetime, and the mighty U.S. military was defeated by an enemy with little more than rifles. Our two current wars [in Afghanistan and Iraq] are much the same, and neither is looking good. And look at the Russians in Afghanistan. . . . Don't tell me that people with nothing but rifles can't take on a modern military."[80] Is guerilla warfare possible? Perhaps, but only with tremendous bloodshed, hardship, pain, and devastation. And the suffering had better be clearly warranted. Guerilla warfare succeeds to the extent that it has popular backing and justification. The Vietnamese would never have tolerated the suffering of their war against the U.S. had they not seen the Viet Cong as fighting for their independence. Afghanis were willing to endure the immense suffering of their war against the Soviet Union because they supported the mujahedeen's cause. Guerilla warfare is indeed possible, but so very extreme and difficult that it is advisable only as a last resort, where the situation is so dire that such combat is warranted—by, for example, the invasion of an occupying army. It is hardly clear that the situation in the United States is so dire, and the public so galvanized against tyrannical forces, that guerilla warfare has any chance of succeeding here.

Furthermore, the Goldwater director reveals a certain naïveté. It was not *merely* by virtue of rifles—literal physical, military force—that the Viet Cong defeated the U.S. military or the Afghanis ousted the Russians. There were other elements to the battle—nonviolent elements that arguably were more powerful than military efforts. In the case of Vietnam, for example, public support for American involvement flagged considerably as the war dragged on and its justification became less clear—and the American media, for the first time, transmitted into living rooms frank and unadulterated images of the war. Our energies for this difficult campaign were greatly sapped by increasing disbelief in its justification.

We should, of course, be concerned that our government might turn tyrannical. And we should be worried that if it does, it has the most powerful military on earth at its disposal. But 300 million guns in the hands of a motley assortment of individuals will not depose such tyranny or deter our ruling class from amassing power—especially since the public at large is hardly united against tyrannical government. Yet gun rights advocates inadvertently raise an important question here, which I will take up in the final chapter: what *would* equivalent force look like today? What power at the people's disposal would be sufficient to hold a tyrannical government in check or, better yet, prevent it from emerging in the first place?

Returning to social contract theory, the philosopher who comes closest to matching the gun rights movement's cynicism and suspicion of central government is Jean-Jacques Rousseau. He constantly reminds his readers that a social contract does not rule out but only delays the inevitable corruption of political institutions. Political authority by its nature tempts those who wield it, and incites them to use their office to amass and consolidate power against the will of the people. Tragically, Rousseau maintains, this danger grows with the size of the nation-state. The power and reach of government must increase with the population it serves, in order to serve the people as they clamor to be served. Over time, the ruling parties wrest power from the hands of the people and deform the political constitution. "This is the inherent and inescapable defect," Rousseau writes, "which from the birth of the political body, tends relentlessly to destroy it, just as old age and death destroy the body of man."[81]

Armed with Rousseau's suspicion when he visited the young United States in the 1830s, the French aristocrat Alexis de Tocqueville was on the lookout for symptoms of political centralization or features that might be conducive to its emergence. Early on in *Democracy in America* he asserts that "democratic nations are most likely to fall beneath the yoke of a centralized administration."[82] This is due in part to the absence of secondary institutions like the church and the aristocracy, which might counter the advances of central government. Without them, Tocqueville writes, "the constant tendency of these nations is to concentrate all the strength of government in the hands of the only power which directly represents the people, because beyond the people, nothing is to be perceived but a mass of equal individuals."[83] Further, he maintains, democratic citizens are eager to vest power in this government above them.

Tocqueville was amazed at the bustling commerce of the cities, how Americans were inspired and empowered to amass private wealth. But he deduced that this passion brought two troubling political consequences. First, devotion to individual wealth-creation meant that citizens demanded significant government services. Central government had to be sufficiently strong to enable commerce by, for example, maintaining roads and postal service, supporting and protecting the national currency, commanding an army and navy capable of eliminating threats to trade at home and abroad. The demands of commerce would help sweep away all of the concerns, voiced by the Anti-Federalists during the constitutional debates, about creating a central government with too much power.

Second, at the same time that government is strengthened to support individual pursuits, citizens increasingly want government to get out of their way and not burden them with its business, so that they might get on with theirs. "Such men," Tocqueville writes, "can never, without an effort, tear themselves from their private affairs to engage in public business; their natural bias leads them to abandon the latter to the sole visible and permanent representative of the interests of the community, that is, the state."[84] He initially marvels at the democratic energy on display in town hall meetings, where citizens from all walks of life offer their political opinions. Aristocrat that he was, Tocqueville did not, in the end, approve of this populism. But no matter—he was sure it would not last. Early Americans were involved in politics out of a sense of personal interest, he observes; their commerce and material well-being depended on the laws in place and the government's ability to enforce them. This same materialism would eventually wear down democratic interest and vigilance.

Tocqueville sensed a noxious combination in the ascendancy of egalitarianism and individualism: "As the men who inhabit democratic countries have no superiors, no inferiors, and no habitual or necessary partners in their undertakings, they readily fall back upon themselves, and consider themselves as beings apart."[85] In short, we will progressively isolate ourselves. Americans will become increasingly wrapped up in their material endeavors, Tocqueville predicts, and wish to be less reliant on anyone else—especially our peers, who hardly stand above us—save for the government that enables our individual pursuits. He invokes a very American suspicion of authority—reminiscent of the suspicion of elites we hear today in the gun rights movement—and yet, he maintains, this suspicion inadvertently strengthens the hand of government. For, so long as government supports our needs and allows us to get on with our business, we would rather consign it authority than our neighbors, who have no natural claim to superiority; rather, they are our rivals in the struggle for personal wealth. So long as government does not overtly or obviously oppress us, we will tolerate it and ignore its advances. Despotism in the democratic state will be a novel entity, Tocqueville claims, for it "would be more extensive and more mild; it would degrade men without tormenting them" and seek "to keep them in perpetual childhood."[86] Further, "the will of man is not shattered, but softened, bent, and guided" by such despotism, which "compresses, enervates, extinguishes and stupefies a people, till each nation is reduced to be nothing better than a flock of timid and industrious animals."[87]

Rousseau and Tocqueville maintain that democracies, like all states, devolve through political concentration. Viewing the young American democracy, Tocqueville deduces that extreme individualism greases the wheels of this process.

Materialism sharpens our individualism and makes us devoted to personal gain, as opposed to personal glory, which is more amenable to civic participation. Egalitarianism ironically urges us to dissociate from others, Tocqueville suggests; if my neighbors and compatriots are neither above me nor below me, what need do I have for them? In the ancien régime, people in different stations relied on one another, and the pieces of society fit together into a seamless whole. Not so in the new world: here, I may be self-determining and self-sufficient. Tocqueville offers a vision of aristocracy that is too rosy. He suggests that the masses should rely on the expertise of the nobility, who are bred and trained for leadership. But the American instinct to reject expertise and authority in favor of self-reliance is, for Tocqueville, at least equally disastrous. It is wonderful so long as it inspires the political attention and interest he witnessed in New England town meetings, but civic involvement is ultimately bound to lose out to capitalistic endeavors and the seductive joys of consumerism. Civic involvement has become a casualty in our own era, when we suffer from "time poverty," as sociologist Juliet Schor put it: Americans put in long work days, combined with increasingly long commutes, and have little time or energy to interact with their peers, work for their communities, or even think much about politics.[88] This state of affairs is fueled by personal ambition, but also by plain greed. As Tocqueville presciently saw, Americans have little interest, and are left with little energy, to be political creatures, and to devote time to thoughtful and concerted political action and interaction. This fragmentation of society into atomistic individuals, each pursuing his or her own endeavor in isolation or in contention with others, renders us vulnerable and ripe for oppression: "What resistance can be offered to tyranny in a country where each individual is weak and where citizens are not united by any common interest?"[89]

There is perhaps no individualism more extreme than that put forth by the contemporary gun rights movement. The NRA argues against the collective reading of the Second Amendment and insists instead upon the individual citizen's right to amass a colossal private arsenal. The organization toils on behalf of individuals' right to shoot intruders in their private abodes without accountability or social judgment. It works to ensure that individuals can act impulsively in private arguments, according to their personal whims, passions, and prejudices. It demands that they be permitted ammunition capable of piercing bulletproof vests worn by police. None of these advances a collective right or concern. It is to further the interests of each individual in being armed to the teeth, with whatever tools, for whatever purpose (provided it is within the law), and to have greater leeway in wielding and employing them. These arms represent a suspicion of the collective, and of the government that would represent the collective good. I argued in the previous chapter how these weapons are a mark of suspicion, and deepen the suspicion of the armed. A gun fundamentally severs its bearer from the community of his peers; it causes others to treat him with trepidation and fear— if they approach him at all. As open carry proponents proudly assert, their weapons are intended to serve as a warning.

Saul Cornell chides contemporary gun rights ideology for promoting gun ownership primarily as "a means for repulsing government or other citizens, not a means for creating a common civic culture."[90] This, he argues, is at odds with the aims and intentions of our Founders. He believes they did envision an individual right to bear arms, but it was never meant to be a right in *isolation*. It was to be linked to a civic function and to collective obligation. Cornell writes,

> The original version of a well-regulated militia was premised on the notion that rights and obligations were inseparable. Arms bearing was a public activity, a way of nurturing and demonstrating one's capacity for virtue. The militia was viewed by the Founders as a vital political and social institution, part of a seamless web that knit the locality, the state, and the national government together into a cohesive political community.[91]

Cornell's argument aptly depicts how the current gun rights movement undermines civic life. Gun rights, as they are currently conceived and championed by the NRA, are the ultimate go-it-alone rights. If our Founders felt that the Second Amendment would help oppose tyrannical government, it is reasonable to wonder how such opposition was ever to be mobilized. It could hardly happen in a nation of armed, isolated individuals, each in charge of a private arsenal. This purpose requires a trained, organized—regulated—force; it implies collective action, purpose, will, and commitment. George Washington grew tired of militias to the extent that they were loose collections of individuals. He wanted a fighting force with cohesion, identity, and organization because he was a warrior, and he knew what war—or the toppling of tyrannical regimes—required.

The gun rights movement pits the individual against society. Collectives are suspect, groups weak, their members sheeplike, obedient, pliant, and ultimately subservient. Collectives breed collective behavior, which is reprehensible to the movement's bold, assertive, fearless, and morally certain adherents. People mired in collective sensibilities wait for the police to bail them out of threatening situations. Free, confident, strong individuals go it alone. Collectives are corruptible, their members easy to manipulate and herd. Only the independent individual is pure and inviolate. Political freedom thus stems from the uncorrupted and incorruptible sovereign individual. To gun rights advocates, that is the center and foundation of liberty. This much is clear from the political vision put forth by Napolitano and LaPierre: the principal political battlefield, anticipated by the Founding Fathers who knew tyranny firsthand, is between the individual fighting to retain his sovereignty, and the collective that would strip it away. This stripping-away takes place through, among other things, government efforts to regulate guns, abetted by those who would cede their freedom for the short-term prospect of personal safety. In the process, such people unwittingly empower tyranny.

Dan Baum writes

> Guns are the perfect stand-in for one of the fundamental, irresolvable, and recurring questions we face: to what extent should Americans live as a collective, or as a nation of rugged individuals? We have the same fight over health care, welfare, environmental regulations, and a hundred other issues. The firearm, though, is the ultimate emblem of individual sovereignty, so if you're inclined in that direction, protecting gun rights is essential. And if you're by nature a collectivist, the firearm is the abhorrent idol on the enemy's altar.[92]

Baum articulates the dichotomy aptly, at least as it is viewed by the gun rights movement. Tyranny has also been invoked in recent debates over health care and environmental regulation. It follows from, and is symptomatic of, collectivism and anything that points in that direction. The gun rights movement offers us radical individualism—the sovereign individual—as the requisite remedy. But its advocates do not perceive, or refuse to admit, how politically debilitating their agenda is. Contrary to what they assert, their sovereign individuals, even armed to the teeth, are no match for the brute power of tyrants. Instead, the NRA and company unwittingly assist tyrants with their (as Cornell puts it) radically "anti-civic vision."[93] The gun rights movement undermines the collective or popular organization that alone might prove effective in countering a government bent on oppression.

CHAPTER THREE

The Face of Oppression

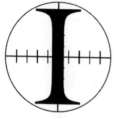

IT is one thing to argue, as I did in the previous chapter, that the gun rights movement does nothing to make us more able to oppose the forces of oppression. It is quite another to argue that, to the contrary, it facilitates the consolidation of power.

I have long wondered how, or why, those in power tolerate a profusion of arms among the populace. If, as gun rights advocates suppose, the U.S. government tends toward oppression and those who rule us are inherently greedy to expand control—and if guns are a nuisance and obstacle to those in power—why hasn't the government stripped us of our guns? Is it because it recognizes the fearsome arsenals some of its citizens possess, and is afraid to approach them? This is highly unlikely. A government listing toward oppression would hardly have moral qualms about shedding the blood of its citizens—and our exceptionally powerful military would have little trouble imposing its will.

There is, of course, a democratic element to consider: a segment of the population clamors for guns, and so the government allows it. For the political class, guns are at best a headache or a moral concern, but they are certainly no existential threat. After one of our periodic massacres, citizens implore their representatives to solve the problem, and representatives respond by proposing new regulations. But the furious declarations of gun rights advocates reverberate and prevail. Why do our politicians tolerate the headache of our gun culture? Why does Senator Tom Coburn solemnly state that guns pose a check on tyrannical government when, as one who signs off on our trillion-dollar defense budget, he knows full well they do no such thing? Why do our representatives perpetuate the exemption of background checks at gun shows, on the premise that criminals will never get background checks—an exemption that gives the criminal class free access to guns? There are few interest groups as wildly adamant about their rights or able to bring as much financial clout to their causes—but lobbying power alone cannot explain gun rights advocates' success. We must consider the direct benefits that individual gun rights offer those in power.

With a bravado typical of gun rights advocates, Charles Cooke writes, "to ask 'Why do you need [a semiautomatic weapon like] an AR–15?' is to invert the relationship. A better question: 'Why don't you want me to have one?' . . . far from being the preserve of two-bit reactionaries, this . . . is a deeply—nay radically—liberal principle."[1] Guns have historically been denied to social undesirables, Cooke argues, and to minorities we have aimed to keep underfoot. Gun ownership would enforce their rights and threaten the status and interests of those in power. This leads Cooke to the dramatic conclusion that "the right to bear arms itself may well be the ultimate right in any free society. . . . Free men who are masters of their government have that right . . . but slaves and subjects do not."[2]

The gun rights movement harbors a deep political cynicism: those in power are not to be trusted. Perhaps they were trustworthy once, but power corrupts. The powerful will look out for their own interests and support democratic interests in name only. If we want our politicians to respect democratic principles, gun rights advocates insist, we must physically threaten them. But if guns actually pose no threat to the ruling class, then this seemingly democratic policy, which forces our rulers to bend to the will of the people on a policy they supposedly detest, must provide them some benefit. What could this be? Another famous political cynic, Machiavelli, provides insight here.

At first blush, Machiavelli seems a powerful ally of the gun rights movement. Joyce Lee Malcolm points out that he was a prominent and influential proponent of citizen militias, and that English political thinkers, who in turn shaped their American peers, were very familiar with Machiavelli's *Art of War*, where he offers his most complete argument for a militia. Malcolm invokes the historian J. G. A. Pocock, who declared that "the rigorous equation of arms-bearing with civic capacity is one of Machiavelli's most enduring legacies to later political thinkers."[3] For Machiavelli, Pocock maintains, arms go hand in hand with political action—they are an extension and representation of the people's political vigilance and involvement, and they bolster the power of "the Many" against "the Few," as Pocock puts it, in "claiming rights within the city."[4] Pocock argues elsewhere that Machiavelli left an indelible mark on the Second Amendment in that it "affirms the relation between a popular militia and popular freedom in language directly descended from that of Machiavelli."[5]

Such language is most readily evident in *Art of War*, where Machiavelli aims, as the preface states, to restore the close relation between "civil and military life" that the ancients once upheld but that in his day, he laments, is lost.[6] His peers, he says, scorn military life—this is due to the poor discipline of his contemporaries, who cannot be bothered to enter into such a rigid life, but also to the corruption of the military. Machiavelli often warns of the dangers of professional armies—what evil won't they get up to when they are idle and must stew in their barracks? How much of our taxes must they consume? As for mercenaries, their unreliability, greed, and cowardice are manifest in numerous instances. How to make citizens more disciplined and deliver a superior fighting force? The solution, Machiavelli says at the outset of *Art of War*, is to create civilian militias. "By establishing a good and well-ordered militia," he writes, "divisions are extinguished, peace restored, and some people who were unarmed and dispirited, but united, continue in unison and become warlike and courageous; others who were brave and had arms in their hands, but were previously given to faction and discord, became united."[7] Enlistment in a militia may improve the character of the citizens—and in turn, amended soldiers make for more faithful and effective armies. "[No] man has ever founded a monarchy or a republic without being well assured that if his subjects were armed, they would always be ready and willing to defend the monarchy or republic."[8]

Note, first of all, that Machiavelli does not conceive of armed citizens independently from organized militias. To that extent, he is in line with Saul Cornell's reading of the Second Amendment. Machiavelli acknowledges the worry that "a great number of armed men must naturally occasion much confusion and disorder and frequent tumults in a country."[9] Organized militias are intended to resolve this concern by instituting discipline, which in turn depends on the quality and fealty of their leadership. Accordingly, Machiavelli stresses that states must therefore take great care in determining who shall command militias—how they shall be selected, trained, and assigned—and how to prevent their corruption.

Second, it is important to recognize that Machiavelli favors arming citizens primarily because of the help they provide the ruling party, if it would effectively prepare for and wage war. He is not interested in using arms to protect citizens' individual rights and freedoms. At best, he seems to think that armed citizens—again, organized into militias—promote the liberty of the state at large. Civilian militias, he writes, "have always been of the highest service to all governments, and have kept them free and incorrupt longer than they would have been without them."[10] So long as the state's fighting force consists of its own citizens, the state and its leadership stand a better chance of remaining incorrupt and independent.

In *The Prince*, his most famous work, Machiavelli suggests a more nefarious purpose for arming citizens. He lays out a host of ways for the incipient monarch to eliminate his foes, consolidate power, and "stand on his own feet," to use a favorite phrase, meaning to remain, as far as possible, independent and invulnerable to fortune. Among his more renowned prescriptions, for example, is that the prince must be prepared to lie and cheat because "rulers who have not thought it important to keep their word have achieved great things, and have known how to employ cunning to confuse and disorientate other men. In the end, they have been able to overcome those who have placed great store in integrity."[11] *The Prince* is notorious for the frankness with which Machiavelli issues his advice. The prince's aims are clear and certain. To attain and consolidate power, he must be cruel on occasion—but when he kills, he must do it viciously and quickly. The prince is rightfully selfish, and greedy for power and glory, but there is an art to political gain. It does not entail unchecked brute force. Machiavelli offers examples of leaders who failed because they resorted to overt and repeated shows of violence. While the prince is no idealist and is strictly amoral, he must in equally strict measure claim or pretend to be idealistic, honest, and faithful. Thus far, Machiavelli's account of executive power matches that of the gun rights movement: rulers have one thing in mind—to expand their control—and they are inherently untrustworthy. We must see through their supposed altruism to understand their true agenda.

Machiavelli urges upon his prince the ostensibly democratic principle that he must seek the support of the masses, but we soon learn this is only because the masses are more numerous and thus more dangerous. It is better to have the people on your side, he tells his prince, than the elites, who are few, fickle, and difficult to please: ultimately, elites are satisfied only when they depose the prince and rise to power themselves. The masses, by contrast, are easy to keep happy. When people are recently freed from tyranny, Machiavelli explains, "all they ask is not to be oppressed."[12] People accustomed to freedom, on the other hand, require something more. The support of the masses—especially those who fancy themselves free—is most at risk in times of war. Yet war is inevitable; the prince must wage frequent war in order to stand on his own feet. Worried for their lot in wartime, chafing under taxation, doubting the leadership if the fight is going badly—this is when citizens are most likely to rebel. They will question the prince's greed and wonder how, or if, it serves their interests. How can the prince survive such crises? He must make sure the people have ample supplies for their sustenance and comfort, also to sustain their livelihoods, professions, and crafts. They must be kept busy making money. And, Machiavelli adds, the prince must make sure that his subjects "are not short . . . of arms."[13]

Why might a prince, worried for his security and authority, and his ability to keep ruling and waging war as he pleases, want his subjects to be armed? Machiavelli even tells us that if a prince newly risen to power—and, as such, necessarily tenuous—should find his subjects unarmed, he must arm them.[14] Why do this if the masses are the most fearsome, potentially explosive party in the state? Machiavelli reasons that possessing arms will more likely make them loyal, even supportive of the prince's cause. Arming the people is a profound sign of trust and allegiance on the part of the prince: he signals he has their interests and welfare in mind—and respects their independence. This is a thrilling vote of confidence.

Conversely, Machiavelli warns, "if you take their arms away from those who have been armed, you begin to alienate them. You make it clear you do not trust them, either because you think they are poor soldiers or disloyal. Whichever view they attribute you, they will hate you."[15] This brings to mind the indignation gun owners express at the prospect of strong gun regulation, that such regulation implies they don't know how to handle their weapons with care and respect. Regulation says they are irresponsible; it lumps them with criminals and lunatic killers. The NRA says to would-be regulators: don't punish upstanding, conscientious gun owners for the recklessness of a few. The organization depicts regulation as a personal insult to millions of Americans.

Machiavelli understands the insult. It is unwise of the prince to disarm his subjects because it sends the message that he deems them deficient in character and strength. They are not worthy of fighting for him, Machiavelli suggests, and are unable to defend their homeland or their homes. Further, such an action says that the prince does not trust his subjects. It tells the people they must be looked out for, coddled perhaps, defended, protected from themselves, and the prince protected from them. Disarming the people suggests they are the prince's natural enemy. Machiavelli does not dispute the accuracy of this assessment, but he maintains that the prince must be careful to communicate strictly the opposite. There is no better way of mollifying the people and drawing them to your cause than arming them.

In one of the more memorable passages of *The Prince*, Machiavelli tells the prince not to bother trying to be loved, since the people are compelled to obedience not through love, but through fear. Above all, he says, a prince must not incur their hatred. Luckily this is easy enough to do: "You will only be hated if you seize the property or the women of your subjects and citizens. . . . [Keep] your hands off other people's property; for men are quicker to forget the death of their father than the loss of their inheritance."[16] Confiscating their weapons has a similar effect. In sum, the people are liable to manipulation so long as the prince leaves them to their selfish designs and does not undermine or overtly challenge their illusion of autonomy. Keep your hands off their women, their money, their weapons, Machiavelli tells the prince. You have your kingdom, leave them theirs. If you allow your subjects the small circle of sovereignty they believe they control—where they, too, "stand on their own feet"—you will be free to do as you like and even count on the people's complicity in your conquests. They will owe you allegiance and devotion to the extent that they are prosperous and feel like masters at home. Take things away from them, especially the symbols of their self-determination, and be prepared to feel the wrath of the sleeping giant. Their demands are simple, their wants few: they will practically bow for the prince to put them under the yoke, provided he satisfies their small demands for autonomy. Far more tricky are the nobles and oligarchs, who know that such autonomy is feeble and hollow, and angle for real self-determination.

Machiavelli offers a more favorable view of the masses' political power and even their virtue in *The Discourses on Livy*, his commentary on the political history of the Roman republic. Here, the masses are not a pawn to be manipulated, but an important power broker whose activity and vigilance are critical to a free state. If *The Prince* offers prescriptions for an authoritarian regime, *The Discourses* offer prescriptions for a republic. Machiavelli opens the latter by stating a conviction similar to that of Rousseau: political constitutions are mortal and liable to dissolution; the best we can hope for is to slow the inevitable concentration of power in fewer and fewer hands. This dissolution was evident in the Roman empire, as the decadence and greed of the emperors and the ruling class slowly sapped Rome's strength. And yet, Machiavelli maintains, Rome is a political model worthy of our attention because it persisted as a republic for several centuries, guarding its citizens' liberty and channeling it into unprecedented imperial glory before succumbing to political centralization. What enabled Rome to do this? Its republican government had a tripartite structure that also inspired our nation's founders. There were the consuls occupying the executive branch, and as there were two of them, they often canceled each other out and limited this office's reach and capacity for abuse; there was the senate, drawn from and representing the interests of the patrician class; and the "plebs," the body of free Roman citizens, composed of merchants and craftspeople, who acted as a collective political force. Machiavelli lauds the friction between the plebs and senate, which "made this Republic both free and powerful,"[17] and describes how the plebs, expressing their collective political displeasure, would terrify the senate: "Look how people used to assemble and clamor against the senate and how the senate decried the people, how men ran helter skelter about the streets, how the shops were closed and the plebs en masse would troop out of Rome."[18]

Such democratic expressions would be deemed too radical for our republic. Machiavelli describes the people going on strike to spite the opposition, something we would find inconceivable. As for the entire populace getting up and leaving the city, that would mean leaving our property behind. And yet, Machiavelli reveals, such protests produced sufficient terror to hold the landed class in check. Machiavelli is thought to be no friend of democracy, but here he captures an essential element of it, central to the freedom it purports to deliver: if democracy is to maintain the liberty and vitality at its core, there ought to be great tension and heated exchange. At times, these conflicts will verge on chaos, which is unacceptable to the ruling class and those vested in the status quo. Real competition between the groups—and the patricians will never willingly cede their power—always carries a risk of violence.

But *The Discourses* is also the story of how the uniquely free and strong Roman republic declined. The political recipe that made it great, Machiavelli laments, enabled Rome to conquer the free peoples around it, with such lingering effects that even in his own day, the Italian people did not know how to be free. How did Rome come to such a sad state? The story of Rome's decline, in Machiavelli's telling, is a story of how the people—the plebs—gradually handed over power to a few who hoarded and gravely mismanaged it. Why did the people let this happen? The transition to empire—though the latter also lasted some centuries—was the nail in the coffin of Rome's freedom, and ultimately its political vitality. Rome's territorial expansion tempted the greed of the few, and its glory blinded the many. Machiavelli tells how the people stopped appointing individuals to the consulate (the executive branch) on the basis of virtue, and began choosing them for their popularity, and ultimately their reputation for power.[19] Roman citizens' ego became wrapped up in the imperial project. "When the citizens had become perverse," Machiavelli says, "only the powerful proposed laws, and this for the sake not of their common liberties, but to augment their own power. And against such projects no one durst speak for fear of such folk; with the result that the people were induced, either by deceit or by force, to adopt measures which spelt their own ruin."[20] These people sound remarkably different from the plebs who expressed their discontent by marching out of the city en masse. Where was their democratic fury? Why were they no longer jealous for their liberty, alert to the advances of the senate, but instead lulled into complicity with the scheming few?

As the empire spread and Rome's enemies were vanquished, Machiavelli says, the people began to feel more secure in their state. Their vigilance dissipated, and with it their interest in the virtue of their leaders. They more readily favored rulers who diminished the power of the people and aligned themselves with the bellicose agenda of the ruling parties. In a passage reminiscent of *The Prince*, Machiavelli argues that a prudent ruler must satisfy his people's demand for freedom, and this demand amounts to "a desire but to live in security."[21] A sense of security, he adds, is easy enough to instill in the people through certain laws and institutions, but also by the ruler's reputed power and the sense of power the people share with him. It is by no means necessary that this sense of security be achieved by, say, actual security, or the independence and freedom of the people themselves. It can be borrowed, a sense of power enjoyed vicariously—which is the most any prudent prince will allow. Meanwhile, he may expand his reach with little disturbance or obstruction.

Few things foster this sense of security better than arms. This is why the prince allows, indeed urges, the people to be armed, though it seems contrary to his interest. Arms encourage the people to feel secure and self-determining, even while the prince knows they are neither. Above all, the people must not be allowed to organize like the plebs wreaking havoc in Rome. They must be kept busy and preoccupied, immersed in their personal endeavors and ambitions, isolated and thus enfeebled. To the extent that the prince succeeds in achieving this state, he gains the added benefit that the people will not grow disgruntled in the first place. They will cease to scrutinize his machinations or pay attention to much that he does. They may become oblivious to the real nature of oppression.

Machiavelli's dark assessment anticipates Tocqueville's concerns for American democracy. In an especially biting passage, Tocqueville complains how proponents of democracy "are constantly excited by two conflicting passions; they want to be led, and they wish to remain free. . . . [They] devise a sole, tutelary and all powerful government, but elected by the people. They combined the principle of centralization and that of popular sovereignty; this gives them a respite: they console themselves for being in tutelage by the reflection that they have chosen their guardians."[22] Tocqueville believes democratic energy cannot be sustained because, at bottom, the people don't care to be involved in politics or participate in government. In a democracy, the people purport to rule. Tocqueville observes early on how he is repeatedly reminded that in America, the people are sovereign—political sovereignty rests in and proceeds from the people. But despite their brave talk, he maintains, the people don't really wish to rule at all. They are perfectly happy to be cared for, and at the end of the day, politics is too much trouble. As many citizens will attest today—many of whom refrain from voting on a regular basis—politics is boring, base, difficult or onerous to keep up with. A lot of research is needed to understand each candidate well enough to vote intelligently and responsibly, and few people have time or interest for that. Politics hinders us from focusing on our own affairs, and the democratic public longs for a respite.

Yet a democratic public may also feel dismayed by its selfish, apolitical tendencies. The people are happy to feel that they have some modicum of political involvement, that they are vigilant participants in the system. But they are secretly grateful to whoever relieves them of the real thing. They are content to *feel* vigilant. As Tocqueville suggests, they wish to be *consoled* for consigning so much power to those who govern—but really, it suits our personal needs and business interests if government is powerful and effective, provides ample public services, provides us with cheap fuel, and keeps us mostly well off.

Guns are one such source of consolation. A pretense to vigilance is at the heart of gun rights rhetoric: the right to be armed is a "loaded gun held to the head of government." That ought to keep our rulers in check and make them wary of expanding power. Gun rights advocates fancy themselves open-eyed realists about the power plays of government—the democratic masses are soft and deluded for the most part, but gun owners are disillusioned and hardened. Like Dan Baum's gun shop owner, they know that there is evil in the world, especially in government, while those poor liberals mindlessly consign government ever more power and control through regulation. For Wayne LaPierre and company, the gun signals vigilance and serves as a political warning. Voting becomes a secondary political act—in fact, if the system is corrupt, as gun rights advocates maintain, voting is irrelevant. Being armed is a superior statement of freedom. Voting may put in power the same cronies or new ones, but guns serve a warning to cronyism itself. Guns are the ultimate act of political defiance, in this view, a real thorn in the side of those who rule. This is precisely why a free people must have this right.

Of course, as I have argued, privately owned guns pose no such threat. Individually armed citizens are more of a menace to one another than to those who hold the reins of our government. But there is something satisfying in the gun rights position. It claims to constitute a powerful political stance with a serious philosophical pedigree. The latter claim is credible and accurate—the gun rights position is born of a tradition of suspecting government and fending off the concentration of power. But the current movement does nothing to advance the philosophical instincts and interests at its root. Instead it gravely undermines them. Gun rights provide a seductive aura of self-determination but no actual political power to advance anything but gun ownership. To the contrary, the gun rights movement diverts many from the real avenues and machinations of political power. Gun rights are an effective smokescreen, Machiavelli might say, that allows the prince to train and marginalize his charges, and get on with growing his personal estate and command.

Gun owners have been a fixture of the Tea Party movement and its angry complaints that the government is too large and invasive and that the president exceeds the bounds of his office. Individuals at some Tea Party protests—especially during the town hall protests against Obama's health care legislation in the summer of 2009—brandished their weapons to underscore their objections. One man at a New Hampshire town hall meeting held a sign suggesting that armed revolt was an appropriate response to health care reform. Sharron Angle, the Republican candidate for a Nevada Senate seat in 2010, famously spoke of "Second Amendment remedies," and agreed that "we have domestic enemies . . . in the walls of the Senate and the Congress," whom, we must assume, would be the likely targets of said remedies.[23] When asked to clarify whom she counted among our domestic enemies, Angle replied, "people who pass these kinds of policies—Obamacare, cap and trade, stimulus, bailouts."[24] Such, in her view, were the signs of encroaching tyranny.

In 2010, *Time* magazine reported on a Second Amendment rally in northern Virginia where scores of protesters showed up armed. The rally had been organized by a group called Restore the Constitution, which apparently had the integrity of the Second Amendment (or a particular reading of it) primarily in mind, but also took the occasion to air other objections to government. The article stated

[As] with the Tea Party supporters, those who were present generally agreed that the government had unconstitutionally overstepped what should be the limits of its power; health care reform and the bank bailouts took the worst oratorical beating. But other grievances varied from speaker to speaker. . . . [An] engineer from Alabama lambasted everything from school lunches to PBS. Others called for a complete congressional revamping. "We're here to tell you something, guys: You're fired!" said Larry Pratt, executive director for Gun Owners of America, pointing across the river.[25]

Notably absent from this litany of charges is the government's War on Terror.

The number of privately held guns in the United States has soared over the past decade. It was widely noted that weapons sales spiked with each of Barack Obama's presidential victories. This was a mystery to many commentators: as candidate and president (at least until the Sandy Hook shootings), Obama uttered hardly a word on gun control. Why were so many stocking up even though the president, in his trademark centrism, left alone the radioactive subject of gun control? The conservative historian Larry Schweikart was not so mystified. He argued it was a sage precaution against expansive government. As Democrats took control of government in 2008, Schweikart explains, "Many Americans worried that the government would spin into an oppressive tyranny of regulations that would impinge on personal liberties."[26] The media attributed "the rise in sales to fears of 'crime and terrorism,'" he claims, but it "had once again failed to understand how gun ownership, as provided by the Founders, was meant to protect Americans from *government*, not from for-eign terrorism."[27] The buying spree was a warning to Obama and his allies: we know your real agenda.

LaPierre spun the spike in sales as a prudent stocking up in the face of the regulations that would surely come from a Democratic administration. For four years, these predictions seemed empty. During Obama's second presidential campaign, LaPierre sought to rally his troops, declaring, to the confusion of many, that gun rights had never been so endangered—the president was merely biding his time and aimed to "hide, shroud, and cloak" his plans to destroy the Second Amend-ment.[28] It must have come as a relief when the president finally spoke out against guns after Sandy Hook: at last, the NRA was vindicated. Here, LaPierre could finally say, is the real face of our Democratic president, eager for regulation, hungry for power, seeking to exert control over law-abiding, freedom-loving gun owners and the unwitting public whose liberty they protect. As gun rights advocates suspected all along, the presi-dent wants to strip the people of their sovereignty.

The NRA was a staunch supporter of Republican presiden-tial candidates in the 2008 and 2012 elections—though the pre-vious Republican administration, freshly removed from power in 2008, had compromised civil rights gravely, in the name of fighting terrorism. And even while LaPierre suggested to Obama that the game was up—gun owners would not tolerate expansive government and its call for greater regulation, greater control over our society—the president was busy dealing far deadlier blows to individual liberties. As many political com-mentators have noted, Obama, who rode to victory on a critique of civil rights offenses involved in the Bush administration's

War on Terror, broadened the War on Terror in ways that might have shocked his predecessor. Contrary to the bold proclamations of the gun rights movement, the massive private arsenal amassed by the American public, augmented after the 2008 and 2012 elections, hardly served as a deterrent against government expansion—and provided no protection against it.

The War on Terror, now in its second decade, has been a crucible for civil libertarians. Critics have bemoaned the expansions of executive power committed in the name of a war that has no clear borders or enemy. The president has claimed the right to detain individuals indefinitely—American citizens or not—if they are merely suspected of involvement with a terrorist organization. The executive branch has denied such individuals the right to trial by jury, a right supposedly extended to all American citizens. It has held foreign terror suspects at the Guantanamo Bay detention camp for years without bringing them even to a military trial—and often without leveling formal charges against them. Furthermore, it has come to light that the president has approved the use of torture to extract information from terror and enemy suspects at our government's secret prisons around the world. In sum, this war has seen our government engage in all manner of activities commonly deemed un-American, or uncharacteristic of the respect we accord human rights and individual freedoms. On our shores, this has entailed what many consider direct assaults on the U.S. Constitution.

The PATRIOT Act, enacted shortly after 9/11, greatly expanded the executive branch's abilities to accumulate information from the civilian population through wire taps on our phone calls, spying on our email and Internet activity, even keeping tabs on the books we borrow, much to the ire of the nation's librarians. The government's ability to circumvent privacy protections and spy on the U.S. public, ostensibly to track down suspicious behavior and prevent terrorist attacks before they occur, has been assisted by the cooperation of the FISA (Foreign Intelligence Surveillance) Court, which operates in secret. The government brings its surveillance requests before a judge in secret, who issues a warrant in secret, whereupon surveillance of the subject may proceed in secret. The methods and justifications in these cases are not open to scrutiny—and FISA judges have hardly proven tough critics for the executive branch, approving over 99 percent of surveillance requests.[29] This prompted one senator to call the FISA court "the most one-sided legal process in the United States."[30]

In an expansion of power his bellicose predecessor did not dare, President Obama claimed the right to assassinate U.S. citizens without due process. When one man discovered that his son, American citizen Anwar al-Awlaki, was on the president's "kill list," he sought a court order barring the president from assassinating him. The judge threw out the case, accepting the government's argument that it had indicted al-Awlaki on the basis of presidential military decisions that no court had the right to review. As journalist Glenn Greenwald wrote, al-Awlaki "was simply ordered killed by the President: his judge, jury and executioner."[31] He was subsequently killed by a drone strike, as was his teenage son, also a U.S. citizen, shortly thereafter (the government claimed this was a mistake). Justifying its assassination of Anwar al-Awlaki without due process, the U.S. government claimed he had abdicated the rights of citizenship by his association with Al Qaeda and vocal support for terrorist activities. "U.S. citizens do not have immunity when they are at war with the United States," government lawyers explained.[32] This is a nebulous determination, not least because the president does not have to reveal his indictments of U.S. citizens in such cases or justify them to a civil court. What constitutes "being at war with the United States"? Attorney General Eric Holder offered this justification for the killing of al-Awlaki: "When individuals take up arms against this country and join al-Qaeda in plotting attacks designed to kill their fellow Americans, there may be only one realistic and appropriate response."[33] Yet al-Awlaki did not "take up arms" against the United States, and many pointed out that his contribution to Al Qaeda was secondary. He did not organize or take part in attacks, though he praised them robustly in social media and advised sympathizers on how they might join the cause. It was argued that he had "radicalized" certain individuals who carried out terrorist actions, and thus incited those attacks.

Even before al-Awlaki's assassination, Greenwald argues, the president several times violated the First Amendment protections of U.S. citizens. He writes, "the First Amendment not only protects the mere 'attending' of a speech 'promoting the violent overthrow of our government,' but also the giving of such a speech. The government is absolutely barred by the Free Speech clause from punishing people even for advocating violence."[34] In addition to violating the First Amendment as well as the Fifth, critics have complained that the administration also defies the Fourth Amendment. Under this amendment, Andrew Napolitano writes,

only judges issue search warrants and only after the governmental agency seeking the warrants presents evidence under
oath of probable cause of crime. Regrettably, that was weak-
ened after 9/11 with the enactment of the Patriot Act. The
Patriot Act—written in defiance of the Constitution and in
ignorance of our history—permits federal agents to write their
own search warrants, just as the king and Parliament had permitted British soldiers to do.[35]

He points out that the Fourth Amendment also obliges the
government to provide clear limits on what and whom it aims
to search, but the 2013 leaks that exposed the government's
collection of individuals' digital data revealed that it ignores
such limits and sifts through the data indiscriminately, looking for signs of suspicion instead. Ironically, when he was a
senator, Obama criticized a provision of the PATRIOT Act
"which allows the government to obtain 'business records'
that are 'relevant' to a terrorism investigation," because it effectively sanctions "government fishing expeditions targeting
innocent Americans."[36] These threats to key provisions of the
Bill of Rights have prompted columnist Peter van Buren to
declare that we have entered the era of "Post Constitutional
America." While that may be extreme, it is undeniable that
the War on Terror has enhanced the president's powers.

Yet LaPierre's legions of gun owners have done nothing
to stop it. Quite to the contrary, LaPierre's doomsaying routinely invokes the rhetoric of the War on Terror, echoing
government warnings about a shadowy, unpredictable, omnipresent enemy. After the Boston Marathon bombings in April
2013, he said, "How many Bostonians wished they had a gun
two weeks ago? . . . Residents were imprisoned behind the

locked doors of their homes—a terrorist with bombs and guns just outside."[37] The government's War on Terror has been a convenient ally in the case for guns. Never mind that the bombing and the subsequent manhunt that terrorized the residents of nearby Watertown was an extremely rare occurrence involving only two assailants who, we learned afterward, were operating on their own. The extreme fear stoked by the incident, thanks to eager media involvement, was too tempting for LaPierre to ignore: individuals must be armed and prepared for suburban shootouts with bomb-toting terrorists—even though this will likely never come to a neighborhood near you.

Our government urges average citizens to be on heightened alert for even the most unlikely scenarios, increasingly marking our public spaces with billboards telling us to look for signs of suspicious behavior. The NRA happily shares this agenda. Gun owners often call on government to "take it to the terrorists."[38] The "terrorist hunting licenses" that proliferated on car bumpers and rear windshields after 9/11 were often paired with NRA stickers—announcing, presumably, that individual gun owners were happy to assist government efforts to eradicate this nefarious enemy. As Nate Silver reminds us, the majority of gun owners are loyal to the Republican Party, which has been the most consistent and vocal cheerleader for government's expanded powers in the War on Terror. In sum, the gun rights crowd has largely abetted the growth of government powers they otherwise abhor.

Gun rights groups position themselves as staunch defenders of the Constitution. They claim to be uniquely and supremely devoted to the document, as it was intended by our Founding Fathers. But it seems clear that they really have just one provision in mind, and a specific reading of that. Conveniently, they maintain that the Second Amendment is the most critical provision, which protects the other liberties laid out in the Bill of Rights. Evidence suggests otherwise. While busily expanding and strengthening gun rights for individual owners, they have allowed other rights to be challenged and undermined by the War on Terror. To understand this disconnect, we must examine how gun rights advocates characterize government abuse of rights, and what, in their view, expansions of power look like.

Following the bloody incidents at Ruby Ridge and Waco, Texas, in the early 1990s, many in the gun rights movement took to warning of a government invasion and occupation of the civilian population, on the pretext of enforcing gun regulations. In an article on the rise of the militia movement during this period, a movement galvanized by gun rights extremists incensed over these incidents, Daniel Junas writes of town meetings across Montana punctuated by warnings of "black helicopters sighted throughout the U.S. . . . and preparation for an invasion by a hostile federal government aided by U.N. troops seeking to impose a New World Order."[39] For LaPierre, Ruby Ridge and Waco presaged a slightly different threat, but one that was no less sinister. In a 1995 letter criticizing expanded gun control legislation, LaPierre declared that "the semi auto ban gives jack-booted government thugs more power to take away our constitutional rights, break in our doors, seize our guns, destroy our property and even injure or kill us. . . . Not too long ago, it was unthinkable for federal agents wearing Nazi bucket helmets and black storm trooper uniforms to attack law-abiding citizens"—but no more.[40] An article in *American Rifleman* two years later decried ATF agents "clad in ninja black" who were nothing more than "armed terrorists" intent on "harassing, intimidating and hurting honest citizens [with] the brute force of unchecked, renegade federal power."[41] Many criticized gun rights groups for their extreme claims. But the bloodshed at Ruby Ridge and Waco represented, in LaPierre's view, the real face of government intervention—the face of a government with totalitarian designs intent on subjugating the populace. A 1993 NRA ad featuring an image of goose-stepping soldiers starkly asked, "What's the first step to a police state?"[42] Apparently, it's gun regulation.

Gun rights advocates conjure oppressive government in physical form: there will be helicopters in the skies and black-clad thugs at our doors. Gun owners wait with semiautomatic weapons to repel them. But it seems the instruments of twenty-first-century oppression will look very different, especially on our shores. As French philosopher Michel Foucault argues, the modern nation-state increasingly exerts control through "disciplinary power," which includes subtle, nearly invisible methods of manipulation.

Disciplinary power, Foucault tells us, resorts not to overt force but to far less conspicuous, more intricate, pervasive, and thorough means. He speaks of a "microphysics of power," where control is exerted through the minute ordering of space, time, and bodies. Disciplinary power entails the realization that new approaches might ensure superior, or as Foucault likes to say, more efficient and enduring methods of control. He traces its emergence through the Enlightenment, when, against the concerns issued by Rousseau and Toc-queville, the ruling interests believed that disciplinary power served them with methods that might "produce states impervious to decline."[43]

At one time, Foucault argues, power exerted itself through horrific displays of violence and torture. With the emergence of disciplinary power, such overt displays disappear, and power angles for new expressions—namely, none—and a new home: it will no longer loom from on high but seek to insert itself inside the daily lives of its subjects. Through the exhaustive ordering of space, bodies, and time, exhibited in the design of factories, schools, prisons, and hospitals, power greatly expands its scope; indeed, the sameness of building designs indicates how power aims to seep into all facets of life. Disciplinary power is anonymous, Foucault argues, and automatic. It has no clear and obvious face, and proceeds through the subjects themselves. It is unverifiable and invisible. As such, it is immensely efficient: it exerts maximum effect with the least immediate or direct effort. One perennial danger of the overt force of the king, expressed for example through public executions, is that it reminds the population that they are oppressed, and who their oppressor is. This becomes intolerable for a people accustomed to freedom, and it may incite rebellion. The ruling interests need a way to achieve domination in harmony with individual liberty. Their agenda must proceed as if by their subjects' voluntary action.

Disciplinary power achieves its aspirations most perfectly, Foucault argues, in the prison design put forth by the eighteenth-century philosopher and social reformer Jeremy

Bentham, dubbed the Panopticon: prisoners are held individually in transparent cells arrayed around a central watchtower, which would be shaded so the watchmen could see out without being seen themselves. The panoptic scheme exemplifies the features of disciplinary power. Authority is anonymous, unverifiable, invisible. It is automatic and enduring, because the prisoners do not know when they are watched but must presume they are watched all the time, so they effectively come to discipline themselves. This is power at its most subtle and efficient. "Panoptic institutions could be so light," Foucault writes.[44] Their design is open and airy, transparent, hardly oppressive in any obvious way. This design can be applied to all manner of structures, on the premise that it is liberating. Office floors can be open and transparent, so that everyone may know what everyone else is doing, and there is no laziness, corruption, or favoritism—but workers can also be spied on more effectively. Better yet, outfit work stations with cubicles, to give employees a modicum of privacy and personal freedom—then they can be individualized under watchful eyes.

It is critical to the panoptic scheme that subjects be individualized. People wither under surveillance if isolated, Foucault points out, and so are easier to manipulate. To this extent, he argues, individualism, so prized in liberal democracies, suits power nicely: people must be isolated from one another to be controlled. "In a disciplinary regime," he writes, "individualization is descending: as power becomes more anonymous and functional, those on whom it is exercised tend to be more strongly individualized; it is exercised by surveillance rather than ceremonies."[45] These are solemn words for the gun rights movement's drive to assert the sovereignty and independence of the individual. The NRA empowers individuals to become one-man armies—and their weapons, I have argued, are an isolating force. This is precisely the result disciplinary power wants.

Bentham did not live to see a Panopticon erected. Not many prisons employed his design to the fullest, but the political lessons of the Panopticon were not lost. The panoptic scheme endures in more devastating fashion than Bentham or Foucault ever imagined, thanks to digital technologies and the surveillance tools they provide those who would watch us.

In the War on Terror, the U.S. government has claimed broad rights to survey the civilian population. The ACLU laments the rise of "America's Surveillance Society" in a report of the same name: since 2001, the FBI has compelled Internet service providers, banks, and others to provide sensitive private information about their clients, all "without prior court approval and without probable cause"; the National Security Agency (NSA) carries out "warrantless surveillance of Americans' international telephone calls and e-mails"; and the American public is subjected to "pervasive video surveillance."[46] "An increasing number of American cities," the report states, "have spent taxpayer dollars to create elaborate camera and video surveillance systems designed to monitor public places such as parks, plazas and sidewalks. Governments are also accessing images collected by privately-owned camera and video systems."[47] Following the Boston Marathon bombing, law enforcement used widespread access to private cell phone videos and photos taken at the site, together with footage from surveillance cameras from businesses, to track down the perpetrators. This seemed a reasonable approach, the Boston police commissioner opined, since the site of the marathon was "probably one of the most photographed areas in the country" that day.[48] By allowing us to record ourselves and those around us abundantly, digital technology fashions a tantalizing network for government to tap into if it wishes.

Digital technology has also given rise to billions of communications—e-mails, tweets, text messages, Facebook updates, and good old phone calls—all of which are available for surveillance. Through such communications, twenty-first-century Americans conduct their increasingly public lives; "private life" conducted on the Internet or through mobile phones is not private at all. The GPS signals in our cell phones make our location perpetually known—and it turns out that law enforcement has access to that information. We happily indulge in these media, of course, because of the wonderful conveniences they provide, but in so doing, we offer government all the information it might care to learn about us. In 2012, *Wired* magazine called the information the NSA aims to collect about us "digital pocket litter":

> Flowing through [the NSA's] servers and routers stored in near-bottomless databases will be all forms of communication, including the complete contents of private emails, cell phone calls, and Google searches, as well as all sorts of personal data trails—parking receipts, travel itineraries, bookstore purchases. . . . It is, in some measure, the realization of the "total information awareness" program created during the first term of the Bush administration—an effort that was killed by Congress in 2003 after it caused an outcry over its potential for invading Americans' privacy.[49]

The *Wired* article was prescient. A year after its publication, a prominent leak by a private NSA contractor revealed that the agency was engaged in just such immense data collection and analysis—"secret blanket surveillance," as Al Gore put it, which he declared "obscenely outrageous."[50] Government officials claimed that the NSA had not violated anyone's civil rights because it was only storing the communications and analyzing the "metadata"—that is, as Hendrik Hertzberg observed in the *New Yorker*, "the time and duration of the calls, along with the number, and potentially the locations of the callers and the called," all of which is analyzed to detect suspicious patterns.[51] The agency, as of 2013, still needs a judicial warrant to inspect the contents of communications it deems suspicious. Yet this is still plenty of information the government is amassing about private citizens. This metadata tells an awful lot about a person: whom he is contacting and associating with, where, and when—where he is parking, where he is going, when he is traveling, and much else. *Washington Post* reporter Barton Gellman argues that government monitoring of metadata is in fact "more intrusive":

> I would much rather someone listen to my phone calls for a month than to have them map who I've talked to, where I went, all my connections for a month, because I can control what I say on the phone. You get a much more revealing picture of people, for example, who are my confidential sources, or whether I'm negotiating to leave my employer and take a new job or a secret business deal, whether I'm having an extramarital affair, whether I'm seeing a psychiatrist. Anything that I might not want to broadcast to the world will be revealed quite clearly from metadata.[52]

As if NSA's efforts were not far-reaching enough, our government has other surveillance tools at its disposal, most notably drone technology, which is returning from foreign battlefields for domestic use. Several government agencies employ drone surveillance with increasing regularity, as does local law enforcement. When the Federal Aviation Administration approved the use of surveillance drones for commercial purposes in 2013, it predicted there would be 30,000 drones (or UAVs—unmanned aviation vehicles) in our skies by 2020 doing public and private work.[53] Government agencies aim to arm drones, too, but have limited their plans to nonlethal weapons for the moment.[54] It seems the options for armed drones are quite chilling. Greenwald highlights the "Switchblade drone," for example, hailed as "the ultimate assassin bug," which "worms its way around buildings and into small areas, sending its surveillance imagery to an i-Pad held by the operator, who can then direct the Switchblade to lunge forward and kill the target . . . by exploding in his face."[55] It should be abundantly clear that civilians armed with semiautomatic weapons are no match for government-deployed Switchblades.

Beyond the remarkable fact of its existence, the emerging surveillance state contains several noteworthy features. For one thing, it is an impressive merger of public and private sectors. The commercial stake many have in the surveillance state means it is sure to grow. Second, expanded surveillance is less and less controversial. The PATRIOT Act has been renewed every three years since its inception, by members of both parties, with limited objection. The American public seems to have accepted the arguments for widespread and intrusive surveillance as a necessary tool in an age of terrorism. Or at least, the public is too preoccupied to care, as people dive into the myriad new technologies that allow them to be watched. Third, the surveillance state is a "one-way mirror," as Greenwald puts it.[56] It gives government deep insight into our activities and behavior while those watching us—who they are, what they want, what they know—remain hidden. This was made abundantly clear, Greenwald argues, when Wikileaks, the international journalistic organization that publishes leaked government documents, posted on its website millions of pages of classified U.S. security documents, and most of the exposed communications were in fact quite banal. "What that reflected," Greenwald explains, "is that the U.S. government reflexively labels everything that it does of any conceivable significance as 'classified' and 'secret.' It keeps everything that it does from us, at the same time that it knows more and more about what we're doing."[57]

Why is the surveillance state a concern? The ease with which it grows and envelops us all suggests that most of the American public is not overly disturbed by it. Tocqueville might say this is because the surveillance state has not—yet—gotten in the way of our private interests. To the contrary, the surveillance state, especially in its private sector incarnations, offers our personal lives and business ventures bountiful convenience. The hardware chain Lowe's, for example, advertises that it can keep track of every purchase you make at its stores—to assist you with future purchasing decisions, of course. The American shopper might be thrilled that retailers can provide their wares in so much greater detail, but who else has access to that information?

It is surprisingly hard to articulate why privacy is so important. Why, in an age of terror, should my private life be sacrosanct? The argument is often made that if you are doing nothing illegal, then you have nothing to hide. Privacy seems like an easy sacrifice in this war, and a tedious encumbrance in the digital age. In our eagerness for new technologies, author Gary Shteyngart cites "a general giddy sense that privacy is kind of stupid."[58] Just imagine the possibilities: if everything is known about you, retailers and businesses can cater to your every desire, at any moment—even desires you didn't know you had! And the government might know we are a danger before we realize it ourselves, and act accordingly. This starts to sound a lot like the soft despotism Tocqueville foresaw for us: everything is provided for us, all our personal wants sated. We may feel fulfilled and empowered by our new digital reality—indeed, its devices are sold on the premise that they enable us to do more, and be freer—but as Tocqueville fears, it threatens to reduce us to a state of "perpetual childhood," where we will require potent political consolation. Claire Cain Miller describes how the Google Now app reads her emails and alerts her, without her asking, to bits of highly personal information: "Now I trust it to tell me whether there is a delay on my route to work (even though I never told it where I live or work). How many steps I walk each month, which recipes I should try, when my e-commerce packages have shipped and whether I need to remember to buy diapers next time I am at the store."[59]

A host of moral and political problems arise with our surveillance society, but I will zero in on the most pertinent one for our discussion, the one the gun rights movement supposedly cares so much about. As our privacy is increasingly broached and we live so much more of our lives in public, we become extremely vulnerable. Many interests might wish to take advantage of us in this state, and government is certainly one. Our government vows that it will not abuse, and is not abusing, its privileged knowledge of our private lives, but this puts us at its mercy all the same, perhaps intolerably so. Imagine what an abusive administration might do with all this information. The possibilities for oppression are immense. The only thing preventing such a turn of events is the character of those in office. But it is just such vulnerability that the Founding Fathers aimed to prevent when they designed our government and laid out our rights—and insisted on protecting us against unreasonable search and seizure. The American people must be insulated from the caprices of those in power, since some are sure to be corrupt. Or worse, the power of office will corrupt them. Greenwald argues that "allowing government officials to eavesdrop on other people, on citizens, without constraints or oversight, to do so in the dark, is a power that gives so much authority and leverage to those in power that it is virtually impossible for human beings to resist abusing that power."[60] Surveillance seems quite harmless to all involved. For those in power, it hardly seems like an abuse. It's so easy to survey the public without much protest, and it's easy to increase this power—exponentially.

Gun rights advocates claim to be a prime defense against a government that would gain too much power over the American public. The Founding Fathers intended that we not be at the mercy of those who rule us, but retain a necessary and basic independence. The surveillance state violates that concern. While LaPierre waves his rifle in the face of the government, it has gained immense leverage over us all. What will it do with all this power? Shall we trust it? Can we trust it? It seems most have decided to ignore the danger. That is their right, but the infrastructure of oppression has been put in place, even if it is not deployed for nefarious ends—yet. Of course, there are some who claim it already does great damage.

Hertzberg says the following of the 2013 leaks that revealed the breadth of the NSA's surveillance operations: "The harm is civic. The harm is collective. The harm is to the architecture of trust and accountability that supports an open society and a democratic polity. The harm is to the reputation, and perhaps, the reality of the United States as such a society, such a polity."[61] Surveillance signals, and sows, mistrust—especially when the surveillance is a one-way mirror. Being watched is inherently corrosive of trust. And it is deeply unsettling that the government is so opaque in its intentions and operations. Foucault would be full of admiration for the emerging surveillance state: it is unverifiable, anonymous, invisible. Indeed, he argued, surveillance can be oppression itself. And it is a form of oppression against which guns are wholly ineffective.

For Bentham, the great virtue of the Panopticon was precisely how it might affect subjects' behavior, and *compel*. Foucault offers the following, ebullient quote from Bentham advertising the benefits of the panoptic scheme:

"Morals reformed—health preserved—industry invigorated—instruction diffused—public burthens lightened—Economy seated, as it were, upon a rock—the Gordian knot of the poor-law not cut, but untied—all by a simple idea in Architecture!"[62] For prisoners, anonymous surveillance is a silent and continuous warning that they must watch what they do, and act as the warden expects. Applied to the workplace, the panoptic scheme might ward off temptations to laziness. In short, surveillance is a manner of imposing behavior on those who are watched, snapping them into line. But it is a soft tyranny—and as such, Foucault maintains, especially pernicious.

It is a kind of oppression we hardly notice or worry about. In the digital age, we willingly subject ourselves to surveillance, and facilitate our surveyors' task. Digital technologies make us feel empowered and free, but silently have the opposite effect. Under surveillance, we come to watch what we do without even realizing it. If we are expressly forbidden to associate with a certain political group, we will feel compelled, and register it as coercion—and that might irritate us. If, however, we are *unsure* if we are watched when we visit certain websites or communicate with certain groups, and suspect we might get in trouble for doing so, we will cease, seemingly of our own volition.

Privacy is essential to freedom because it allows us to indulge in eccentric behavior without fear of judgment or incrimination. From discussion of bold, sometimes crazy ideas, brave new political notions are born. Privacy lends an openness and courage to the political arena, a necessary dynamism—it empowers political thinkers and agents at the most basic level. Thus it is essential to democracy, or at least to the aspirations of democratic regimes: if you would embolden citizens to be politically active at every level of society, you require the utter freedom privacy affords. "[Secrecy] and privacy are prerequisites" to political activism and protest, Greenwald argues.[63] What is political opposition to look like, how is it to behave, if it knows it is constantly watched and followed?

Guns do little to protect our freedom in this respect. They are no remedy for the oppression that may be at hand. The surveillance state grows and compels whether we are armed or not. In fact, the gun rights movement inadvertently assists the surveillance state by urging adherents to beware government oppression in a wholly other form—a form in which oppression, in our time, is less likely to emerge.

Greenwald says of the surveillance state, in an assessment that is eerily evocative of guns: "You can acculturate people to believing that tyranny is freedom, that their limits are actually emancipations and freedom, that is what this Surveillance State does, by training people to accept their own conformity that they are actually free, that they no longer even realize the ways in which they're being limited."[64] Guns are likewise a cultural fixation that offers the illusion of freedom—and makes us vulnerable to manipulation, abuse, and oppression. They invite us to feel free and indomitable, while blinding us to the ways in which we are limited and dominated. Accordingly, Machiavelli tells us, those in power are all too happy to see us armed. They nod their heads in approval when Cooke claims guns are the ultimate right of a free people—as LaPierre says, the true mark of liberty! Cooke and LaPierre fail to grasp that modern nation states do not need physical force to put us underfoot. They can achieve oppression in ways that cannot be opposed or hindered by mere guns.

CHAPTER FOUR

Guns and the Threat to Democracy

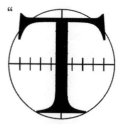

"HE dispersion of physical power in society is both a cause and an affirmation of dispersion of political power."[1] So says gun rights proponent and Cato Institute fellow David Kopel. Guns are essential to democracy, in his view: they give real power to the people. We cannot retain popular sovereignty without privately owned guns, generously dispersed. Guns back up the vote, if you will—they ensure that we are heard, our will heeded, and our sovereignty preserved.

Democracy, gun rights advocates like to remind us, is founded on a violent moment. Power must be ripped from the hands of elites, who do not share it willingly or happily. It must be taken forcibly, through revolution. Gun rights advocates, clearly mindful of Americans' own revolutionary moment, verily worship the Founding Fathers and claim to pose a similar revolutionary threat against standing government today. As they have it, the revolution is ongoing: those whom we elect must be chastened, their ambitions contained. Guns bolster the people's democratic confidence and are a reminder of our revolutionary power, and destiny.

Further, Kopel declares, guns distinguish the particularly American brand of democracy, the most enduring of modern democracies and the inspiration and advocate for emerging democracies around the world. The archetypal heroes of various nations, he argues, are highly indicative:

> The armed Canadian hero is a government employee (the mounted policeman); the armed Japanese hero is an aristocrat (the samurai). Unlike the British knight (with expensive armor), the Japanese samurai (with handcrafted, exquisite sword), or the Canadian mounted policeman (carrying a government-issued handgun that ordinary persons were not allowed to carry), the classic armed American hero—the cowboy—sported a mass-produced Colt .45 that could be bought at a hardware store. The cowboy's Colt revolver was known as the great equalizer . . . because firearms make a smaller, less powerful person functionally equal to a larger person.[2]

That is to say, guns underscore the fundamental equality of American democracy. They ensure that citizens remain equal, and equal to those who hold power. They ensure that the people remain vigilant, mindful citizens, unlike citizens of other so-called democracies, who naively assign control to a new aristocracy of bureaucratic elites. Kopel suggests we shouldn't expect any better from Europe or Japan, steeped as they are in feudal traditions. Only the American experience is democratic through and through. Americans had to be self-reliant from the start, out on the frontier protecting themselves and upholding justice, and guns are central to that experience. Thanks to our gun culture, we on these shores are more resilient democrats, less inclined to slip into submissiveness. The gun debate is thus the central struggle of democracy. "What is ultimately at stake" in the fight over gun control, Kopel argues, "is the same question that precipitated the American Revolution: whether the American people are the sovereigns in their own country or whether they should be ruled from above, for their own good, according to the supposedly benevolent commands of the elitist rulers of a top-down, European-style society."[3]

Wayne LaPierre, expressing similar sentiment, states that the Second Amendment offers "the purest and most precious form of freedom because it is the one freedom that gives common men and women uncommon power to defend all freedoms."[4] Gun rights are the one freedom that guarantees all the others. They are the backbone of democratic power: the "First Freedom," as the title of the NRA's magazine indicates. Legal scholars Joshua Horwitz and Casey Anderson point out that gun rights groups strive to make "freedom" synonymous with gun rights: the NRA organizes a "Freedom cruise" where vacationers can be regaled by gun rights apologists and strategists, and it urges its members to "Vote freedom first," subjugating all other freedoms to gun ownership.[5] To the extent that gun rights are limited in any manner, the NRA says liberty is threatened, as measured in its magazine's "Freedom Index." Horwitz and Anderson point out that this includes measures as seemingly apolitical and innocuous as not hunting mourning doves. When voters in Michigan declined to permit such a hunt, the NRA's index registered a grave injury to our freedom.[6] Increasingly, the NRA argues that we are freer to the extent that gun rights are absolute. Regulation is politically sinister, by definition undermining and threatening freedom.

Author Joan Burbick explains that gun rights groups see the Second Amendment as the "teeth in the Bill of Rights," providing the force that protects and preserves all other rights.[7] The amendments in the Bill of Rights were "ranked in random order," Charlton Heston claims, and the Second Amendment was meant to be first. "Among freedom of speech, of the press, of religion, of assembly, of redress of grievances," he said in a speech to the National Press Club, freedom of gun ownership "is the first among equals. It alone offers the absolute capacity to live without fear. The right to keep and bear arms is the one right that allows 'rights' to exist at all."[8] In the same speech, Heston also explained to the media, whom he deemed unfairly disdainful of guns and their owners, that "our Constitution provides the doorway for your news and commentary to pass through free and unfettered. But that doorway to freedom is framed by . . . muskets."[9] Many citizens do not wish to have a gun; perhaps they sneer at them and scoff at gun owners, or are afraid to own one themselves. Such people, like the smug media, Heston wishes to say, are unwitting beneficiaries of the work performed by gun owners, whose presence ensures that we enjoy any freedom at all.

By this logic, as guns grow more pervasive and subject to fewer regulations, we become more free. Guns carve out the necessary space for us to act and exist as free, democratic citizens—they secure the space for speech, expression, assembly, and protest. There is no freer society than an armed society. And an armed society, where all manner of arms are present and visible in everyday settings—schools, malls, theaters, offices, government buildings, churches—is the goal of the current gun rights movement.

The existence of gun-free zones has become a topic of debate. While they were conceived with good intentions, to safeguard our most vulnerable locations, gun rights advocates maintain that the effort has backfired: gun-free zones advertise themselves to would-be shooters as places where they will encounter little or no resistance. That's why, the argument goes, Adam Lanza targeted Sandy Hook Elementary School—he knew he would not be hindered there. Gun rights advocates point out that James Holmes, the Batman-obsessed shooter who targeted a packed midnight screening of the Batman film *The Dark Knight Rises*, could equally well have gone to six other theaters in Aurora, Colorado, that were showing the film that night. Why did he choose that one theater, when two other potential targets were actually closer to his home? It turns out, John Fund writes in *National Review*, that the theater he chose was the only one of the seven that "posted signs saying it banned concealed handguns carried by law-abiding individuals."[10] Fund suspects that was the deciding factor for Holmes. The Sikh temple in Oak Creek, Wisconsin, attacked by shooter Wade Michael Page in August 2012 was also a gun-free zone, as gun rights groups reminded us at the time. The president of the temple was armed with only a butter knife, and heroically employed it to save others before he was shot and killed. If, however, the temple had permitted guns, some argued, members of this religious minority, often mistaken for Muslims and targeted for prejudice since 9/11, could have protected themselves better.[11]

As law professor Glenn Harlan Reynolds wrote in an opinion piece in *USA Today* following the Newtown shootings, "Policies making areas 'gun free' provide a sense of safety to those who engage in magical thinking, but in practice, of course, killers aren't stopped by gun-free zones. As always, it's the honest people—the very ones you want to be armed—who tend to obey the law. . . . Gun-free zones are premised on a lie: that murderers will follow rules."[12] Citing a study by the celebrated gun rights researcher John Lott, Reynolds claims that the vast majority of mass shootings take place in gun-free zones. He reminds us of cases where victims with access to guns were able to stop mass shootings early on. Lott's findings were no mystery, or mere coincidence, Reynolds maintains. They support Lott's broader claim that more guns mean less crime.

It is a favorite saying of the gun rights movement that "An armed society is a polite society." I have long taken this to mean that arms ensure that citizens will think twice before provoking a confrontation or acting offensively. Gun rights advocates reveal a further meaning, that guns force bearers to behave responsibly: the more people that are armed, the more they will act responsibly, both with their weapons and in their dealings with others. Lott provides data and studies that claim to back up this assertion. Where guns are more pervasive and gun ownership less onerously regulated, he has argued, there is less crime. Gun control groups call for tighter regulations in the belief that they will make us all safer, but Lott turns that argument on its head. Gun rights advocates cite him frequently. Lott's is the decisive word on the subject, they maintain, providing scientific proof of the crime-fighting and freedom-preserving virtues of an armed society.

In his 2000 book *More Guns, Less Crime*, Lott presents the findings of his study of nearly three decades of crime data from jurisdictions across the country—states, cities, counties—and the impact of various gun control laws on crime. The data compel him to assert that states that pass "shall issue" nondiscretionary concealed carry laws have the most success in combating crime.[13] Such laws, he writes, are "the most cost-effective means of reducing crime. The cost of hiring more police in order to change arrest and conviction rates is much higher, and the net benefits per dollar spent are only at most a quarter as large as the benefits from concealed-handgun laws. Even private, medium-security prisons cost state governments [more]."[14] Dollar for dollar, in Lott's view, arming responsible, trained citizens will produce more effective crime fighting and deterrence. Concealed handguns are also "the great equalizer among the sexes" because they offer women the means to fend off rapists or, if they are battered, to shoot or warn off their abusers.[15] Lott maintains that his studies reveal a halo effect of concealed carry laws: "Citizens who have no intention of ever carrying concealed handguns . . . get a 'free ride' from the crime fighting efforts of their fellow citizens," as evidenced, for example, by the "drop in murders of children following the adoption of [nondiscretionary concealed handgun] laws. Arming older people not only may provide direct protection to these children, but also causes criminals to leave the area."[16]

One of the more remarkable features of Lott's work is his use of stirring narratives where guns helped individuals fend off violent criminals—or where the lack of guns meant the opposite. One such story concerns an eighty-year-old man in West Baltimore who was strangled to death after his home had been invaded. It turns out that this man, James Edward Scott, had had a gun, but after he shot a previous intruder, police took it away—presumably in observance of local gun laws (though Lott does not say). Lott quotes a neighbor as saying "If [Scott] would have had a gun, he would be OK."[17] Other neighbors noted that the old man's house had been broken into many times, and he had often been harassed while working in his yard. According to Lott, this case shows that "our legal system cannot provide people with all the protection that they desire," and actually undermines our security insofar as it prevents individuals "from defending themselves."[18]

Yet this case also suggests that individual gun ownership is not an enduring solution for security and is quite flimsy even as a temporary solution. Clearly, other factors need to be addressed first if we would promote Scott's safety and that of his neighbors—and the children on his street. Lott says that guns in the hands of private citizens cause criminals to flee an area. But Scott lived in a rough part of town: his home had been burgled repeatedly, and he was harassed outside his house. West Baltimore is notoriously dangerous, and his neighborhood is the kind that spawns criminal behavior. The dearth of viable employment options and the abundance of negative social factors lead residents into lives of crime—which, in Baltimore, principally means the drug trade. If Scott had had a gun, it would hardly inspire criminals to "leave the area." In Baltimore, where gang members are already well armed, they will know sooner or later that they only require a more powerful weapon if they wish to invade the old man's home. Mr. Scott's gun would not deter any desperate drug addict from breaking into his home. Would he have saved himself on that fateful night if he had had a gun? Perhaps. But because his home was obviously a target in the neighborhood, he most likely would have been outgunned or outmaneuvered sooner or later. Hardened, resolved, well-armed criminals— or strung-out drug addicts—are hardly fearful of guns in the hands of private citizens. The latter are no more than an inconvenience, and no real obstacle to what criminals do or want. In Baltimore's most desperate neighborhoods, where opportunity is bleak and social afflictions vicious, armed citizens will not suddenly cause criminals to wise up, get a job, or move out. If we would really aim for less crime, which Lott claims is the objective of his book, there are broader social conditions that must be addressed. Scott's gun is no better than a tenuous and temporary salve. I don't think for one second he would say it made his life safer, and evidence suggests the contrary. It was a last resort in a desperate situation.

Of course, Lott's solution suits libertarians like David Kopel, as well as the gun rights crowd. He does not broach the messy, expensive, and arduous task of fixing the education system in poor urban centers like Baltimore. Smaller class sizes, better trained and compensated teachers, more thoughtful curricula and testing, and updated facilities would help produce graduates better prepared for the workplace. That would be a boon for inner-city neighborhoods, relieving residents of having to resort to the drug trade, and help them escape the poverty that inspires so much crime. A better set of economic incentives for employers would improve the job opportunities for such graduates. Barring that, we might consider arming and training urban police forces better, and giving them more personnel and funding. Many police officers will tell you that we must also address the nation's drug problem. The United States consumes fully a third of the illegal drugs on the planet, and the drug trade is at the heart of much crime. Baltimore, for example, allocates few resources to drug treatment even though nearly one in ten residents is addicted to drugs. Lott's solution—just arm citizens—is simple and straightforward, and cheaper than any alternative. It avoids complex, expansive social policy. It teaches individual responsibility. And it scares criminals straight.

But if we do not address the real drivers of crime, then individually owned guns are at best a stopgap solution. They may occasionally save some lives, but they do not on the whole make us safer. In a world where more and more people must walk the streets armed, I wager, they would hardly consider themselves safe. Guns are a sign of insecurity—at the very least, they are no deterrent to criminals who are resolved, ruthless, and well armed. If we do not address the underlying causes of crime, it is not hard to see that a plethora of guns is a toxic ingredient added to the mixture.

I have presumed thus far that Lott's study stands up: that it is basically correct in asserting that guns offer citizens a modicum of improved safety, even if it is at best tenuous and temporary. It turns out there is much wrong with his work.

In an article in the *Stanford Law Review*, legal scholars Ian Ayres and John Donohue attack the work of Lott and David Mustard, Lott's collaborator on a paper that prefigured *More Guns, Less Crime* and which provides the book's basic premise. One famous example Lott cites is that of Suzanna Hupp, who in 1991 survived a massacre in a Texas cafeteria in which her parents and twenty-one other people died. Hupp had a gun in her car but was barred from carrying it on her person (this was before concealed carry was legal in Texas). Had she been able to carry her weapon into the restaurant, she claimed afterward, she might have stopped the killer and saved her parents' lives. Ayres and Donohue counter that if more people in the restaurant had been armed when the shooter started his spree, it may well have "added one or more victims" to the death toll.[19] Many gun owners bridle at the suggestion that they might contribute to the carnage—they consider themselves especially responsible, careful individuals—but as we saw in the Empire State Building shootings in August 2012, when police officers inadvertently injured several bystanders while trying to halt a shooter, even trained individuals make errant shots in the heat of the moment.[20] Ayres and Donohue write that "while Lott and Mustard have energetically catalogued the situations in which armed citizens have protected themselves or others, they never acknowledge cases on the other side of the ledger where the presence of guns almost certainly led to killings."[21] Lott's reliance upon statistical analysis to anchor his argument is supposedly the decisive element, but Ayres and Donohue are not alone in taking issue with that aspect of Lott's work. After examining Lott and Mustard's data and extending their dataset over time, Ayres and Donohue conclude that "the statistical evidence that [concealed carry] laws have reduced crime is limited, sporadic, and extraordinarily fragile. Minor changes of specifications can generate wide shifts in the estimated effects of these laws."[22]

Lott, through two colleagues, issued a response to Ayres and Donohue in which he extended the dataset and claimed to save his thesis. Ayres and Donohue, examining Lott's rebuttal, discovered "severe coding errors that, when corrected, thoroughly obliterated the attempt to confirm the *More Guns, Less Crime* thesis. Similar coding errors . . . have cropped up elsewhere in Lott's work."[23] Chris Mooney, writing on the controversy in *Mother Jones*, says that "a charge of coding errors, while not unheard of, is embarrassing, since it implies that only by using mistaken data can Lott preserve his thesis. The errors might have been accidental, but since the *Stanford Law Review* exchange, Lott has continued to defend the erroneous work."[24] In 2004, the National Academy of Sciences weighed in on the controversy and found that Lott was not justified in drawing the conclusions that he did. In its press release, the National Academy of Sciences stated: "There is no credible evidence that 'right-to-carry' laws . . . either decrease or increase violent crime."[25]

The credibility of Lott's claims has been thrown in doubt by other strange incidents. "Pressed by critics," Mooney explains, Lott "failed to produce evidence of the existence of a survey, which supposedly found that '98 percent of the time that people use guns defensively, they merely have to brandish a weapon to break off an attack'—that he claimed to have conducted in the second edition of *More Guns, Less*

Crime."[26] Lott said he lost the survey data when his computer crashed. In a later work, *The Bias Against Guns*, public health researcher David Hemenway writes, Lott claims that changes in state gun laws resulted in "a 72 percent [reduction] in Indiana's violent crime rate and a 102 percent reduction in Indiana's auto theft rate." But this is another case of dubious statistics, for Hemenway points out that this would have required "a crime miracle . . . a negative car theft rate, which must mean thieves returning cars."[27] Perhaps the most bizarre turn of events came when an avid online supporter of Lott's work—one "Mary Rosh"—turned out to be Lott himself. As the editor-in-chief of *Science* magazine commented, "In most circles, this goes down as fraud."[28]

In their edited book *Reducing Gun Violence in America*, Johns Hopkins public health researchers Daniel Webster and Jon Vernick provide summaries of several studies on the impact of widely available and unregulated guns on crime and safety. Their findings undermine many of Lott's arguments, and certainly his overarching suggestion that more guns make for a safer society. Examining the data, the authors of one of the book's chapters state that "the U.S. is not a more violent country than other high-income nations. Our rates of car theft, burglary, robbery, sexual assault and aggravated assault are similar to those of other high income countries." But "when Americans are violent, the injuries that result are more likely to prove fatal" thanks to the easy access to guns.[29] "For example," these authors continue, "the U.S. rate of firearm homicide for children 5 to 14 years of age is thirteen times higher than the firearms homicide rate of other developed nations, and the rate of homicide overall is more than three times higher."[30] This runs counter to Lott's supposition that more guns in the hands of responsible adults would make our children safer; the contrary is occurring. The authors say their findings reveal that "states with higher rates of household firearm ownership had significantly higher victimization rates for men, for women, and for children," and that "gun ownership was most strongly associated with an increased risk of homicide by a family member or intimate acquaintance."[31] Guns don't reduce crime, but they do transform it—and not for the better. They make violent outcomes more likely.

These researchers also dispute Lott's suggestion that guns are the great equalizer of the sexes. They report that "a gun in the home is a particularly strong risk factor for female homicide victimization, with the greatest danger for women coming from their intimate partners."[32] Lott might be right in theory, that women could conceivably use guns to protect themselves if the weapons are available in the home, in their purse, or on their body, but it seems he is not right in practice, and it is easy to see why: if there is a gun in the home, the batterer is just as likely to use it as the victim—indeed, the batterer, with a tendency toward violence and abuse, is more likely to use it if available. Further, a gun is at least as likely to escalate an instance of abuse as to defuse it. If the batterer sees a gun raised on him, he may simply know better for next time and prepare himself accordingly. In a situation with repeated, nonrandom encounters, it is silly to think that a gun makes one "safer." It largely elevates the degree of personal risk.

Webster and Vernick provide a host of studies from other nations, such as Australia and Great Britain, which have both succeeded in reducing violent crime and firearm mortality by imposing greater restrictions on guns. In his essay on Brazil's experience regulating firearms, Antonio Rangel Bandeira writes that "of the nearly 30 countries that have promoted voluntary disarmament, none is a dictatorship. Democracies seek to reduce the level of armament in their society, depending instead on good police and a strong rule of law to achieve public safety."[33] Bandeira appears to be mindful of arguments put forth by American gun rights groups: regulation, he argues, is carried out *by* and *in* democracies and has not led to totalitarianism, contrary to NRA predictions.

There is no shortage of arguments and studies like those compiled by Webster and Vernick. It does not take much imagination to understand why these researchers found what they did: more guns in the hands of more people, and regulated loosely, equal more gun-related deaths and greater temptation for violent criminals or violent avengers. These are deadly tools that children might get their hands on and experiment with. Or they might emulate the characters they see on television and in video games. Guns needlessly escalate violent encounters; what might culminate in a fistfight instead may lead to a shooting. Brandishing a weapon in the heat of an argument elevates the dispute to another level. It is a definitive, and ominous warning that peaceful negotiation and persuasion may be beyond reach. Gun advocates value their weapons on precisely this account: the gun on my hip says "don't mess with me." But it also tells the other party that this person is not of a mind to negotiate. If he is to be dealt with roughly—by a criminal or an adversary—it will have to be with a gun. A visible gun amounts to a dare; it says, "if you want to challenge me, this is how." And in an armed society, that challenge is more likely to come.

Lott suggests a correlation between permissive concealed carry laws and greater safety, but public health researchers maintain that looser gun laws mean more violent crime, and more gun-related deaths, including suicides. I suspect that gun rights advocates would say that the gun-related deaths in America, excluding suicides, are by and large not the work of *trained* and *responsible* gun owners but of negligent folk, or better yet, criminals. What Lott really tells us, then, is that more guns in the hands of *trained* and *responsible* gun owners will make for fewer gun-related deaths. As LaPierre might say, we just need more trained and responsible gun owners to make society safer. Yet even trained individuals—police officers—sometimes make grave mistakes. It is difficult to imagine what level of training would have made the Aurora movie theater safer when James Holmes barged in, threw two teargas canisters, and unleashed a barrage of bullets. The armed, responsible individuals—"good guys with guns," in LaPierre's famous phrase—would have been shooting at a target obscured by smoke and darkness, in a crowded, frenzied room. Gun rights groups suppose that "bad guys" are readily identified, but they are not. In the 2011 shooting at a shopping center in Tucson, Arizona, where eight people died and Representative Gabrielle Giffords was gravely injured, it turns out that one individual in the crowd actually had a gun and drew it to kill the shooter. But he identified the wrong man and nearly pulled the trigger on an innocent bystander.[34]

More guns mean more gun-related mistakes, even if they are owned by people with training. For example, Adam

Lanza, the Newtown shooter, got his weapons from his mother, who frequented shooting ranges and had earned NRA training certificates.[35] He used his mother's guns to kill her before going to Sandy Hook Elementary School. Gun rights advocates like Harlan Reynolds object to increased regulations on the ground that they are an affront to responsible gun owners. Gun rights advocates also complain that public health studies on gun-related violence suggest that guns are symptomatic of some kind of disease, or brand their owners as sick in some way. Reynolds calls gun-free zones "an insult to honest people."[36] Increased regulation and gun-free zones do not necessarily imply that gun owners are dishonest, just that they are human and liable to the occasional mistake, or more important, that their weapon might fall into the hands of people who *are* dishonest and prone to mistakes. When the latter persons are armed, the presence of armed and honest NRA members will not make us appreciably safer. The honest gun owner is liable to be gunned down too, especially when he draws his weapon on the shooter—making himself target number one and endangering everyone near him.

Armed individuals in public, the NRA tells us, are our best hope for a modicum of security in the event of a mass shooting. The problem is, as guns proliferate unregulated, mass shootings may well increase. We thus find ourselves in an odd predicament where the NRA's argument rings true because we are perpetually facing worst-case scenarios. A 2013 article in the *American Journal of Medicine* states that "abundant gun availability facilitates firearm-related deaths. Conversely, high crime rates may instigate widespread anxiety and fear, thereby motivating people to arm themselves and give rise to increased gun ownership, which in turn, increases availability. The resulting vicious cycle could, bit by bit, lead to the polarized status that is now the case with the U.S."[37]

The NRA might say that armed individuals in the darkened Aurora movie theater, even shooting errantly and hitting innocent bystanders, are at least better than nothing in the midst of a massacre. This argument works well in a dangerous world: guns are our best, last resort. Of course, the NRA has also done a great deal to *bring about* this dangerous world. In a world where criminals are armed well—even neighbors you might argue with on the street—and mass shootings are possible in even the most unlikely places, a gun seems increasingly like a good idea, as the last measure to ensure one's personal safety. The NRA is not wrong in this regard, it's just remarkable how the organization has been so successful in helping to create that world where its arguments ring true. A highly armed society like ours is bound to be dangerous—and in a dangerous society, where rule of law is increasingly eroded and deadly violence more likely, a gun is increasingly the only thing providing a chance of personal security. But who wants to live in that world? And why must we think such a world is inevitable? Almost every other democracy has less deadly violence than the United States. The NRA's claim that a dangerous world is inevitable seems valid only if arms are widespread.

It is possible that "guns save lives," as gun rights advocates claim, but they bring no enduring safety. At best, they maintain a tense, fragile substitute, like the electric détente when two warring gangs hold each other off with pointed weapons. When two groups deter one another in this manner, I don't think we are justified in calling that peace, or security. The NRA's recipe is not that for a civil society, just the best we can hope for in the "Mad Max" world that LaPierre likes to invoke. But in our American democracy, we have higher ambitions.

According to NRA logic, because one cannot predict when and where insane killers will show up, it makes sense for people to be armed all the time, everywhere. We must carry guns in our restaurants and bars, hospitals and churches, government buildings and private workplaces—anywhere an attack could conceivably occur. But even if this were not a false security, the price is too high. An armed society, where guns and gun ownership are unlimited, threatens rights that are essential to democracy.

One way to understand guns' threat to freedom and democracy is to imagine their effect on academia, where we nurture the civic values our citizens are to embody. Following several mass shootings over the past few years, the debate concerning guns in our schools and on our college campuses has proven especially rancorous. After the Virginia Tech massacre in 2007, when a student embarked on a campus shooting rampage that left thirty-two people dead and seventeen wounded, there were loud calls for students and professors to be armed in the classroom to halt such attacks in the future. After the Newtown shootings, LaPierre unveiled the NRA's master solution: the National School Shield, which called for placing police officers or armed guards in every school in America or, barring that, arming teachers and school staff.

The answer to gun violence in our schools and on our college campuses, according to the gun rights crowd, is more guns, not fewer. Several jurisdictions have followed this advice.

Reynolds points out that it took police twenty minutes to show up at the scene of the shooting in Newtown. "Five minutes is forever when violence is underway," he writes, "but 20 minutes—a third of an hour—means that the 'first responders' aren't likely to do much more than clean up the mess."[38] We need armed individuals on the scene if we have any hope of halting a massacre. One Texas superintendent instituted a policy of arming staff and teachers in his rural school district years before the Newtown incident. At the time, he justified his decision by saying that "our people just don't want their children to be fish in a bowl. . . . Country people are take-care-of-yourself people. They are not under the illusion that the police are there to protect them."[39] Arming teachers and staff in our schools, then, is a sign of self-reliance, a traditional American virtue.

But there are several problems with the NRA proposal. A practical concern is that it is extremely expensive. Many have wondered where the personnel would come from to place armed guards in each of the nation's 100,000-plus schools. It is an especially galling measure for school districts that are forced to make deep budget cuts elsewhere. The *Washington Post* profiled efforts by the Butler County school district in Pennsylvania to roll out the NRA's recommendations: "Butler County had cut 75 teaching and administrative positions in the past five years because of a shrinking budget, but now the district of 7,500 students couldn't hire armed guards fast enough."[40] Yet it is worth asking if armed guards are even an effective solution. There was an armed guard at Columbine High School on the day of its fateful shooting, and though he fired at the assailants, he failed to stop them. Furthermore, the guard's presence failed to deter the shooters. They selected this target, it seems, because they bore a grudge against the school and their peers; they could not have acted out their morbid finale in any other setting. Further, like Adam Lanza at Sandy Hook, the shooters were very well armed and prepared. How is an armed guard supposed to stop such people when they are truly bent on their task? How much training, preparation, and vigilance will guards require? And how is an armed guard to protect an entire school? If he or she is placed at the front door, the shooter may simply bypass the main entrance and shoot his way through a classroom window or blow open a locked side door.

Is the answer then *more* armed guards? Should we outfit our schools with bulletproof glass? Banish windows entirely, or put a gun in the hands of every teacher? By suggesting that we simply arm our schools, the NRA would put us on a path that grows steadily more untenable and oppressive to freedom. The NRA's solution is always more guns: if there is a shooting, it's because not enough guns were there, or enough trained shooters. But where does this end? Critics of the School Shield program argue that it would turn our schools into "armed fortresses," and it is not clear that is good for anyone except for the businesses arming our schools.[41]

There is no shortage of such businesses. A Colombian company has designed bulletproof backpacks for schoolchildren, and also bulletproof safety vests that it hopes schools will store in their classrooms in case of a "ballistics emergency."[42] An

American manufacturer has started selling bulletproof white-boards for the classroom, which teachers might use to protect themselves and their students. Hardwire LLC also produces "bulletproof clip boards . . . as well as a bulletproof insert that can be placed in a child's backpack . . . [and] a bullet-stopping cover that can be affixed to a classroom door."[43] Many schools have started installing "Sally Ports," the secured entrance system typically found in prisons. But at what cost will we turn our schools into fortresses? What is the cost to education, to our children's emotional development, and to democracy?

Consider a recent *New York Times* report that increased police presence in schools has led to "a surge in criminal charges against children for misbehavior that many believe is better handled in the principal's office," such as "scuffles, truancy and cursing at teachers."[44] Those who are not trained teachers or school administrators may well misjudge student behavior and deal with it in a fashion that escalates the confrontation at hand. One criminologist states that "there is no evidence that placing officers in the schools improves safety . . . and it increases the number of minor behavior problems that are referred to the police, pushing kids into the criminal system."[45]

The *Washington Post* reported that the school district in Butler County, Pennsylvania, had "unarmed guards . . . hired after Columbine," "metal detectors . . . installed after Virginia Tech," and "the intercom and surveillance system . . . updated after Aurora."[46] Following the Newtown shooting, Butler County's superintendent deemed those measures insufficient and decided to introduce armed guards. The article goes on to describe one such hired guard in his new post—Frank Cichra, a former cop: "He loaded one bullet into the chamber so he could fire instantaneously in case of an attack and 11 more into a magazine. He sat at a desk facing the glass doors, his eyes scanning the parking lot. A sergeant had told him once that a good state trooper operated like a traffic light on yellow, always on edge, anticipating whatever might come."[47] This is a useful if worrisome metaphor. How "on edge" should he be for the next Adam Lanza? The *Post* article describes Cichra at his post, greeting and inspecting students as they file in. One ten-year-old girl sets off the metal detector, which prompts Cichra to sift through the contents of her lunch bag: "String cheese. Goldfish cracker. Chocolate milk."[48] It is no victory for freedom when armed guards check our children's lunch bags after they have had to enter school through metal detectors. Such developments should give us pause, but instead, the NRA urges us to arm everyone—in the name of freedom.

As if anticipating the adverse impact of his presence on the school's educational mission, the *Post* article states, Cichra "had decided the best way to carry a gun in an elementary school was to act nothing at all like a person carrying a gun," even removing the cover of the book he read at his post, *American Sniper*, which depicted an automatic rifle.[49] "The kids don't need to be seeing that," Cichra said.[50] Why not? Because, as Cichra senses, guns are inimical, even antithetical, to the purpose of our schools. As one superintendent in Massachusetts put it, "To have an armed guard at every school completely sends the wrong message . . . about what schools are about."[51]

Why this is, I will consider shortly. But first it is important to note that gun rights groups are upping the ante in higher education too, urging states to allow students as well as faculty to carry weapons on college campuses. This movement picked up steam after the Virginia Tech shooting, and as of 2013, *USA Today* reports there were "twenty-three states that allow individual colleges or universities to decide if they'll ban concealed weapons on campus" and six that "allow firearms on public university campuses."[52] The NRA is lobbying state legislatures across the country to adopt the policy of the latter six states. Though some legislatures rebuffed those efforts, many lawmakers have vowed to keep pushing for such bills.

The arguments in favor of "campus carry" are largely the same as those for armed guards in our schools: if students and faculty have guns, they will be able to protect themselves and others in the event of a mass shooting. Campus carry bills, advocates argue, signal that colleges are no longer gun-free zones and will deter likely shooters. Yet, there are additional concerns, unique to college campuses. Some worry that it is unwise to introduce guns where young adults sometimes engage in rowdy, drunken behavior, and in their drunkenness might escalate minor arguments into major firefights. Objecting to North Carolina's campus carry bill, one student body president wondered "What about tailgating where alcohol consumption is taking place? Or the fact that theft is the most common crime committed on campus?"[53] Legal scholar Adam Winkler says he has pondered the prospect of an angry student drawing a gun on him if he should issue a failing grade. He admits, however, "there is little evidence to support my gut feeling. Utah, for example, has not seen an increase in campus gun violence since it changed its law in 2006."[54] Still, Winkler maintains, guns on campus are not likely to make much difference in mass shootings. They will not be a deterrent, especially if the shooter is mentally ill or harbors a vendetta against the school, a professor, or his classmates. "Even if a student with a gun can use it to defend against a mass murderer," Winkler writes, "it's hardly clear that anyone, including the armed student, is made safer. Policemen or other students with guns might not be able to differentiate among gunmen, putting the person defending herself at risk of being shot by mistake. Even well-trained gun owners suffer enormous mental stress in a shootout, making hitting a target extremely difficult."[55] In the best case, guns are not likely to make much difference either way with respect to safety. A worst-case scenario is if college-age adults do start to use guns frequently and negligently to resolve disputes or express anger. In the best case, Winkler believes, guns will be seen seldom, if at all, on campus—nor will they really do much to stop determined shooters, or make mass shootings much better. But he believes that none of that is the real objective of the campus carry movement:

> The true motivation is to remove the stigma attached to guns . . . [and] build broader public acceptance of guns. Exposure can breed tolerance. . . . The strategy, however, is risky. Teenagers might begin to see carrying a gun as a mark of adulthood, like smoking and drinking. Without the maturity of age, they might turn to violence too quickly. Gun rights advocates are willing to take these risks because colleges are where the next generation of America's leaders will be produced. What better place to affect people's attitudes about guns than the very institutions responsible for teaching our most cherished values and ideals?[56]

Perhaps Winkler goes too far in accusing gun rights groups of tolerating increased violence in exchange for greater acceptance of guns. I am inclined to give them the benefit of the doubt and assume that they truly believe that more guns equals more safety. Yet Winkler raises valid concerns. Do we want our youth to grow accustomed to guns, perhaps using them routinely to deal with confrontations or perceived offenses? Is it compatible with democracy that guns are part of our everyday methods for dealing with social challenges? And what impact might guns have on the classroom and the sensitive project at hand there?

In the *Stanford Law Review*, Jason Nance offers an assessment of the many security measures used in American schools, including the additional ones recommended by the NRA: "Strict security measures, particularly when used in combination, create a prison-like environment resulting in a deteriorated learning climate for students."[57] He finds that they impose an atmosphere of fear and hostility, suspicion of the outside world, which threatens to seep into the school community itself.

> Strict security measures sour students' attitudes, produce barriers between students and educators, and frequently are a cause of discord within the school community. The use of these measures sends a message to students that they are not to be trusted, that they stand accused of wrongdoing. In fact, some studies cast doubt on whether strict security measures effectively reduce school crime at all. For example . . . [one study found] that schools' reliance on metal detectors, locked doors, locker checks, and security guards may lead to more disorder, crime, and violence.[58]

Why more disorder and not less? Because, Nance explains, these security measures conspire to send the message that the schools' "primary mission is to control students rather than educate them."⁵⁹ People—especially rebellious teenagers—chafe or act out against efforts to monitor, regulate, and subdue them. Further, these measures tell our children that we live in a society at war, one that is unfree to that extent, and that a kind of battlefield mentality is needed to graduate into it.

The constellation of security measures risks leaving an especially deep mark on young children. It teaches them instinctively to mistrust the world. This outlook may be fine with certain gun rights advocates, who as we saw in Chapter 1 believe we are in the midst of a catastrophic social breakdown—yet it is a debilitating outlook for young minds. This is not to say we should teach our kids to trust everyone; to be sure, there are predators out there. But we should not want our children to be consumed by mistrust. We want them, as far as possible, to be liberated from the terror that predators would sow. Armed guard Frank Cichra gets this, hiding the book cover with the gun on it—"kids don't need to be seeing that," he says. He's right. It is not that kids shouldn't know there are guns in the world, and killers, too. But they do not need to be reminded of this all the time, to be told that the world is an awful place where they should be instinctively wary of everyone and anyone, because killers can pop up anywhere and anytime.

Such basic, pervasive, instinctual mistrust is destructive of democracy. It is naïve to accept this blanket suspicion and recommend it, as LaPierre does, and think that it has no larger effect. The cynicism of the gun rights crowd may be the greatest danger it poses: mistrust corrodes society and is not consistent with a viable democracy. Democracy requires a basic openness among its citizens; it demands a fundamental faith that those who are not like us are still accessible, intelligible, not malign: we can reach an accommodation with them.

The famed education theorist Paolo Freire called mistrust a major tool of oppression. Freire was interested in educating the children of oppressed populations with a view to politically empowering them, teaching them to act and behave as invested, willful citizens such as democracy requires. In his most important work, *Pedagogy of the Oppressed*, Freire deplores what he calls the "banking concept" of education, whereby students are deemed fit only to fill up with useful information, digested via rote learning, so that they might become cogs in the machine of society, or in some cases, members of an existing oppressive system.[60] Freire wished that schools might produce individuals who could think critically for themselves, demand their rights, and freely choose their own paths. To that end, he favors a "dialogical theory of education," which he describes as follows: "problem-posing education, which breaks with the vertical patterns characteristic of banking education, can fulfill its function as the practice of freedom only if ... the teacher-of-the-students and the students-of-the-teacher cease to exist and a new term emerges: teacher-student with students-teacher."[61] Dialogue carried out in this manner, problem-posing engaged in collectively by students and teachers, produces a community of questioners in the classroom. It introduces a horizontal relationship—a fundamental equality that will later be politically significant for emergent citizens. Most colleges in twenty-first-century America take Freire's approach—it's how they already conduct learning in the classroom: faculty are urged to create a de-centered classroom where students are not intimidated by professors lecturing from the podium, but rather, engaged in discussion—and direct questioning—by professors who are seated at the same table as students, and who encourage students to speak their minds and experiment with their thoughts. Obviously, Freire's account does not map neatly onto, say, the kindergarten classroom. Children that age need a disciplinary figure, and democracy should not necessarily reign in kindergarten. But, Freire would say, his basic theory bears important intuitions even there: we must still strive to make young students responsive and critical learners, and teach them as far possible horizontally and collaboratively. They are not simply to be lectured to.

The horizontal relationship Freire prescribes for education is of interest because gun rights advocates claim to be invested in a similar project. That is to say—as Kopel suggests at the opening of this chapter—they see their weapons as a means of asserting themselves politically, assuring themselves some political power, and leveling the playing field, as should be the case in a democracy. The gun is how we drag the ruling parties down to our level and forcibly remind them that in a democracy, the people are in power. By its rhetoric, the gun rights movement also declares its intention to combat vertical relationships of power, in favor of horizontal ones.

For Freire, however, the key to achieving this horizontal relationship, not only in the classroom but in society, is dialogue, and dialogue "requires an intense faith in man, faith in his power to make and remake, to create and re-create, faith in his vocation to be more fully human. Faith in man is an a priori requirement for dialogue; the 'dialogical man' believes in other men even before he meets them face to face."[62] There can be no dialogue—no real, substantive exchange—without some basic openness and optimism toward others and the world. Freire urges a loving embrace of humanity that gun rights advocates spurn, and yet he reminds us of a basic point about education—specifically, education aimed at producing a certain type of citizen: equality and political action are undermined to the extent that dialogue is impaired or prevented. And dialogue requires, and in turn produces, trust that mobilizes the power of the people. He writes, "it would be a contradiction in terms if dialogue ... did not produce this climate of mutual trust, which leads the dialoguers into ever closer partnership in the naming of the world. . . . To glorify democracy and to silence the people is a farce."[63] Democracy requires dialogue, which means it requires both the courage to speak out and an openness to hear others. It presupposes some shared identity, that everyone is at least committed to the democratic project. That is what unites us, even if we see eye to eye on nothing else. Democracy implies a basic willingness not to dismiss others out of hand.

What is striking about the gun rights movement, by contrast, is its tendency to write people off. It has an instinctively dismissive approach to segments of the population—criminals, the mentally ill, "bad guys." Liberals too: they can't be partners in dialogue because they don't understand the guns they would regulate. Anyone who recommends gun regulation of any kind is an "enemy of freedom," according to the NRA—and why should anyone talk to an enemy of freedom? As Freire would have it, this is firmly at odds with the aspirations of a system that would cultivate citizens to share a stake in the running of society. To a great extent, the gun rights movement has already abandoned the democratic project: it has decided that portions of society cannot be negotiated with, and government can be negotiated with only by threat of force. In so far as this influential movement has abandoned democracy, it drags the rest of us down with it.

Here it is worth considering the thoughts of John Dewey, who is perhaps the premier philosopher of education in democracy. Dewey believed that the primary purpose of the school is to teach children to be members of society. Skills can be learned elsewhere, but the opportunity to learn how to be active, contributing, peaceable, constructive members of a diverse society is limited, especially when children are otherwise ensconced in family life, which is naturally hierarchical, not democratic. In his essay "My Pedagogic Creed," Dewey states: "I believe that . . . the school is primarily a social institution. Education becoming a social process, the school is simply that form of community life in which all those agencies are concentrated that will be most effective in bringing the child to share in the inherited resources of the race, and to use his own powers for social ends."[64] What new elements, and what new energies, have we concentrated in our schools over the past few years? A major change has been in concentrations of security—fear—and defensive measures. Which in turn proves a powerful lesson for our children.

If they are miniatures of society, as Dewey maintains, our schools provide an important service for the NRA. Schools that are armed and fortified teach children that the world is a dangerous place—they teach students to see manifold defensive gestures as second nature. It's similar to what Winkler detects in the campus carry movement, namely, a program that will accustom our youth to the NRA's dark vision of the world, and to the notion that one should be armed to enter it.

Sounding rather like Freire, Dewey complains that much education in his time "fails because it neglects this fundamental principle of the school as a form of community life. It conceives the school as a place where certain information is to be given."[65] Schools thus neglect their primary moral role. They should not, Dewey believes, impart specific moral values, but they should promote the development of individuals who are morally concerned and conscientious. He writes, "the moral education centers upon this conception of the school as a mode of social life, that the best and deepest moral training is precisely that which one gets through having to enter into proper relations with others in a unity of work and thought."[66] Schools provide a venue where children learn to be with one another, work with one another, and achieve common goals—with all the diplomacy and cooperation those things entail.

Schools provide for the socialization of our children, according to Dewey—not where they might be indoctrinated in a certain set of values, but where they might learn to live in a pluralistic society, one that does not have prescribed goals, but goals that must be decided upon in a community, articulated, and pursued.

Socialization aims to impart certain habits, Dewey maintains; that is its focus, and in our case, these would be habits of interest to a democratic society. "A democracy is more than a form of government," he writes; "it is primarily a mode of associated living, of conjoint communicated experience."[67] The classroom teaches this experience. It is where we will train citizens in a democracy and craft their political instincts—to make them demanding of their rights, for example, also sensitive to the rights of others, and mindful of maintaining the harmony of the whole. "An undesirable society . . . is one which internally and externally sets up barriers to free intercourse and communication of experience," Dewey writes. "A society which makes provision for participation in its good of all its members on equal terms and which secures flexible readjustment of its institutions through interaction of the different forms of associated life . . . is democratic."[68] By "flexible readjustment of its institutions," Dewey means the peaceable transformation of major institutions of power, so that they might better reflect the people's needs and interests. School teaches the essential democratic message that this is achieved not through violence but through communication. In a democracy, schools ought to dispose children to have such habits first and foremost.[69]

A democracy, Dewey maintains, is distinguished by peaceful negotiation—which doesn't mean it is not tense, just not violent; it is also marked by peaceful transitions of power and peaceful transitions in the nature, character, and shape of its ruling institutions. Though born in violent revolt, democracy eschews violence in its inner workings and directs constituent members to achieve change through dialogue and negotiation, collaboration and cooperation. This requires a habitual openness on the part of youth, a willingness to work with others, an interest in others, and a modicum of trust that others might be fruitful partners—that the world outside is worthy and liable of change. With its vision of a fallen world, and the fortresses it would make of our schools, the NRA stands in opposition to this project.

Freire and Dewey remind us that democracy takes root in our schools. As we render them forbidding places, we are likely to see the results in the kind of citizens—and human beings—we produce. We must not take this prospect lightly. What is especially disturbing about this development is that it is not necessary—our schools don't need to be fortresslike. We are choosing to take this route rather than regulate gun ownership, limit the number of weapons out there, and make it harder for people to acquire them. We have chosen instead to turn our schools into bunkers, at great expense—while education funding dwindles—in order to accommodate an alleged absolute right to own guns. It is also a key feature of democracy, a guiding principle of our Founding Fathers, that rights that unduly infringe upon the lives and interests of some, or many, must be curtailed. People may engage in the pursuit of happiness however they like, provided that whatever they deem necessary to that pursuit does not inflict harm or intrude forcefully on the lives of others.

Guns do that. Gun rights, as the NRA currently champions them, are greatly intrusive. The proliferation of guns in our society leads to much collateral damage—innocent bystanders are literally killed. Further, as is evident in their schools, their proliferation alters the way *all* of us must live.

It is necessary to consider, as well, the impact of guns on college campuses. While it is true that guns on campus would be concealed, their legalized presence, perhaps in great numbers, would change things, and not for the better. Their presence certainly won't help advance the goals of the college classroom and may well hinder them. The mission of the liberal arts college is to foster creativity and intellectual courage among students; it is to make them open, curious, outgoing citizens. Accordingly, the college classroom is a refuge of sorts—alternatively, a laboratory—where controversial, sometimes incendiary ideas are aired. Ideally, there are no banned books in the college classroom. If someone endorses a reprehensible idea, he or she must be defeated in argument and persuasion. College classrooms are supposed to be lively, sometimes raucous, though I realize that is less often the case than it should be. Nevertheless, colleges remain specially zoned places for intellectual experimentation, and moral and political questioning. Guns are inimical to this project and spirit. Sometimes emotions run high in the college classroom, when ideas are tested and opinions championed or disputed. Sometimes offense is taken, and given. Is it outrageous to consider that some individuals might reach for a gun? One college in Texas recently witnessed a gunfight between arguing students.[70] Perhaps it is not such an outrageous concern after all. Guns in the classroom might encourage professors to keep the conversation tepid, or incite students to watch what they say, how they say it, and to whom. To that extent, guns reveal a troubling ability to chasten speech.

Hannah Arendt suggests as much when she writes that "violence is mute."[71] She tells us that the ancient Greeks, who provided an inchoate model of democracy and touchstone for all others that followed, considered even the mere threat of violence to be a pre-political form of communication and control.

To the inhabitants of the *polis*, violence is how barbarian peoples deal with one another, not peoples who hope to approach the highest fulfillment of human nature. As Aristotle held, this fulfillment involves politics; humans are more than just social animals—they are political animals. Humans do more than live in common so as to satisfy their needs. They are also drawn to talk with one another, debate and contemplate the highest principles and most important questions: What is justice? What is freedom? What is happiness? What is virtue?

For the Greeks, Arendt says, politics is the locus of speech and action—*lexis* and *praxis*.[72] It is where deeds are carried out that are unrelated to and unconstrained by necessity, and we are free to negotiate nonviolently. Violence is the preferred way of dealing with necessity and nature, but not fellow citizens who are free and equal. Indeed, in the properly political realm, Arendt holds, citizens are free insofar as they are equal: they are not below or above someone but on equal footing. According to the Greeks, Arendt explains, to be equal "meant neither to rule nor to be ruled."[73] Politics is dominated and distinguished by communication and persuasion, enacted through either literal speech or communicative deeds, such as protest. "In acting and speaking," Arendt writes, "men show who they are, reveal actively their unique personal identities," and "this disclosure of 'who' in contradistinction to 'what somebody is . . . is implicit in everything somebody says and does."[74] Accordingly, Arendt likes to say, in the political realm, speech and action are revelatory.

Political debate, and the questioning of political ideas and ideals, carried out in a community of peers, is what sets apart the human race, and the *polis*. If communities do not provide a space or occasion for the discussion and consideration of such essential issues, Arendt argues, they are somewhat less than human. They provide less of what humans intrinsically yearn for. The Greeks, Arendt says, were drawn to the public realm by their desire for immortality; this could not be achieved in private, on one's own. They sought out the company of their peers where they might assert their devotion to eternal principles—and be remembered. Politics is a necessarily *agonal* enterprise, Arendt explains, prone to conflict and contest. Principles that would be eternal and universal are not easily compromised. They will, by their nature, stoke the most heated debate.

In recent years, guns have made prominent appearances at political rallies, most notably at protests against the bill that would become the Affordable Care Act in the summer of 2009. Few policy developments in this country have been as successful as healthcare reform in stoking strong emotions, mostly on the right—so much so that some individuals felt they needed an additional element to express their extreme displeasure. The media were dumbfounded at the sight of armed protesters; many commentators did not know what to make of them, or what they signified, beyond suggesting a threat to President Obama's life if he was in the vicinity. In two of those incidents, the president was indeed nearby, and though police officers warily eyed the armed protesters, they could not take away the weapons, arrest the protesters, or send them away, thanks to local open carry laws. These incidents, however, show how guns stand opposed to the notion of protest in a democracy.

In August 2009, the president traveled to Phoenix to deliver a speech promoting healthcare reform. The large crowd gathered outside the venue included both supporters and critics of his plan. Some of the critics were armed. One man who drew much media attention was neatly dressed, with an AR-15 (a semiautomatic weapon) slung over his shoulder and a holstered handgun on his hip. When approached by reporters who wanted to know why he felt the need to bring—and display—his weapons at this gathering, the man revealed little. He identified himself only as "Chris," and explained his actions by saying: "Because I can do it. In Arizona, I still have some freedoms left."[75] The media reported that the man started arguing with many opposing protesters. Police warily shadowed him throughout.

A week earlier, an armed individual had shown up for the president's appearance in New Hampshire. He wore a holstered handgun on his thigh and carried a sign declaring "It is time to water the tree of liberty." This invoked Jefferson's line: "The tree of liberty must be refreshed from time to time with the blood of patriots and tyrants."[76] His sign ostensibly called for armed revolt or assassination, but the police did not remove him from the scene, even though the president was close by; they said they were legally barred from doing so. The man, who identified himself in this instance—his name was William Kostric—was not overtly angry or unruly, though his sign surely suggested otherwise. He also stood alone. When asked what was intended by his solo armed protest, Kostric stated: "I wanted people to remember the rights that we have and how quickly we're losing them in this country. It doesn't take a genius to see we're traveling down a road at breakneck speed that's towards tyranny."[77]

Law enforcement officials were not amused by either protest. They complained that these were needlessly provocative gestures that threatened to divert their attention and energies away from protecting the president. One police officer said of an armed protester, "Just by his presence and people seeing the rifle, and people knowing the president was in town, it sparked a lot of emotions."[78] A political scientist, reflecting on the armed protesters in Phoenix, said, "When you start to bring guns to political rallies, it does layer on another level of concern and significance. It actually becomes quite scary for many people. It creates a chilling effect in the ability of our society to carry on honest communication."[79] By raising the issue of speech, this comment cuts to the heart of the matter. Guns silence—they frustrate free speech, even while the NRA boasts that guns protect and bolster it. Guns by their very presence issue a threat, and to that extent, they cut off communication, or indicate that its end is near. Consider the man in New Hampshire: his sign and weapon did not indicate that he had shown up at the president's speech with an open mind. To the contrary, they declared that his mind was made up—definitively—and that only revolt was in order. He had already determined that the time for speech was past. It is provocative enough to carry a poster saying "It is time to water the tree of liberty." It is quite another and more urgent matter to display these words while also displaying a gun. Kostric did not engage in dialogue—protesters did not approach him to enter into debate—and it is easy to see why. Who would want to? His weapon was message enough.

Who would think Kostric would be open to anything other than an affirmation of his existing beliefs?

The protester in Phoenix engaged opponents, but his weapon sent a similar message. It probably discouraged opponents from getting too worked up or responding too angrily. Ironically, the displays of guns at these protests raised most people's degree of alarm at the same time that they likely subdued many who might have wished to engage the armed protesters. Few people would be willing to say what they really think to armed individuals in those situations. "They're intimidating people like it's a western saloon," said one Secret Service agent about the armed protesters.[80] Guns defeated the purpose of the public gatherings in both cases: they subdued some of the louder voices in favor of healthcare reform and indicated the level—and extremes—of the opposition. The guns also underscored the divide between the camps, making the possibility of dialogue more remote.

Kostric insisted that his carrying a gun was symbolic, his intent peaceful, and that he should not be seen as a threat—at least, not on that day, at that protest.[81] Armed protesters have issued similar statements at other events in recent years, including Tea Party rallies. At the Second Amendment rally across the Potomac River from Washington in Virginia in 2010, where many people carried guns, the preponderant message was that the Obama administration had overstepped its constitutional bounds and needed to be stopped—even by armed resistance. "We're serious. We're going to do whatever it takes," one man declared.[82] Apparently realizing the tenor of his statement, he quickly added "that he didn't mean anyone would get blown up or shot."[83] Another protester offered the ominous prediction that "in these next two years, it's not gonna be like any other two years you've ever seen. And I think there will be blood. They can have mine."[84] Kostric has issued chilling threats, too, such as in an online defense of drug dealers killing cops who enter their homes: "If people can't wake up and see why it's immoral to trespass and destroy someone's property, kidnap and lock them in a cage for growing a plant in their backyard, then perhaps a body count is what's required for change."[85] This sums up what is worrisome about armed protesters: they seem all too comfortable with the prospect of body counts as a means of bringing about change.

At a 2010 Tea Party rally in New Mexico, an armed protester carried a sign saying "Bring it on, Obama."[86] Another said he carried his gun to express his extreme displeasure with what he perceived as a dawning Communist takeover of the U.S. government. "I'm not trying to start a war," he explained. "I just want to make a point."[87] It's hard to imagine, in this context, what that point might be, short of war. A gun at a protest is a physical threat, not a verbal or procedural one; the man and his companions wished to issue a threat to the president with their guns. These protesters may be more threatening still if we consider that their guns are loaded. When the group Moms Demand Action for Gun Sense in America staged a rally in Indianapolis in 2013, they were met by a counterprotest that included demonstrators armed with AR-15s. One of the counterprotesters, asked if his gun was loaded, said that of course it was: "Any weapon that is not loaded is just a rock or a club."[88]

Our democracy has always preserved a place for radical voices. To the consternation of many, we even allow avowed racist organizations like the Ku Klux Klan to stage public marches. But guns add a new and radical element to the mix, an element that is at odds with the idea of political discussion and risks destroying our culture of assembly. At an emotionally charged rally, how are you supposed to talk to someone with a gun? How are you to feel comfortable and free to march with an armed protester looking on—his gun a not-so-subtle threat to your political position, perhaps, and an expression of extreme anger? Gun rights groups might retort, let everyone be armed. According to their reasoning, guns protect and affirm speech; if you are afraid to speak out in public, a gun will restore your courage. I have tried to imagine what would have happened if people on all sides of the issue had been armed at the Obamacare rallies. How might Kostric have reacted if armed Obamacare apologists stood defiantly in front of him? Would there be any exchange of words—or any need for it? The scene sounds more like a standoff than political assembly—who would dare speak out in that setting, and what would you say? What need is there to say anything? And what if heated arguments did occur? If shots were fired, what would happen next?

This leads to another reason guns are inimical to protest: they might incite police to react roughly, as has happened many times in the past, even when rallies were nominally or largely peaceful. What if the protesters had been armed at the Democratic Convention in Chicago in 1968—where police, goaded by the defiant mayor, were already itching for a confrontation—or in Seattle in 2000, when police battled anarchists smashing store windows? What if the Occupy Wall Street protesters had stashed guns in their tents before the

New York City Police Department descended on Zuccotti Park to disband their encampment? We cannot imagine guns in each of these cases because the police never would have allowed such protests in the first place. Police typically justify rough treatment of protesters by saying the latter had become unruly, violent, abusive, and posed a threat to the larger community. In many cities in 2011, police departments broke up Occupy camps on the grounds that they were becoming dangerous. Guns in the hands of protesters only strengthen the police's case for subduing protest.

Further, consider the prospect of armed protesters in the face of our increasingly militarized police. Many observers of the Occupy movement commented on the militaristic approach taken by police, especially in disbanding the protests. A *New York Times* article entitled "When the Police Go Military" offered a summation: "Riot police officers tear-gassing protesters at the Occupy movement in Oakland, Calif. The surprising nighttime invasion of Zuccotti Park in Lower Manhattan, carried out with D-Day like secrecy by officers deploying klieg lights and a military-style sound machine. And campus police officers in helmets and face shields dousing demonstrators at the University of California Davis with pepper spray."[89] The article went on to say that such actions stem from years of police department build-up during the War on Terror. Facing the possibility of a domestic terror attack and showered with money from the Department of Homeland Security, police departments across the country have bulked up on military gear—even in small towns—and shown greater readiness to employ SWAT teams for all manner of incidents, including nonviolent protests.[90] In his book

The Democracy Project, activist David Graeber writes of the anomalous presence of a SWAT team at a small Occupy protest soon after the Zuccotti Park sweep. Cato Institute fellow Timothy Lynch complains of an increasingly "militaristic mind-set" among police, apparent in "the way they search and raid homes and the way they deal with the public."[91]

Lynch goes on to explain that "the more police fail to defuse confrontations but instead help create them—be it with their equipment, tactics or demeanor—the more ties with community members are burned. . . . The effect is a loss of civility, and an erosion of constitutional rights, rather than a building of good will."[92] The journalist Radley Balko quotes a New Hampshire resident critical of his town's plan to purchase a BearCat (a kind of armored vehicle) for its police department: "It promotes violence. . . . We should promote more human interaction rather than militarize."[93] A militarized police, according to Lynch, endangers civility on both sides. Sending a SWAT team to a nonviolent, gun-free protest is an uncivil gesture by the police; it is an expression of deep suspicion. At the very least, it is a demonstrative threat to the protesters not to get out of hand—or, as Graeber argues, if the protesters are obviously peaceful, a SWAT team is a heavy-handed attempt to threaten them into protesting less vocally—or just less. Further, as Lynch suggests, militarized police are more likely to create than defuse confrontation.

It is difficult to imagine how armed protesters, in the face of a SWAT team, could make the situation better for the protesters and uphold their right to speech. An armed protest facing a SWAT team is a combustible mixture; the presence of guns provides a perfect excuse for the police to crack down.

Police were happy to disperse Occupy camps on far lesser grounds, including supposed public health threats. Imagine what they would do in the face of AR-15s. Even if they did not physically confront armed protesters, what would protest look like under those circumstances? I can't imagine that it would be anything we could describe as free. To the contrary, it would be unbearably tense, electric, and ultimately muted as a result of the weaponry. But of course, police would outlaw protest in the first place, if protesters were armed. We can only exercise the right of assembly if assembly is nonviolent. When guns are present, especially among protesters, both assembly and free speech quickly vanish.

Arendt sees a convergence of freedom and equality, speech and action: only in the political realm, devoted to speech and action, purged of violence, are we wholly free and equal. I believe Arendt is correct: political freedom is gravely threatened by an armed society. I have pointed out how guns are inimical to free speech. It is worth considering their impact on equality, too.

Gun rights advocates argue that guns are crucial to the assertion and maintenance of equality in society; they ensure that our rulers do not rise too far above us and reduce us to slavery. Further, guns ensure parity among our peers—in particular, parity with the criminals who would overpower us. Gun rights advocates like to cite various incarnations of the nineteenth-century slogan for Colt revolvers: "God created men equal, Colt made them equal." The Colt website offers a politically provocative alternative: "Abe Lincoln may have freed all men, but Sam Colt made them equal."[94] The site goes on to say that "this post–Civil War slogan would have been music to Sam Colt's ears, had he lived long enough to hear it."[95] It certainly fits with NRA arguments that freedom and equality are mere ideas without guns—guns make them real. But what is the equality guns would deliver? And how exactly would guns make us equal?

I would point out, first, that equality vanishes as soon as some are armed and others are not. The armed protesters described above are not equal thanks to their guns; they stand apart. They are not one with the crowd. Their guns distinguish and alienate them. Furthermore, their weapons seem to represent an effort to elevate their message above the din of the protests, perhaps even shock others into silence. Who would speak back? Who would angrily put them down? Perhaps opposing protesters might decide to arm themselves, to right the balance of power and speech. What kind of equality would that restore? Would it be a kind of equality worth having, or tolerating? Again, it would be the miserably tense equality of a violent standoff, not the kind where anyone is free. And in a democracy, that is not equality worth pursuing.

Let's move beyond the confines of the protest or assembly, and consider the "equality" of an armed society more broadly. The NRA claims that guns help ordinary citizens attain parity with armed criminals and an armed, predatory government. Advertisements for the Tavor Semi-Automatic Rifle say it will "restore the balance of power."[96] Perhaps—but the balance achieved would hardly last. If I require a gun to achieve equality with criminals in my neighborhood, I should probably leave the area, since this is not a kind of equality I can survive for long. Sooner or later, armed criminal gangs will outgun me if they want. Guns are largely useful to the extent that they make me *more* than equal. Though they suggest otherwise, gun rights advocates don't typically envision that their brave confrontations with the criminal element will involve crooks who are very well armed—with semiautomatic weapons, for example, or body armor and night vision goggles. When, in his emotional defense of the castle doctrine, LaPierre describes how a person is justified in using a gun on a criminal who breaks his window and enters his home in the middle of the night, the underlying presumption is that the intruder is not armed—certainly not with an AR-15. If he were, it would be the height of stupidity to rush at him, gun in hand, daring to see what firepower he has. Gun rights proponents don't really want to engage in gun battles with hardened, perhaps better equipped criminals. They imagine they will always have an advantage, that the sight of guns will scare off their assailants.

This is the real selling point of guns: they give an individual an *advantage* over others. If that advantage is seen to be diminished, then we are justified in purchasing a lighter, quicker, more powerful weapon, or several of them, to regain the upper hand. This is the thinking: we are told that ordinary citizens must be able to buy semiautomatic weapons because today's criminals are increasingly well armed. But these arguments come from people who do not typically, or ever, engage in protracted battles with criminals wielding AR-15s. Those who do, like the police, know better—they know the nature of the equality gained when all parties are similarly well armed. Residents of neighborhoods plagued by violence know better, too. In areas where it is readily evident that guns provide no advantage over active and present criminals, residents are re-ceptive to gun control. They harbor no illusions as to what an armed equality with the criminal class looks like, who wins in most cases—and to what state it reduces everyday life.

The notion that guns are conducive to equality is delu-sional, or at least deeply misguided. It is reminiscent of the terrible equality Hobbes invokes in the state of nature, which he counts a "war of each on each." For Hobbes, in nature, we are free to pursue any and all desires—men are also equal in power. We are all equal in the ability to get what we want, more or less, and in our ability to dispose of those who stand in our way. This equality is what makes nature so terrifying, according to Hobbes: everyone is to be feared, everyone sus-pected. If people were unequal with respect to power, this might allow for the emergence of basic societies, and order—the powerless would line up behind the strong. It is the stand-off created by a violent equality that makes life "nasty, brutish, and short."[97] Thus we must hasten to depart nature, Hobbes maintains, and enter civil society, where we no longer have to advance our interests and assert our equal rights at the point of a sword, and may achieve a modicum of peace, stability, and security.

In civil society, we exchange armed equality for unarmed equality. In civil society, as our Founding Fathers saw it, equality among our peers and with our government is to be achieved and enforced by law. This is what John Adams meant when he said that "ours is a government of laws, not men." No individual will should rule and get its way; we must be ruled by indifferent, impersonal law. Men are not required to ensure their safety and secure their rights by brute force but by the protection of the laws. This is the great relief that civil society offers. Yet it is difficult to maintain a state of affairs where rights and equality are protected by law, and gun rights advocates are correct to suspect that they are perennially threatened. Individual interests chip away at our rights, subvert the law according to their design, and must be fended off and kept in place. But the proper response is to do this effectively, and not to embrace viscerally appealing remedies that, while offering the illusion of defending our rights, in fact erode them further.

CHAPTER FIVE

Power and Democracy

ow compatible is the gun rights movement with democracy? The movement's claim that a profusion of privately held arms is the defining feature of our democracy forces us to reckon with its insurrectionist element. This is where gun rights arguments ultimately lead: a threat of armed revolt against standing government. We are told that guns were not enshrined in our Constitution to protect our right to hunt or defend ourselves, but principally so that the sovereign people can depose corrupt governments when necessary. Any government that proposes to take away or regulate our guns, gun rights advocates argue, betrays its tyrannical streak. Gun-grabbing is key evidence that our government has despotic designs and must be reminded that the people can and will remove it—violently if need be.

Yet not only does this argument elicit numerous complications, it has been invoked in such a way that it runs counter to and even undermines the spirit of democracy. In one memorable incident, during the 2010 Nevada Senate race, Republican candidate and Tea Party favorite Sharron Angle said in a radio interview, "Thomas Jefferson said it's good for a country to have a revolution every twenty years. I hope that's not where we're going, but, you know, if this Congress keeps going the way it is, people are really looking towards those Second Amendment remedies and saying, my goodness, what can we do to turn this country around?"[1] Congress has to be stopped, Angle suggested, and by arms if necessary. What in particular was she objecting to? She abhorred the massive government bailouts for the banks and auto industry, also any hint of legislation on climate control, and of course gun control. But President Obama's landmark bill on healthcare reform, which the Democrat-controlled Congress narrowly passed in 2010, provided her principal complaint. These were signs, she and her supporters argued, of a government growing in size, control, and intrusion into Americans' daily lives—a government moving rapidly toward socialism. That is the tyranny Angle had in mind, which might necessitate armed revolt.

When questioned about her comment, Angle's spokesman assured reporters that the candidate was not "advocating for a revolution."[2] Yet Angle had made similar remarks before. She told a Nevada newspaper that "it's almost imperative" that Republicans take Congress: "The nation is arming. . . . What are they arming for if it isn't that they are so distrustful of their government? They're afraid they'll have to fight for their liberty in more Second Amendment kinds of ways. That's why I look at this as almost an imperative. If we don't win at the ballot box, what will be the next step?"[3] Her opponent, Democratic Senator Harry Reid, circulated a response saying that Angle's "rhetoric that if she doesn't win at the ballot box people should go to the bullet box undermines the democratic process."[4] By allowing Reid to depict her as a reckless extremist, Angle permitted him to eke out a narrow victory. It is clear that Angle tried to walk a fine line with such comments; they struck a chord with her angry base, and yet everyone knew they were a bit over the top. But not much.

John Chachas, whom Angle had defeated in the Republican primary, said, "it's not necessarily an ill-advised campaign message, especially to her base" and that her popularity "speaks volumes . . . to how imposed upon people in rural America feel by these things passed on a national level."[5] The Republican former governor of Nevada, Bill List, issued a similar statement: "People are far more riled up about what's going on out there than I've ever seen in my lifetime."[6] What exactly does this say about Angle's call for insurrection? That it's metaphorical? Merely a colorful way of expressing the extreme anger out there? Or that people are so furious that they might actually reach for their guns?

In a democracy, this curious expression of anger conveys a threat of a special kind. Its force lies in the threat to transcend or subvert the democratic process as such, because the voters to whom it appeals see those in power doing the same. Far from disabusing her followers of that notion, Angle thrived on it, and inflamed her supporters on claims that the president and his allies were bent on socialist tyranny.

Angle's attempts to distance herself from her bellicose language were understandably half-hearted. Her comments spoke to and followed from the Tea Party movement's anger in 2010. They were among the more extreme and remarkable expressions of Tea Party hostility, but hardly unexpected. When some people complain that the nation is becoming a tyranny, and many of them believe the principal intent of the Second Amendment is to enable them to overthrow tyranny, it is hardly strange that they might raise the prospect of armed insurrection. Angle was not alone. A Republican congressional candidate in Alabama aired an ad in the 2010 campaigns in which a George Washington impersonator, after hearing a list of Obama's offenses, declares, "Gather your armies!"[7] In the run-up to the 2012 elections, a Republican newsletter in Virginia called for "armed revolution" if Obama were reelected, claiming that he was an "ideologue unlike anything world history has ever witnessed or recognized" and that "this Republic cannot survive 4 more years underneath this political socialist ideologue."[8] The threat of violence simmered just below the surface of the Tea Party movement. When people showed up at Tea Party rallies dressed in Revolutionary era garb with rifle in hand (or not), the implicit message was one of rebellion—the time for democratic, peaceful mediation was almost past.

The first complicating issue of Angle's threat is that she wants to remind Reid, the President, and the Democrat-led Congress that the American people are ready to overthrow tyrannical government, but as columnist Jay Bookman writes, "how do you define 'tyrannical government'?" He continues:

"To my mind, it would be a government that cancels elections, that refuses to allow the peaceful transfer of authority, that uses military force to keep itself in power or that tries to defy judicial limits on its power."[9] To the contrary, he explains, "to cite 'Second Amendment remedies' as a way to 'correct' the acts of a duly elected Congress and duly elected president . . . [is] deeply antithetical to concepts of freedom."[10] Angle suggests that she and at least some of her allies, the people whose wrath she channels, will not accept an election whose results they dislike, and they are not obliged to accept it—indeed, she suggests they are obliged to object strenuously, perhaps even with force.

Scholar and critic Stanley Fish finds the suggestion of "Second Amendment remedies" un-American, in that "it sets itself against one of the cornerstones of democracy—the orderly transfer of power."[11] Transfer of power is to be effected and managed by and in law, not force. An appeal to "Second Amendment remedies" suggests that some have decided they will no longer abide by the results of elections and are now effectively outside the republic. Fish notes that those who call for "disorderly transfer of power" don't mean to subvert the democratic system. To the contrary, they believe they are doing something eminently in the spirit of American democracy: saving it. Our republic has gotten corrupt, they believe, and Harry Reid and Barack Obama are symptoms of that corruption. Their agenda hastens us toward a socialism that is tyrannical and hostile to freedom. Of course, Fish points out, echoing Bookman, the major question facing this claim is "who gets to decide that tyranny is imminent, and by what measures is the imminence of tyranny determined?"[12] That is to say, what are tyranny's key features, and what evidence tells us it is near? The main complaint behind so much Tea Partiers' wrath, which in their eyes nearly justified armed revolt, was the president's healthcare reform legislation. But it does not clearly measure up to any of the criteria Bookman mentions above, which might justify popular revolt: government abuse of power, military oppression of the people, revoking voting rights, or changing the results of elections—all of which we are accustomed to seeing in the developing world, where countries struggle to accept democracy and democratic institutions. A healthcare reform based on a free market approach that requires people to purchase health insurance in order to expand the numbers of insured Americans is not an obvious example of oppression. Its most vocal and angry critics saw it as evidence of socialism: it is reminiscent of socialized medicine, with its goal of universal coverage, and would require all of us to pay for this expansion. But even a single-payer program like those found in "socialist" countries is hardly alien to democracy.

How shall we know that tyranny is upon us? Who is supposed to say? Who is the responsible and respected party we should heed in these matters? Surely no government-sanctioned source can qualify, because it is government that we must suspect. Who shall it be, then? This is the problem, Fish observes, for which Second Amendment supporters have no good answer. In theory, in a democracy, it should be the people themselves, or at least a large segment of the people, who recognize the tyranny in place and decide that revolt is in order. This would evidently reflect the will of the people—a suitably and safely democratic principle. But supporters of

Second Amendment remedies cannot claim such a degree of popular recognition of tyranny. Angle's nod toward armed revolt showed her extremism, political commentators said, which ultimately alienated voters and ensured her loss. If there is no popular will for revolt, this means that gun rights extremists who threaten insurrection perceive a threat the rest of us do not see. They would save us from ourselves, as we naively, ignorantly stand by while Obama and his Democratic cronies amass power and advance their socialist agenda. I think this is quite close to how gun rights extremists see things. They are uniquely aware of abuses to the system, uniquely vigilant, uniquely prepared to face up to tyrannical government. The rest of us are "sheep," while gun rights proponents are the sheepdogs who would protect us.

But this only complicates their call for armed insurrection. It means that only a small minority of voices, a minority of judges, is charged with issuing the call to upend tyranny. And why should we believe those voices? Many of these would-be insurrectionists, especially those in the Tea Party camps, cited Obamacare as the dawn of socialism and a likely justification for revolt. But it is hardly clear that socialism, by definition, merits revolt: plenty of nations around the world are far more socialist than the United States, and few people would say such societies—Denmark and the Netherlands, for example—are pits of oppression. A duly elected socialist government, should such a thing come to pass, would still be a duly elected government.

Furthermore, Obamacare, for all its faults, is not socialist. True, some Americans will persist in thinking so, and a portion of them will also believe that socialist European nations are tyrannical. But to most Americans, the call for armed in-surrection is hardly convincing. The other major complaint of the Tea Party—the bailout of the Wall Street banks—is similarly unconvincing, both in its depiction as "socialist" policy and as evidence of expanded government power. The American government bailed out the veritable center of glob-al capitalism with few strings attached and only a modest increase in government oversight or control of the banking industry. As the claims for tyranny are unmerited, as the Tea Party and friends are objecting to policies that are not obvi-ously oppressive but, at worst, just bad policies, it seems their calls for revolt are extreme. "Second Amendment remedies" sounds, at the end of the day, closer to the desperate mutter-ings of a dangerous fringe element than the sage warnings of uniquely perceptive "sheepdogs" whom we should trust to protect and guide us.

The cause of armed revolt is undermined when it is in-voked for such mundane affairs as a mandate to purchase health insurance. Locke maintains that it should be reserved for only the most dire, most obvious offenses, predicaments that are broadly recognized, not for the continual hectoring of an extreme element. It is dangerous to invoke rebellion repeatedly for the slightest perceived offense. As Locke ar-gues, the threat of rebellion goads government into abridging law and turning to violence. It tells the government that a portion of the electorate is seriously contemplating violence, and that it must respond in turn. After all, one ardent gun rights supporter and militia movement sympathizer, who harbored deep anger against the government—Timothy McVeigh—bombed the Alfred P. Murrah federal building in

Oklahoma City in 1995, and killed 168 people. As a result, our government will not take the threats of insurrectionists lightly. Some gun rights extremists will respond, approvingly, that the government had better take them seriously, but this is naïve. It urges the government to be oppressive. It is another case where the gun rights advocates make their predictions come true: they fret about oppressive government, but by waving their weapons threateningly in the face of government, Locke says, they invite the state to respond with force.

Furthermore, Locke would tell us, those who make calls for rebellion must have little or no idea what would follow. Angle, by her language, suggests a simple solution—that we can simply swap out legislators and legislation at gunpoint. Or that we can violently depose Congress and insert new representatives, or a whole new government, and get on with business. But that is not how revolutions work, of course. The casual historian or observer of overseas rebellions will tell you that revolution is treacherous. It creates a vacuum of power and risks throwing the nation into protracted chaos. Angle, however, suggests to the voters that a violent uprising is a fine idea—it is a practical, even productive expression of their anger. Nothing could be farther from the truth. What gun rights extremists have lost sight of is that armed revolution is the *last* and *least desirable* course of action.

The call for insurrection is careless, irresponsible. This is ironic, because it is issued by gun rights proponents who describe themselves as eminently responsible. It is irresponsible because it invokes a perilous course of action— for uncertain gain—to assuage the anger of a few. Even worse, it gravely endangers the democratic tradition whose very loss it laments.

As Joshua Horwitz and Casey Anderson put it, "When gun owners assert that they are ready to use their firearms to vindicate their political views, they are really saying that they are unwilling to abide by the American political tradition that the people without guns can tell people with guns what to do."[13] I might put the problem this way: politicians like Angle suggest to everyone that violence is an acceptable way of transacting political business: you may need to issue physical threats to get what you want on occasion. Some people may act out those threats. After all, what good are threats if they are not made real once in a while? Calls for insurrection risk upending the aim of politics as such: that social change, great and small, will be achieved by purely peaceable means—short of war. Threats of violence, even mere suggestions of violence, do not help the political process in the least. They only make things worse.

Horwitz and Anderson argue that the NRA's goal "is not just to change policy, but to debase civic discourse."[14] As evidence, they cite Wayne LaPierre's apocalyptic claims that global forces are coming after our guns, following U.N. efforts to limit the flood of weapons to war-torn and crime-plagued nations in the developing world. We might also consider his dire warnings of Mexican drug cartels crossing our borders to sow mayhem, and the hurricanes that will plunge our cities into chaos after a bankrupt federal government is powerless to protect us. LaPierre leans heavily on such dark forecasts, but they are ultimately inhospitable to democracy. If we are on the verge of apocalypse, we cannot wait for democratic institutions to analyze problems and debate solutions. We must not have patience for democracy at all—following

LaPierre's logic, it would be unreasonable, even naïve to do so. Further, there can be no compromise or negotiation when disaster approaches. At that point, your opponents are more than opponents—they are enemies, albeit unwitting ones, but in no case should they be tolerated.

The greatest threat the current gun rights movement poses to our democracy is that it would undermine rule of law. Naturally, gun rights advocates claim the opposite: they say guns are essential for law and order, and the greater observance of laws. With their weapons, gun owners ward off criminals and deter criminal behavior; they may also stymie crimes in progress before law enforcement professionals show up. And of course, the gun rights movement maintains it would be the protector of the law against any prospective despot. Cato Institute fellow David Kopel writes, "In much of the world, the armed masses symbolize lawlessness; in America, the armed masses are the law."[15] This begs the question: why should armed masses spell lawlessness elsewhere but not here? What is that additional element ensuring that armed Americans are law abiding, unlike armed citizens everywhere else? Kopel suggests it has something to do with the fact that Americans "do not trust the police and government to protect [us] from crime" and that "America places more faith in its citizens than do other nations."[16] In other words, because we are given more responsibility, we are more upstanding with our guns and less liable to become an unruly mob. Simply by trusting us, our Constitution renders us more trustworthy. It seems *National Review* columnist Charles Cooke's argument is also implicit here, namely, that the armed American populace has been charged with an auxiliary role in keeping the peace, and it takes that duty seriously. Greater responsibility is inherent in the kind of freedom we Americans enjoy.

Kopel's argument seems to be an expansion of the gun rights advocates' notion that gun ownership makes people more conscientious. Recall the suggestion that we should put guns in the hands of more black youths in our ghettos, on the premise that this will make them more responsible.[17] I think we have good reason to suspect both that claim and Kopel's. There are always outside features or prior foundations that dispose us to act a certain way. A gun is no magic pill that suddenly makes a person responsible—and a mass of guns heaped on a population does not magically make it grateful and awestruck by the trust placed in it. If gun ownership makes a person more responsible, it likely enhances the nascent responsibility that was already present; and if it makes that person reckless, it is only exacerbating antisocial tendencies that were already there. As gun rights advocates like to say, "Guns don't kill people—people kill people." Guns are instruments of existing behavior. They are not themselves responsible for crime, gun rights advocates mean to say. The majority of gun owners are an upstanding lot, not corrupted by their weapons. But if we accept this argument, we must also accept the reverse: guns are not of themselves responsible for good behavior in individuals either. They cannot transform personal behavior—or make someone "good"—and ensure that an armed society will be more polite than it already is. The problem is, a profusion of guns—and people resorting to them—eats away at that foundation that ensures that the lawful among us remain lawful.

Fish says it is a "commonplace of democracy" that "ours is a government of laws not men. . . . A government of men is one in which laws issue from the will and desires of those who happen to be in authority. In a government of laws the preferences of men (and women), even those holding high office, are checked by the impersonal requirements of an impersonal law."[18] Under a government of laws, and in a democracy dedicated to egalitarian principles, citizens are also "checked by the impersonal requirements of an impersonal law," and may not interpret the law in their individual manner—in the heat of the moment. This is what distinguishes rule of law as such: citizens defer to this immaterial entity, this invisible code, and expect their peers to do the same.

Horwitz and Anderson relate the following story about rock musician and strident gun rights advocate Ted Nugent, which they borrow from the pages of *Rolling Stone* magazine. In a 2007 concert, Nugent came on stage "decked out in full-on camouflage hunting gear" and "wielded two machine guns while raging, 'Obama, he's a piece of shit. I told him to suck on my machine gun.'"[19] After some foul epithets directed at Hillary Clinton, Nugent concluded his rant by screaming "Freedom!"[20] Machine guns are instruments of war; they are intended for taking on a similarly armed enemy. Nugent strode brazenly on stage with those weapons because he knew he would not be shot down by someone in the audience. He would not have done it so casually and gleefully in that setting where machine guns are common, and commonly used, like a war zone. People who suffer through the daily threats and toils of war would, I wager, be more serious about the prospects of toting and flaunting their weapons; at the very least, they know what it might well bring in return. In a war zone, a gun is no symbol of freedom but a symbol of constraint, compulsion, and necessity. It is an instrument for survival. Nugent's act insults all those who live under the brutal realities of war, while he swings machine guns on stage and screams about freedom. He is free—but he is wholly ignorant of what makes him so.

When he lugs his weapons on stage, Nugent is inadvertently expressing his faith in the rule of law. He assumes that it extends over his audience and that no one will draw a weapon on him. Like many gun owners, he will claim the contrary: they will aver that their guns are the condition of their safety. Nugent will say he *needs* his guns to be free. But it is not guns that provide either safety or freedom—and they never will. It is rule of law. Thanks to widespread, unspoken, and nonviolent deference to law, Nugent and company are safe. They can wave their weapons and carry them down the street, and not be shot—something that is *not* the case in real war zones, where rule of law is gone.

To the extent that individuals credit their personal weapons with ensuring their safety, they ignore the rule of law. For those who inhabit lawless areas, or areas where rule of law is weak, a gun does not make one secure. It is not the cure-all, safeguarding one's life, but a temporary measure at best. James Scott, the elderly man in Baltimore I described in the previous chapter who fought a constant battle against criminals in his besieged neighborhood, was a case in point. His life was by no means safe and secure, and his gun never made it so. It merely helped him survive. It boggles the mind that gun rights advocates might idolize this man's case or cite it as some kind of model. His experience is to be lamented, and prevented. God help anyone who must live by the gun. It is a fearful, miserable existence.

We cannot take lightly the prospect of Nugent and company flaunting their weapons in public. It is no harmless, innocent act, but one that affects us all. A society that is progressively more armed, exposing weapons in public and appealing to them with greater regularity, is one that erodes the rule of law. As more people are armed in public, it sends the message that rule of law is weak. LaPierre would doubt-less say that message is accurate. I argue it is not: violent crime rates have plunged in America in recent decades, and the na-tion is safer than it once was. As for those areas where people can walk about armed—the shopping mall, the diner, college campuses in some states—they are safe because rule of law is strong there. If gun owners say they are safer in such places thanks to their guns, they are simply wrong. But so long as gun owners, abetted by LaPierre, sow the message that rule of law is weak, and burden rule of law with doubt and suspicion, more and more people may come to harbor similar suspi-cions. They will arm themselves, too. This is of course LaPi-erre's game plan: fill everyone with fear that rule of law is threatened or has vanished, and more people will buy guns. It is a tragic game plan, however, for one of the key ingredients of rule of law is a silent trust that it works. Rule of law re-quires our faith in it, a broader belief and acceptance. It is one of those social phenomena that falls apart when that belief no longer pertains.

This is precisely what Stand Your Ground threatens to do. It is an open refusal to defer to law, to defer to a common judge, as Locke puts it, and to insist that others do the same. As more individuals prosecute law themselves in Stand Your Ground states, confronting perceived threats in public, others will decide that they must be similarly armed, and prepared at the very least to deal with would-be George Zimmermans roving the streets, committing travesties of justice. What if someone thinks *you* look suspicious? Stand Your Ground will embolden others to act like Zimmerman himself, extirpating "bad guys." If enough people make frequent appeals to Stand Your Ground, everyone else may reasonably doubt whether rule of law covers them at all.

To a great extent, trust in rule of law is coextensive with trust in government, that the government can effectively carry out rule of law, see that justice is done, and protect the civilian population. "[When] government cannot provide security, it is failing at its most basic function," Horwitz and Anderson write, and then we are justified in lacking faith in government.[21] And yet, they maintain, gun rights groups have steadily undermined the government's ability to provide security. "Gun rights enthusiasts often claim that private citizens need to arm themselves because the police are unable . . . to come to their aid when criminals attack," Horwitz and Anderson explain, "yet these same gun supporters work tirelessly to make sure that law enforcement will lack the tools it needs to reduce gun violence."[22] For example, gun rights groups routinely block efforts to close the gun show loophole or to expand background checks. The NRA likes to say that instead of creating new gun laws and new gun regulations, the federal Bureau of Alcohol, Tobacco, and Firearms must work harder to enforce "the laws that are already on the books." But through its intense lobbying efforts, the NRA has crippled the agency's ability to do just that.

There is perhaps no greater evidence of gun rights efforts to undermine the government's ability to combat gun crime, and prevent guns from falling into the hands of criminals and the mentally ill, than the NRA's success in hobbling the very government agency charged with this task. In 2006, the ATF was removed from the Treasury Department and made a stand-alone agency, which effectively allowed the ATF to be more vulnerable to NRA attacks and marginalization. This move meant the agency's director had to be approved by Congress. And for seven years hence, Congress blocked presidential nominees for the post, at the NRA's behest, leaving the agency without a permanent director. Senators blocked President George W. Bush's nominee to head the agency because they deemed him "hostile to gun dealers."[23] A 2012 *Washington Post* investigation points out that one of the senators in question "was a member of the NRA's board of directors."[24] President Obama's nominee was "stalled in the Senate for two years," the *Post* reports, "because [the nominee] raised the ire of the gun lobby with comments it has characterized as anti-firearm."[25] Congress finally approved a permanent director in August 2013. In the meantime, the ATF budget has stagnated, preventing it from expanding its staff, even while the number of privately held guns has soared, and private sales thrived. In a *Mother Jones* expose on the beleaguered agency, Alan Berlow writes that the ATF "employs about 5,000 men and women, approximately the same number of staff it had a decade ago; about half are special agents assigned to conduct criminal investigations. That's a force about the size of the Harris County, Texas, Sherriff's Department."[26] By contrast, Berlow explains, the budgets, and staff, of other law enforcement agencies have grown significantly: "Since 1972, the Drug Enforcement Administration's staff has more than doubled, while the FBI's is up by two-thirds. The ATF's current budget of $1.15 billion, is little changed from the $900 million it received 10 years ago."[27] This means the agency "is able to inspect only a fraction of the nation's 60,000 retail gun dealers each year," according to the *Post* investigation, "with as much as eight years between visits to stores."[28]

Furthermore, Congress has barred the ATF from creating a central computer database to track gun sales and gun ownership. Berlow points out that the NRA objects to such a database on the premise that it "could be used by a tyrannical government to confiscate firearms."[29] Absence of such a database—which would be quite easy to arrange and manage— makes the ATF's job much larger. Berlow explains:

> With a centralized database, an ATF agent in possession of a gun found at a crime scene could simply plug the gun's serial number into a computer and identify the name of the dealer who sold the weapon, along with the name of the first purchaser. Without a database, agents must often embark on a Rube Goldberg-style odyssey, contacting the gun's manufacturer or a gun's importer who will direct the agent either to a middleman who sold the weapon to a dealer or to the dealer himself, who can identify the first buyer. Dealers are required to keep records of each firearm transaction. Frequently, however, the records are on paper, and dealers can't locate particular ones quickly. At the same time, there is no law requiring consolidation of wholesale weapon transfers—those sales by

the manufacturer or middleman—which means ATF inspectors have no way of knowing whether a dealer's ledgers accurately represent all of the guns he has bought or if he is illegally selling guns off the books.[30]

The ATF has not been similarly stymied in monitoring who owns machine guns, for example. Thanks to the 1934 National Firearms Act (NFA), anyone who owns such weapons must have their names entered into a centralized federal registry. Contents of this database "have never been divulged outside of a legitimate law enforcement inquiry," a former ATF official tells Berlow, and "the NFA has effectively removed these guns from the criminal marketplace."[31]

Adding insult to injury, the 1986 Firearms Owners' Protection Act (FOPA) greatly altered the definition of a firearms dealer, who would then require a federal license—and subject clients to a background check. Berlow says the law "exempted 'collectors,' people engaged in 'occasional sales' and those selling guns from 'personal collection' regardless of its size, all of which greatly expanded the universe of unlicensed sellers."[32] One former ATF agent says that once FOPA came into being, "we'd arrest a guy with hundreds of guns, all with price tags on them, and he'd say they were part of his collection, and the tags were to let his family know what they were worth in case he died."[33]

Legislative efforts by former Kansas Republican Representative Todd Tiahrt further complicated the ATF's job. Berlow states that "85 percent of traced crime guns had changed hands at least once before being recovered by law enforcement, and none of those secondary buyers were run through the NICS [background check] system."[34] In 2003, Tiahrt added a requirement that the FBI "destroy information contained in Brady or NICS checks within 24 hours. When a felon purchases a gun," Berlow explains, "he commits a new felony. But now the FBI has only 24 hours to figure that out. In effect the FBI is required to destroy evidence of a crime."[35] This prompted another retired ATF agent to tell Berlow that "obviously, bringing the record retention down to 24 hours would preclude any significant investigation. . . . One might as well not even bother."[36]

Horwitz and Anderson complain that the NRA has sponsored legislation whereby the ATF is "limited . . . from sharing certain trace data with local law enforcement, creating hurdles that impede efforts to identify and investigate corrupt gun dealers and illegal traffickers, and most trace data cannot be released to Congress or the general public. . . . Without access to this type of information, the public can no longer learn which dealers are among the 1.2 percent of federal firearms licensees who sell 57 percent of the guns traced in criminal investigations."[37] Again, the contemporary gun rights movement works to create the very conditions in which its arguments pertain. It strives to create a society where personal security must be ensured by the barrel of a gun—because guns, and armed criminals, are plentiful, and law enforcement has been rendered impotent to keep them in check.

The twentieth-century English political philosopher Michael Oakeshott calls rule of law "the greatest single condition of our freedom, removing from us that great fear which has overshadowed so many communities, the fear of the power of our own government."[38] Ostensibly, Oakeshott shares the same concern about predatory, expansive government as gun rights advocates, and yet he maintains that rule of law, not guns, is our best defense. A general observance of rule of law—by ruler and ruled alike—preserves freedom. He explains:

> [Government] by rule of law . . . is itself the emblem of that diffusion of power which it exists to promote, and is therefore peculiarly appropriate to a free society. It is the method of government most economical in the use of power; it . . . leaves no room for arbitrariness; it encourages a tradition of resistance to the growth of dangerous concentrations of power which is far more effective than any promiscuous onslaught however crushing; it controls effectively without breaking the grand affirmative flow of things; and it gives a practical definition of the kind of limited but necessary service a society may expect from its government, restraining us from vain and dangerous expectations.[39]

Rule of law is the most effective—*economical*—way for government to exercise power. It imposes an agenda that is limited, impersonal, and credible. It creates the least intrusion and constitutes the most secure foundation for authority. Rule of law is also the most *economical* means to keep government limited. It is far more effective in this effort, Oakeshott believes, than any "promiscuous onslaught." Why? Presumably because violence serves as an invitation for government to abandon its adherence to rule of law and react in kind. Violence is hardly economical, but messy, ineffective, and counterproductive. It urges those who govern us to lapse into arbitrary rule, as is their perennial temptation. A free state is one where power is strictly impersonal. Liberty requires diffusion of power, Oakeshott maintains, and there is no greater diffusion than when power proceeds from rule of law.

How shall we ensure that government remains limited, and hews to rule of law? How to ensure, short of armed insurrection, that government does not slip into arbitrariness but remains respectful of the will of the masses? Though we tend to ignore its virtues, nonviolent protest has succeeded repeatedly over the years. This raises the prospect that nonviolence is more effective in achieving the stated goals of the gun rights movement. Martin Luther King, Jr., writes in his essay "The Social Organization of Non-violence" that "there is more power in socially organized masses on the march than there is in guns in the hands of a few desperate men. Our enemies would prefer to deal with a small armed group rather than with a huge, unarmed but resolute mass of people."[40] King's nonviolent movement, then, was not merely idealistic: it was politically astute. As Mahatma Gandhi envisioned it, nonviolence is eminently effective—and thus tremendously powerful—in helping aggrieved groups attain their aims.

It is worth first considering the pitfalls of violence, as King understands it. "[To] meet hate with retaliatory hate would do nothing but intensify the existence of evil in the universe," King writes. "Hate begets hate; violence begets violence; toughness begets greater toughness."[41] Individuals who take up violence against their government, for example, will be less able to extract demands, openness, and sympathy from their adversary. Violence renders government tougher, resistant, closed. Aggrieved groups that engage in violence against the government are characterized as terrorists—and governments typically do not negotiate with terrorists. Violence is an invitation to alienation. Aggrieved groups hope to alert the public to the justice of their cause and elicit sympathy, if not solidarity. In the face of violent action, noted community organizer Saul Alinsky explains, "the masses of people recoil with horror and say, 'our way is bad and we were willing to let it change; but certainly not for this murderous madness—no matter how bad things are now, they are better than that.'"[42]

Government would rather face armed individuals, perhaps even armed groups, than unarmed masses. Threats of violence issued by these individuals and groups warrants a forceful response in turn, and risks putting us in a cycle of violence ending in tyranny. I have argued that gun rights groups effectively create the world in which their arguments hold true. In this context, this means they prod the government to be the despot they claim to oppose. Violent reaction is a temptation for rulers. In war, it is easy to bypass the onerous rules, process, and traditions of democracy—it is easy to ignore civil rights. And as gun rights advocates repeatedly say, they know government is itching to do this. But if so, this means violence plays directly into the hands of those who govern us, who wish to expand their power and impose arbitrary rule. If we would urge them in a different direction, nonviolence is far more effective.

Describing the Gandhian rationale for nonviolent protest, author and activist David Graeber writes that it "is meant to create a stark moral contrast: it strips bare the inherent violence of a political order by showing that, even when faced by a band of non-violent idealists, the 'forces of order' will not hesitate to resort to pure, physical brutality to defend the status quo."[43] Hannah Arendt says that political action is *revelatory*. In this case, and as Graeber suggests, nonviolent protest would reveal—expose and illuminate—tyranny. If nonviolent protest elicits rough treatment, and perhaps an outsize or obscene response, this shows the ruling parties for what they are and reveals their violent appetites and tendencies. Alternatively, nonviolent protest is an effort to hold government to the high standards the people expect of a democratic government. If you face the government with violence, you may expect violence in turn; you effectively announce what you esteem its true nature to be. But if you protest lawfully, that makes clear you expect a lawful response in turn. Accordingly, Thoreau's theory of civil disobedience plays a key role in the nonviolent movement. As legal scholar Bernard Harcourt sums up Thoreau's view, "civil disobedience accepts the legitimacy of the political structure and of our political institutions, but resists the moral authority of the resulting laws."[44] To the extent that it draws from Thoreau's theory of civil disobedience, nonviolent protest aims *not* to throw into question the larger political structure. If this structure is a democracy, nominally devoted to the equal rights of all citizens, Thoreau maintains, the nonviolent protester wishes to encourage the democratic state to live up to its name. The nonviolent protester who follows Thoreau's advice aims to achieve something constructive, not destructive. Thoreau realizes that justice, freedom, and equality can be achieved only within the confines of the state. If democratic protest undermines the state, it undermines its cause.

Such is the virtue of nonviolence: it works to change the state without destroying it. It works to change the political order without abandoning order as such—and without abandoning the hope for justice in that order. In his famous "Letter from a Birmingham Jail," King writes that "One who breaks an unjust law must do so openly, lovingly, and with a willingness to accept the penalty. I submit that an individual who breaks a law that conscience tells him is unjust, and who willingly accepts the penalty of imprisonment in order to arouse the conscience of the community over its injustice, is in reality expressing the highest regard for law."[45] Nonviolent disobedience, King argues, sends the message that one believes in the state, and the law; it says that one is not lawless, angling for anarchy, or pursuing purely selfish goals. Nonviolent disobedience expresses a hope for justice. The genius of this approach is that it is protest in the spirit of rule of law. It affirms law, and the rule of law. To that extent, the practitioners of nonviolent protest may stand a better chance of gaining respect and sympathy, and having their cause heard. As King might say, the justice of their cause will slowly but surely become evident.

If nonviolent protest affirms the political order, violent protest—insurrection—is a rejection of the system, a declaration that it is rotten to the core and must be thrown out. Nonviolent protest is affirmative and not threatening to the basic order of the state, while violence rejects the state. The former can be worked with—it announces that it is open to conversation and negotiation. Nonviolent protest is thus compatible with democracy. As Thoreau and King characterize it, it is the form of protest inherent to democracy. Insurrection makes no similar concessions; it rejects conversation. In so doing, a violent stance makes its purported goals more remote.

As we have seen, gun rights advocates describe themselves as realistic. They recognize evil in the world and assert that guns are an appropriate preparation and response. They suggest they are uniquely courageous in facing up to these threats, while their policy opponents are cowardly and naïve to push for vain regulations. Gun control supporters, the NRA maintains, misunderstand reality; they think threats can be mediated, when in truth they can only be met with force.

It is a key feature of the nonviolent movement, however, that it believes its approach is eminently practical. King writes that "true non-violent resistance is no unrealistic submission to evil power. It is rather a courageous confrontation of evil by the power of love, in the faith that it is better to be the recipient of violence than the inflictor of it, since the latter only multiplies the existence of violence and bitterness in the universe."[46] According to King, nonviolence is confrontation with an eye to what is politically possible; it is confrontation with a view to making your opponent more, not less, open to negotiation. It is a politically savvy way of generating public interest and sympathy, as opposed to causing the public to retreat in fear. Sharron Angle may have fired up her base with her insurrectionist notions, but she alienated many potential supporters.

Yet nonviolent protest requires uncommon courage. Gandhi states that "passive resistance cannot proceed a step without fearlessness," since it may expose the protester to imprisonment, humiliation, and beatings.[47] You put yourself at the mercy of illegitimate authorities, in full knowledge that you are provoking them to reveal their depravity. It is to take on a sacrificial stance, as King put it, but not passively—it is not to submit, but to expose, and in exposing, fight—and in fighting within the law, strive for justice. The gun rights movement fails to grasp, or convey, what it means to object constructively—or, I contend, with real power.

In case anyone should doubt the power of nonviolent protest, and its impact on the ruling class, extreme government response attests to that. The Occupy movement's power was made apparent by the massive militarized police presence at protest camps across the country. Speaking at a much diminished Occupy protest in New York after the Zuccotti Park camp had been disbanded, Graeber opened his remarks by observing the massive police presence surrounding them: "That SWAT team over there tells you everything you really need to know."[48] In his estimation, the police presence indicated fear, suspicion, and self-doubt on the part of the ruling class. Meeting a paltry number of Occupy protesters with such vastly disproportionate force told Graeber that the powers-that-be recognized that these protesters, though they carried no weapons, constituted a credible threat. It told him that, in an indirect fashion, the ruling interests recognized the legitimacy and danger of the protesters' complaints.

The Occupy movement was preponderantly nonviolent.[49] In its methods, approach, and goals, the movement's organizers invoked guiding principles of Thoreau, King, and Gandhi. The movement urged our democratic state to live up to its values, highlighting the nation's deepening inequality and the increasing influence of moneyed interests in choosing elected officials. "There's nothing that scares the rulers of American more than the prospect of democracy breaking out," Graeber declared at the protest that day.[50] There is nothing more

terrifying to encroaching oligarchy than democratic goals being realized, and power shared or liberally dispersed among the
population. For Graeber, the ruling interests convey and admit
this fear when they issue forth SWAT teams. Indeed, what else
should we conclude when we consider how, as Harcourt describes, "the peaceful voices of Occupy . . . were buried beneath
the hype and frenzy of our police state, the legions of black clad
riot police with batons, the images of a few violent clashes, and
the frightening images of our new normal urban militarized
security?"[51] In the wake of the Occupy movement, offering testimony to the power of its tactics, President Obama quietly
signed into law a far-reaching bill that forbids many forms of
protest in public spaces.[52] In a broader and more obvious sense,
the nonviolent Occupy movement affected the president and
the larger political discussion by enshrining the terms "the 1
percent" and "the 99 percent" in our lexicon, and burning into
the national consciousness the widening gap between rich and
poor. Though the Occupy movement did not produce any legislative victories (at least not directly), *Washington Post* blogger
Chris Cillizza points out, it had a significant impact on the 2012
presidential election. "[The] idea that the one percent got
rewarded while everyone else got the shaft was at the center
not only of Obama's positive message (that he was a fighter for
the middle class) but of his negative message against former
Massachusetts Gov. Mitt Romney as well. . . . Obama became
the middle class champion while Romney was cast as protector
of the wealthy."[53]

Hannah Arendt writes that "popular revolt against materially
strong rulers . . . may engender an almost irresistible power

even if it foregoes the use of violence."[54] Here she invokes what she feels is a critical distinction between strength and power. Strength is a property of individuals, while power is a property of groups: "Power springs up between men when they act together and vanishes the moment they disperse" and "is to an astonishing degree independent of material factors."[55] Strength, by contrast, relies on instruments. It is exemplified by the tyrant who has many such tools at his behest—but no power. "[Whoever] isolates himself and does not partake in such being together," she writes, "forfeits power and becomes impotent no matter how great his strength and how valid his reasons."[56] One's strength, and the instruments that support it, can paradoxically bring impotence—they can be the driving force of impotence, ensuring that one is disempowered while real power lies elsewhere, in the community. This arrangement brings to mind guns and their isolating effect, how they sow mutual mistrust among people, armed and unarmed alike. Guns are a force of social fragmentation, driving us into isolated camps, away from real social power.

In her short book *On Violence*, Arendt writes that "power corresponds to the human ability not just to act but to act in concert," for "when we say of somebody that he is 'in power' we actually refer to his being empowered by a certain number of people to act in their name.[57] Violence, inflicted by those who possess strength, is highly individuating. It can be exacted by individuals, and with devastating effect—think of the suicide bombers who kill hundreds. Violence isolates, smashing communities, separating individuals, alienating us from one another in our pain and fear. As such, Arendt claims, "violence can always destroy power" but can never give rise to it.[58] In fact, she adds, "rule by sheer violence comes into play where power is being lost."[59] That is, when a regime turns to brute force to exert its will and ensure obedience, this is a sign that its authority is waning; it must compel by threat of violence because it no longer commands respect. And once a regime relies on violence, its days are numbered, according to Arendt—it betrays vulnerability. The turn to violence is, in other words, a symptom and expression of weakness. "[Impotence] breeds violence," she writes, and a "loss of power becomes a temptation to substitute violence for power."[60] One can command from such a perch for a time, but it is tenuous and by no means free.

We tend to equate strength and violence with freedom and power, Arendt maintains, but we do so in vain. Violence does not make one free, but to the contrary, renders a person vulnerable to force and compelled to live in fear. The tyrant, Arendt might say, reaches for his weapons and armies in order to secure, assert, and expand his freedom, but foils his aim in the process: he must fear violent reprisal until the end of his days. Guns are subject to the same logic. They offer a false sense of power. What's more, Arendt urges us to consider how guns themselves are symptoms of impotence, or rather, expressions of a sensed loss of power—sensed not overtly, perhaps, but just beneath the surface. How might this be the case? What social or political impotence might the robust gun rights movement express?

Many commentators have noted striking similarities between the grievances of the Tea Party and the Occupy movement, even while they seem polar opposites and endorse different approaches to their grievances. At bottom, both political movements objected to the government response to the 2008 recession—in particular, to the bailout of the banks whose risky behavior was a prime cause of the recession. This was, both movements agreed, a severe violation of the principle of fairness. Some were aided unfairly—including those who bore an outsize share of the culpability for the crisis—while others were burdened unfairly. On the latter point, the Tea Party and Occupy diverge: the Tea Party maintained that the hard-working middle class should not be burdened for the indiscretions of wealthy financiers, the mistakes of homebuyers facing foreclosure, or the general laziness of the poor. The Occupy movement wished to lift the burden on middle class and poor alike, and urged that the rich carry their fair share. Still, both movements highlighted how growing numbers of Americans had come to feel that the cards were stacked in favor of select portions of the population. Traditional values of diligence, honesty, and responsibility were no longer rewarded, but greed and deceit were.

Economist Joseph Stiglitz points out that "for most American families, even before the onset of the recession, incomes adjusted for inflation were even lower than they had been a decade earlier."[61] The recession wiped out much of the wealth of the middle class and the poor. Millions of Americans who had the bulk of their net worth tied up in their homes found those homes in foreclosure, and millions more faced unemployment or chronic underemployment. As the dust from the great recession of 2008 settled, a further insult was laid bare. As Annie Lowrey reports in the *New York Times*, "the top 10 percent of earners took more than half of the country's total income in 2012, the highest level recorded" in the past century, and "the top 1 percent took more than one-fifth of the income earned by Americans, one of the highest levels on record since 1913."[62] The wealthy minority not only did not suffer during the recession, it made out better—while the rest slipped further down the economic ladder.

Because few were convicted or found culpable of the reckless behavior that brought about the economic crisis, and because many at the center of it were given preferential treatment, or at least handled kindly, Stiglitz writes, "views that our political system is rigged are even stronger than those that our economic system is unfair."[63] Prime evidence of the former, he argues, is the Citizens United decision of 2010, which permitted corporations to shower political candidates with money. Though critics' worst predictions did not come true—namely, that the corporate interests backing Romney, for example, would overwhelm the opposition with their financial power, and single-handedly spirit him to victory—the 2012 presidential election proved to be the most expensive ever, with spending on the order of $6 billion.[64] It is no mistake that ordinary Americans feel political influence is so far out of reach, the exclusive domain of the rich—indeed, the domain of a further minority still, the exorbitantly rich. It is a cycle that deepens the general sense of disempowerment, according to Stiglitz: "Political rules of the game have not only directly benefited those at the top, ensuring that they have a disproportionate voice, but have also created a political process that indirectly gives them more power," insofar as the process contributes to a broader "disillusionment with politics and distrust of the political system."[65] As people recognize that their role in the political system is diminished, so they are even less inclined to take part in it, or pay attention, and instead focus on themselves and their own concerns. In this respect, *Citizens United* is doubly damaging, Stiglitz argues, for it performs a literal act of disenfranchisement, granting disproportionate power to the few, and in the process, frustrates the masses from exercising whatever political influence remains. It encourages and accelerates a progressive retreat from the democratic process—from politics itself—on the part of the masses, who would be the backbone of democracy.

As if commenting on our plight, Arendt writes that the "glorification of violence is caused by severe frustration of the faculty of action in the modern world."[66] That is to say, glorified violence is symptomatic of political impotence, our inability to act politically and convey political power. This glorification of violence is not an act of frustration and despair but a substitute—it is an alternative means of expression, which, as Arendt would point out, seems potent—but is not. During the 2008 presidential campaign, candidate Obama told a group of donors in San Francisco—remarks that, when leaked to the public, sparked an uproar on the right—that working-class voters in middle America "get bitter, they cling to their guns or religion or antipathy to people who aren't like them or anti-immigrant sentiment or anti-trade sentiment as a way to explain their frustrations."[67] Reflecting on these comments, journalist Dan Baum believes that Obama's point "wasn't so much that stressed out blue-collar folks were clinging bitterly to their guns and religion" but "that guns and religion were keeping them from feeling bitter about the indignities inflicted upon the middle class."[68] What indignities does Baum have in mind? "Many of the partially educated, rural, middle-aged guys in the bulge of the gun-guy demographics hadn't seen a real wage increase since 1978," and that was merely one of several trends: "Job security: gone. Employer-provided health care: gone. Pensions: gone. House: underwater. [Gun guys] had their livers pecked out while women, immigrants, blacks and gays all seemed to have become groovier, sexier and more dynamic players in American culture than they were."[69] The gun-owning demographic was especially afflicted by the recent economic crisis, and long-term economic trends. It is a portion of our society that finds its lot precarious in many ways—and grasps for security in some corner of life. For an individual whose existence is otherwise filled with insecurity, guns offer the illusion of control—as Tocqueville might say, the illusion of security. Baum believes he understands the solace guns provide when he writes of the revelation he received from concealed carry: "I had the skill, courage and maturity to manipulate a device of boundless lethality and keep its power safely contained. What bolstered my self-esteem was my ability to live alongside a firearm day in and day out, without ever harming anybody. The gun made me useful, relevant, special."[70]

On a less noble note, Baum suggests that gun culture is also strongly reactionary. The people who cling to their guns increasingly find themselves faced with insecurity unfamiliar (so they think) to their forebears and long for the days when insecurity was something suffered by others (namely, the poor and minorities). Gun culture, Baum would remind us, is predominantly white and male, its most avid adherents older and blue collar—precisely the population that once had it particularly good in America but that, thanks to several economic, social, and political revolutions, has seen its influence and status diminished, and its once certain rewards reduced or taken away altogether. This explains the anger of gun owners, Baum believes—the anger that seems so anomalous and mystifying to those on the left. It's an anger that indicates that the issue is about more than just guns. It's the anger evident in the speeches of former NRA spokesman Charlton Heston, who liked to point out how gun owners are scorned by the liberal media and political establishment—told to "sit down and shut up," as he put it. Heston understood that gun owners were casualties of a revolution; they are a besieged demographic, whose rights and interests have been eclipsed and whose welfare is receding—and with the symbols of their indignation and alarm in hand, would stand up and scream "Stop!" For Heston, the gun was less about reserving the right of rebellion and more about asserting one's refusal to give ground in the social divide.

Echoing and expanding upon Baum's critique, Leonard Steinhorn claims that gun culture reacts to and reviles a reversal of fortune, and also a reversal of values:

> [Now], in our knowledge economy, we admire and awe the brainy elite and erstwhile geek whereas the musclebound working man has become déclassé. Adding insult is that liberal intellectuals that used to venerate blue collar virtues have now embraced and acclaimed the exact group that yesteryear's working class rejected as unmanly, effeminate, gay men, thus turning the masculinity power structure of old upside-down.[71]

A remarkable political trend of the past decade is the acceptance of homosexuality across broad swathes of America. At the end of 2013, even the deep red state of Utah was pressed to legalize gay marriage. This is a stunning change when you consider that gay marriage was political kryptonite for liberals not long ago—so much so that Republican strategist Karl Rove sought to put it on state ballots during the 2004 presidential elections in order to galvanize the Christian vote. Ten years later, gay marriage has become a rallying cry for Democrats. Gun culture is an attempt to reassert the primacy of masculine virtues, Steinhorn argues, and buying a gun affirms one's strength as a man. Prime evidence of this, he explains, is the ads devised by arms manufacturers: "Glock guns give men 'confidence to live your life.' The Walther PPX handgun is 'Tough. Very Tough.'"[72] The manufacturer of Bushmaster semiautomatic weapons was widely criticized after the Sandy Hook shootings (Lanza used a Bushmaster in that incident) when the media highlighted the company's ad campaign, which showed pictures of the weapon alongside the words "Consider your Man Card reissued." Before this campaign was summarily terminated after Sandy Hook, "you could learn on the 'Man Card' section of Bushmaster's website that 'In a world of rapidly depleting testosterone, the Bushmaster Man Card declares and confirms that you are a man's man.'"[73]

Paired with the dramatic reversal in fortune for middle-class white men is the humbling fact that they find themselves increasingly dependent on government. The Tea Party, largely born out of anger at government expansion, reserved special ire for the social safety net. Of course, in a great irony, many of those same angry Tea Party proponents have found themselves reliant on government assistance—including, in its economic insecurity, the gun guy demographic. For those who like to consider themselves free and self-determining, this is galling. *New York Times* reporters Binyamin Appelbaum and Robert Gebeloff capture this well in a 2012 story on Tea Party supporters in Chisago County, Minnesota. The reporters encounter a remarkable number of Tea Partiers "who describe themselves as self-sufficient members of the American middle class and as opponents of government largess" even while they "are drawing more deeply on that government with each passing year."[74] Chisago County leans Republican, Appelbaum and Gebeloff point out, with a large population of Tea Party adherents. Even so, government benefits in the county increased 69 percent between 2000 and 2009, and "across the nation, the government now provides almost $1 in benefits for every $4 in other income."[75] Republicans, and their vocal Tea Party cohorts, are not wrong to ring the alarm on growth in government spending—but it is strange that they benefit so greatly from what they would deny others. Appelbaum and Gebeloff cite a study by Dartmouth professor Dean Lacy, which shows that

> support for Republican candidates, who generally promise to cut government spending, has increased since 1980 in states where the federal government spends more than it collects. The greater the dependence, the greater the support for Republican candidates. Conversely, states that pay more in taxes than they receive in benefits tend to support Democratic candidates.[76]

One of the residents Appelbaum and Gebeloff interviewed, a Mr. Gulbranson, relies on several thousand dollars each year from the earned income tax credit. His tight finances prompted him to sign up his children to receive free school breakfast and lunch at federal expense. Medicare paid for his mother's surgery, which he could not have otherwise afforded. In spite of all this, he stated, "I don't demand that the government does this for me. I don't feel like I need the government."[77] Another resident, whose disabled daughter is the beneficiary of numerous government-funded programs for her care and education, as well as "for trained attendants to stay with her at home while [her parents] work," claimed he would like the government to do less. He said his daughter did not need all the benefits provided for her. A tattoo artist complained that so much government support was being wasted— for instance, on tattoos. Government beneficiaries, he complained, are "getting $300 or $400 tattoos, and they're wearing nice new Nike shoes that I can't afford. . . . I guess I shouldn't say it because it's my business, but I think a tattoo is a little too extravagant."[78]

Evident in these statements is an impulse that can only be described as self-destructive: these people are so angry at government support and those who benefit from it that they would rather hurt themselves than see it continue. Of course, the struggling Tea Party supporters in Chisago County say they feel self-sufficient and self-determining. They think they are still autonomous or should be, or they yearn desperately, perhaps myopically, to be independent again as they fancy they once were. But they have fallen far short and are bitter as a result. Appelbaum and Gebeloff write that as "more middle-class families . . . land in the safety net in Chisago and similar communities, anger at the government has increased alongside. . . . They say they want to reduce the role of government in their own lives. They are frustrated that they need help, feel guilty for taking it and resent the government for providing it. They say they want less help for themselves."[79] The authors evoke a growing sense of helplessness among those who staunchly see themselves otherwise. They reveal a strong undercurrent in society where growing numbers of Americans (especially conservatives) suspect they are living a lie: they glorify self-reliance but are propped up by government support. In fact, government support runs so deep—it is so vast and expansive in twenty-first-century America—that we hardly recognize it: farm subsidies ensure lower food prices for us all; tax breaks for oil companies (effectively subsidies) provide us with the lowest gas prices in the industrial world; federal mortgage guarantees keep interest rates low, enabling millions of Americans to own homes; our bloated defense budget sustains large segments of the economy and puts millions of people to work. It is inconceivable, and deeply unpalatable, to do away with government support. It is far better to assert one's longed-for independence—or extreme displeasure at its demise—by other means. Such as owning a gun.

In many respects, Thomas Jefferson seems an ally of the modern gun rights movement. Saul Cornell points out that Jefferson was unique among his peers, notably in the writing of the Virginia Constitution, in that he did not believe the right to bear arms should be linked to a civic duty to serve in a militia but should be unlimited and unqualified. He was persuaded by the Italian Enlightenment philosopher Cesare Beccaria, Cornell explains, who "was the first modern theorist to argue that when firearms are outlawed, only outlaws will have firearms."⁸⁰ Jefferson wished to include in the Virginia Constitution the simple and expansive statement that "no free man shall be debarred the use of arms," but as this "proved too bold for his contemporaries," Cornell writes, he "quickly emended his draft language to narrow the scope of this right."⁸¹

Jefferson, we must recall, is also credited with that incendiary phrase gun rights advocates are fond of citing: "The tree of liberty must be refreshed from time to time with the blood of tyrants." He desperately wanted the American people to retain their revolutionary spirit, Arendt maintains, which is why he was so pleased upon hearing of Shays' Rebellion in the early republic, where Massachusetts farmers and Revolutionary War veterans violently objected to the vast debt they found themselves in, and marched to close the courts where they would be prosecuted for their delinquency. Jefferson remarked that we should not go twenty years without similar rebellions. "The very fact that the people had taken it upon themselves to rise and act was enough for him," Arendt writes, "regardless of the rights or wrongs of their case."⁸²

And yet, Arendt points out, and as his later letters reveal, Jefferson had a change of heart regarding rebellion—a change of heart that carries significant implications for the contemporary gun rights movement and ultimately provides an impressive rebuttal to it. Jefferson voiced his approval of Shays's Rebellion in Paris, where he was serving as ambassador to France, two years before the start of the French Revolution. At that point, Arendt argues, he was prone to fallacious thinking about the nature of political action: he conceived it "exclusively in the image of tearing down and building up."⁸³ He belonged to a generation that had performed remarkable political feats. They had successfully rebelled against a monarch, erected a democratic republic, and written constitutions for the various states and the federal government. Jefferson could not be blamed, at that point in his life, for clinging to a violent concept of political action, which is why he was not dismayed by the news of violent rebellion in his homeland—he considered it the font of democratic energy. Later, Arendt maintains, the French Revolution disabused him of this notion. The constant upheaval proved fatal to the bold aspirations of its instigators and early apologists, leaving much bloodshed in its wake and ultimately landing France in the lap of the imperialist Napoleon. When Jefferson "had learned his lesson from the catastrophes of the French Revolution, where the violence of liberation had frustrated all attempts at founding a secure space for freedom," Arendt writes, he "shifted from his earlier identification of action with rebellion and tearing down to an identification with founding anew and building up."[84]

Jefferson's change of heart is evident in an 1816 letter to one Samuel Kercheval where he mentions two key notions in some detail: the ward system, and the recurring constitutional convention. Of the former, he tells Kercheval that we ought to "divide the counties into wards of such size as that every citizen can attend, when called on, and act in person. . . . [M]aking every citizen an acting member of the government, and in the offices nearest and most interesting to him, will attach him by his strongest feelings to the independence of his country and its republican constitution."[85] Jefferson reveals that he is thinking primarily of New England townships, where citizens would take part in the public business of the town, and make policy, public spending, and taxation decisions for their own jurisdiction. These townships, he writes, "have proved themselves the wisest invention ever devised by the wit of man for the perfect exercise of self-government, and for its preservation," where "the whole is cemented by giving to every citizen, personally, a part in the administration of the public affairs."[86]

Arendt explains that Jefferson developed grave doubts about the future of the American republic, and its success in preserving our freedom. He had "a foreboding of how dangerous it might be to allow the people a share in the public power without providing them at the same time with more public space than the ballot box," she writes, and perceived a "mortal danger to the republic" insofar as "the Constitution had given all power to the citizens without giving them the opportunity of *being* republicans and of *acting* as citizens."[87] Retaining power but having no real means to exercise it leaves the citizenry ripe for manipulation by private interests who wish to channel that power for private gain. Jefferson offered the ward system as an attempt to provide an enduring public space of freedom, where each of us might act as republicans, take on the business of politics, and know it intimately—and know our freedom intimately, too, so that we might be vigilant, and jealous to guard it. "Each ward would thus be a small republic within itself," he writes in a letter to John Cartwright some years later, "and every man in the State would thus become an acting member of the common government. . . . The wit of man cannot devise a more solid basis for a free, durable and well-administered republic."[88]

According to Arendt, Jefferson's plan would perform two essential services. First, it offers us that space to be political beings, as is our elemental yearning, and the necessary condition for freedom and happiness. Second—and crucially—the ward system ensures and continually nurtures the legitimacy of the state. "[While] in all authoritarian government," Arendt explains, "authority is filtered down from above, in this case authority would have been generated neither at the top nor at the bottom, but on each of the pyramid's layers; and this obviously could constitute the solution to one of the most serious problems of all modern politics, which is not how to reconcile freedom and equality but . . . equality and authority."[89] In a ward system, as Arendt has it, authority is generated at each level, in that the imprint of the people is carried upward to each successive level of government. This would provide considerable defense against perceived crises of legitimacy—including those that motivate the gun rights movement.

Jefferson also tells Kercheval that

> Some men look at constitutions with sanctimonious reverence, and deem them like the arc of the covenant, too sacred to be touched. They ascribe to the men of the preceding age a wisdom more than human, and suppose what they did to be beyond amendment. . . . I am certainly not an advocate for frequent and untried changes in laws and constitutions. I think moderate imperfections had better be borne with; because when once known, we accommodate ourselves to them, and find practical means of correcting their ill effects. But I know also that laws and institutions must go hand in hand with the progress of the human mind. As that becomes more developed, more enlightened, as new discoveries are made, new truths disclosed, and manners and opinions change with the change of circumstances, institutions must advance also, and keep pace with the times.[90]

It is interesting to note Jefferson's dismissal of those who would insist on a fixed and set meaning of the Constitution, as if we are forced to accept it as it was written by the Founding Fathers—even while their intent may no longer be entirely evident to us, and the context of their words is quite different indeed. In making it a critical element of their argument that we are *obliged* to observe gun rights simply because they are enshrined in the Constitution, gun rights advocates are wont to treat the Constitution as that divine document which Jefferson deplores. At the same time, however, Jefferson reveals the lessons he has taken from the French Revolution, namely that radical change can be more damaging than its promised or anticipated reward. He thus urges us to live with "moderate imperfections" rather than risk dooming the whole edifice. He is mindful of the serious nature of revolution—whose prospects, in the days of Shays' Rebellion, he perhaps took too lightly. Revolution is necessary, but we must strenuously avoid the violence that so often deforms, it. To this end, Jefferson proposes that we "provide in our constitution for its revision at stated periods."[91] These periods, he later advises, should be every nineteen years, or when a new generation comes to occupy the majority. A constitutional convention will be called, and its delegates and reforms approved ultimately by the wards themselves. Jefferson describes how the mayor would apprise his ward of these reforms and convey their decision upward to the county court, which would in turn pass it on to higher levels of government. The "voice of the whole people," he writes, "would thus be fairly, fully, and peaceably expressed, discussed and decided by the common reason of society. If this avenue be shut to the call of sufferance, it will make itself heard through that of force, and we shall go on, as other nations are doing, in the endless circle of oppression, rebellion, reformation."[92]

In Jefferson's view, our republic requires official, sanctioned methods for radical change. The violence of revolution is destructive of, not conducive to, freedom. The gun rights movement fails to grasp this—or it chooses to ignore it. Much like the nonviolent movements led by King and others, Jefferson aims to enable radical change within the rule of law. Once rule of law is undermined, so are all possibilities for political freedom. Arendt says of Jefferson that he knew that "the violence of liberation" frustrates "attempts at founding a secure space for freedom." This sums up nicely my diagnosis of an armed society: the violence of liberation, such as the gun rights movement claims to endorse, would destroy the space of freedom. Pervasive arms inhibit free speech, and make assembly and democratic protest ultimately impossible.

A free state does all it can to preserve and protect a secure and fruitful space of freedom, where residents may act as empowered political creatures. A free state looks for legal and political means to enact radical change, when such change is needed, from a population that is vigorously and broadly engaged. As this is made more remote, Jefferson suggests, we must expect basic political urges—the urge to be free and autonomous—to emerge in unwelcome ways, in violent acts that threaten to undermine the state as such.

The contemporary gun rights movement, in its fury, in its extreme and often irrational demands, exemplifies the political decline Jefferson feared. It is symptomatic of widespread political disenfranchisement in a cultural democracy—a state that, though it is hardly committed to democratic principles with any seriousness, routinely tosses them about as a matter of course. Is it any wonder some take the charge of autonomy seriously—literally—angrily, and reach for the gun? In so doing, however, they reveal their ignorance of the real substance and power of autonomy.

The gun rights movement would author a demise of democracy, yet, it is also a symptom: it signals a decline of democracy at hand, precipitated by larger, entrenched forces. Any attempt to regulate guns in America, and limit their destruction, must therefore be accompanied by greater political changes, innovations, and reforms, which make the state more transparent and our democracy more responsive to the wishes and needs of the people in whom, at least in theory, sovereignty rests. We must have the courage to be a democracy, to hear the voices of all—even those we fear, or suspect—and demand a forum for our voices in turn.

Notes

PREFACE

1. Barack H. Obama, State of the Union Address, February 12, 2013, *Whitehouse.gov*, http://www.whitehouse.gov/the-press-office/2013/02/12/remarks-president-state-union-address (accessed January 21, 2014).

2. Lydia Saad, "Americans Want Stricter Gun Laws, Still Oppose Bans," *Gallup*, December 27, 2012, http://www.gallup.com/poll/159569/americans-stricter-gun-laws-oppose-bans.aspx.

3. "Broad Support for Renewed Background Checks Bill, Skepticism about Its Chances," *Pew Research Center*, May 23, 2013, http://www.people-press.org/2013/05/23/broad-support-for-renewed-background-checks-bill-skepticism-about-its-chances/.

4. "State Gun Laws Enacted in the Year Since Newtown," *New York Times*, December 10, 2013, http://www.nytimes.com/interactive/2013/12/10/us/state-gun-laws-enacted-in-the-year-since-newtown.html.

5. Melanie Michael, "Popcorn Defense: Can Accused Florida Movie Shooter Use 'Stand your Ground?'" *KSDK.com*, January 15, 2014, http://www.ksdk.com/story/news/nation/2014/01/15/popcorn-defense-can-accused-florida-movie-shooter-use-stand-your-ground/4488939/.

6. Sean Sullivan, "Everything You Need to Know about 'Stand Your Ground Laws,'" *Washington Post*, July 15, 2013, http://www.washingtonpost.com/blogs/the-fix/wp/2013/07/15/everything-you-need-to-know-about-stand-your-ground-laws/.

7. Sabrina Tavernise and Robert Gebeloff, "Share of Homes with Guns Shows 4-Decade Decline," *New York Times*, March 9, 2013, http://www.nytimes.com/2013/03/10/us/rate-of-gun-ownership-is-down-survey-shows.html.

8. Dan Baum, *Gun Guys: A Road Trip* (New York: Alfred A. Knopf, 2013), 160–161.

9. Judith Butler, "Violence, Mourning, Politics," in *Precarious Life: The Powers of Mourning and Violence* (London: Verso, 2004), 28.

10. "Unconcealed Guns Can Unsettle, but They're Often Legal," narrated by Sandy Hausman, *NPR*, January 30, 2013, http://www.npr.org/2013/01/30/170652470/unconcealed-guns-can-unsettle-but-theyre-often-legal.

11. Sean Trende, "What Colorado's Recall Results Mean for Dems," *Real Clear Politics*, September 11, 2013, http://www.realclearpolitics.com/articles/2013/09/11/what_colorados_recall_results_mean_for_dems_119913.html.

12. Joshua Horwitz and Casey Anderson, *Guns, Democracy and the Insurrectionist Idea* (Ann Arbor: University of Michigan Press, 2009), 226.

13. Wayne LaPierre, speech delivered at the Weatherby Foundation International Hunting and Conservation Award Dinner, Reno, Nevada, January 22, 2012, http://www.pbs.org/newshour/rundown/2013/01/lapierre-responds-to-obamas-inaugural-address.html.

14. Baum, *Gun Guys*, 65.

15. Hannah Arendt, *The Human Condition* (Chicago: University of Chicago Press, 1958), 26.

CHAPTER 1. THE CULTURE OF FEAR

1. Wayne LaPierre, press conference, Willard Intercontinental Hotel, Washington, D.C., December 21, 2012, http://home.nra.org/home/document/nra-press-conference.

2. LaPierre, press conference, December 21, 2012.

3. Kristin M. S. Bezio, "Stop Blaming Video Games for America's Gun Violence," *Christian Science Monitor*, February 12, 2013, http://www.csmonitor.com/Commentary/Opinion/2013/0212/Stop-blaming-video-games-for-America-s-gun-violence.

4. Congressman Frank Wolf website, "Wolf Again Supports Warning Labels on Violent Video Games, January 24, 2011, http://wolf.house.gov/press-releases/wolf-again-supports-warning-labels-on-violent-video-games/.

5. Liza Gold, "Gun Violence: Are Violent Video Games to Blame?" *Fairfax Times*, September 25, 2013, http://www.fairfaxtimes.com/article/20130925/OPINION/130929392/1065/gun-violence-are-violent-video-games-to-blame&template=fairfaxTimes.

6. Elisabeth Hasselbeck on "Fox and Friends," *Fox News*, September 17, 2013, https://archive.org/details/foxnewsw_20130917_100000_fox_and_friends.

7. Drew Desilver, "A Minority of Americans Own Guns, but Just How Many Is Unclear," *Pew Research Center, June 4, 2013*, http://www.pewresearch.org/fact-tank/2013/06/04/a-minority-of-americans-own-guns-but-just-how-many-is-unclear/.

8. "Gun Homicides and Gun Ownership Listed by Country," *Datablog* (blog), *Guardian*, June 22, 2012, http://www.theguardian.com/news/datablog/2012/jul/22/gun-homicides-ownership-world-list.

9. Sydney Lupkin, "U.S. Has More Guns—and Gun Deaths—Than Any Other Country, Study Finds," *Medical Unit* (blog), *ABC News*, September 10, 2013, http://abcnews.go.com/blogs/health/2013/09/19/u-s-has-more-guns-and-gun-deaths-than-any-other-country-study-finds/.

10. Lupkin, "U.S. Has More Guns."

11. Lupkin, "U.S. Has More Guns."

12. "FastStats: Assault or Homicide," *Centers for Disease Control and Prevention*, updated December 20, 2013, http://www.cdc.gov/nchs/fastats/homicide.htm; FastStats: Suicide and Self-Inflicted Injury," *Centers for Disease Control and Prevention*, updated December 20, 2013, http://www.cdc.gov/nchs/fastats/suicide.htm.

13. David Gura, "Background Check: What It Really Takes to Buy a Gun," *Marketplace, American Public Media*, February 7, 2013, http://www.marketplace.org/topics/business/guns-and-dollars/background-check-what-it-really-takes-buy-gun.

14. Gura, "Background Check."

15. Jen Christensen, "How the Violent Mentally Ill Can Buy Guns," *CNN*, February 5, 2013, http://www.cnn.com/2013/01/30/health/mental-illness-guns/.

16. Michael Cooper, Michael S. Schmidt and Michael Luo, "Gun Law Loopholes Allow Buyers to Skirt Checks," *New York Times*, April 10, 2013, http://www.nytimes.com/2013/04/11/us/gun-law-loopholes-let-buyers-skirt-background-checks.html.

17. Corinne Jones, "Background Checks on Gun Sales: How Do They Work?" *CNN*, April 10, 2013, http://www.cnn.com/2013/04/10/politics/background-checks-explainer/.

18. Michael Bloomberg, interview by Bob Schieffer, *Face the Nation, CBS*, July 22, 2012, http://www.cbsnews.com/news/face-the-nation-transcripts-july-22-2012-aurora-mayor-and-police-chief-mayor-bloomberg-pm-netanyahu/3/.

19. Frank Main, "Getting a Gun in Chicago Quick and Easy," *Chicago Sun-Times*, August 25, 2012, http://www.suntimes.com/news/crime/14618767-418/getting-a-gun-in-chicago-quick-and-easy.html.

20. Main, "Getting a Gun in Chicago Quick and Easy."

21. Lupkin, "U.S. Has More Guns."

22. "Firearms-Control Legislation and Policy: Australia," *Library of Congress: Law Library of Congress*, updated February 28, 2014, http://www.loc.gov/law/help/firearms-control/australia.php.

23. "Firearms-Control Legislation and Policy: Australia."

24. "Firearms-Control Legislation and Policy: Australia."

25. "Firearms-Control Legislation and Policy: Australia."

26. Lupkin, "U.S. Has More Guns."

27. "Firearms-Control Legislation and Policy: Canada," *Library of Congress: Law Library of Congress*, updated February 28, 2014, http://www.loc.gov/law/help/firearms-control/canada.php.

28. "Firearms-Control Legislation and Policy: Canada."

29. "Licensing Gun Owners and Purchasers Policy Summary," *Law Center to Prevent Gun Violence*, posted August 23, 2013, http://smartgunlaws.org/licensing-of-gun-owners-purchasers-policy-summary/.

30. "Licensing Gun Owners and Purchasers Policy Summary."

31. "Sales of Multiple Guns Policy Summary," *Law Center to Prevent Gun Violence*, posted December 9, 2013, http://smartgunlaws.org/multiple-purchases-sales-of-firearms-policy-summary/.

32. "Safe Storage and Gun Locks Policy Summary," *Law Center to Prevent Gun Violence*, posted September 1, 2013, http://smartgunlaws.org/safe-storage-gun-locks-policy-summary/.

33. "Safe Storage and Gun Locks Policy Summary."

34. Tavernise and Gebeloff, "Share of Homes with Guns Shows 4-Decade Decline."

35. Nate Silver, "Party Identity in a Gun Cabinet," *Five Thirty-Eight: Nate Silver's Political Calculus* (blog), *New York Times*, December 18, 2012, http://fivethirtyeight.blogs.nytimes.com/2012/12/18/in-gun-ownership-statistics-partisan-divide-is-sharp/.

36. Richard Legault, *Trends in Gun Ownership* (El Paso, Tex.: LFB Scholarly Publishing, 2008), 112.

37. "Gun Rights and Gun Control—September 2010," Pew Research Center, http://www.pewresearch.org/files/old-assets/pdf/gun-control-2011.pdf.

38. Manny Fernandez, "Oklahomans Prepare for a New Law that Will Make Guns a Common Sight," *New York Times*, October 30, 2012, http://www.nytimes.com/2012/10/31/us/oklahoma-prepares-for-open-carry-gun-law.html.

39. Fernandez, "Oklahomans Prepare for New Law."

40. John Pierce, "Why Open Carry Gun Laws Work," *U.S. News and World Report*, April 15, 2010, http://www.usnews.com/opinion/articles/2010/04/15/why-open-carry-gun-laws-work.

41. Fernandez, "Oklahomans Prepare for New Law."

42. Fernandez, "Oklahomans Prepare for New Law."

43. Tom Jackman, "Today Is 'Gun Owners Support Starbucks Day,' for Virginians Who Openly Carry Guns in Public," *The State of NoVa* (blog), *Washington Post*, February 22, 2013, http://www.washingtonpost.com/blogs/the-state-of-nova/post/today-is-gun-owners-support-starbucks-day-for-virginians-who-openly-carry-guns-in-public/2013/02/22/a82d25c8–7c6d-11e2-a044–67685653 6b40_blog.html.

44. Fernandez, "Oklahomans Prepare for New Law."

45. Manny Fernandez, "An Entry Reserved for Those with Guns," *New York Times*, March 8, 2013, http://www.nytimes.com/2013/03/09/us/guns-get-a-pass-at-texas-capitol.html.

46. Fernandez, "An Entry Reserved."

47. Fernandez, "An Entry Reserved."

48. Joel Achenbach, "This Gun Rights Backer, Armed with His Glock and His Blog, Is Always on Alert," *Washington Post*, February 2, 2013, http://www.washingtonpost.com/national/health-science/this-gun-rights-backer-armed-with-his-glock-and-his-blog-is-always-on-alert/2013/02/02/2467d81e-6c87–11e2-ada0–5ca5fa7ebe79_story.html.

49. Achenbach, "Always on Alert."

50. Achenbach, "Always on Alert."

51. Baum, *Gun Guys*, 307.

52. Baum, *Gun Guys*, 307.

53. "Author Says Arming Urban Youth Might Stem Violence," *U.S. News and World Report*, March 8, 2013, http://www.usnews.com/news/articles/2013/03/08/author-says-arming-urban-youth-might-stem-violence.

54. "Arming Urban Youth Might Stem Violence."

55. "Arming Urban Youth Might Stem Violence."

56. Baum, *Gun Guys*, 157–58.

57. Steven Pinker, *The Better Angels of Our Nature* (New York: Penguin Books, 2011), 117.

58. Joel N. Shurkin, "Mystery of New York's Crime Rate Remains Unsolved," *Inside Science News Service*, February 13, 2013, http://www.insidescience.org/content/mystery-new-yorks-falling-crime-rate-remains-unsolved/937.

59. Richard Simon, "Washington D.C. Finishes 2012 with Fewer than 100 Murders," *Los Angeles Times*, January 1, 2013, http://articles.latimes.com/2013/jan/01/nation/la-na-nn-washington-dc-2012-homicides-20130101.

60. Federal Bureau of Investigation, *Crime in the United States 2011*, Table no. 1, http://www.fbi.gov/about-us/cjis/ucr/crime-in-the-u.s/2011/crime-in-the-u.s.-2011/tables/table-1.

61. Bureau of Justice Statistics: Office of Justice Programs, *Special Report: Violent Victimization Committed by Strangers, 1993–2010*, by Erika Harrell, December 2012, http://bjs.gov/content/pub/pdf/vvcs9310.pdf.

62. James Dao, "Baltimore Streets Meaner, but Message Is Mixed," *New York Times*, February 9, 2005, http://www.nytimes.com/2005/02/09/national/09baltimore.html.

63. Dao, "Baltimore Streets Meaner."

64. David Heinzmann, "Homicide Numbers Reveal Stark Contrast: African-Americans Hardest Hit by Spike in Violence, Deaths in Chicago," *Chicago Tribune*, July 12, 2012, http://articles.chicagotribune.com/2012-07-12/news/ct-met-chicago-homicide-demographics-20120712_1_homicide-victims-homicide-numbers-police-data.

65. Heinzmann, "Homicide Numbers Reveal Stark Contrast."

66. "How Urban Violence Fits into Gun-Control Policy," narrated by Scott Simon, *NPR*, January 19, 2013, http://www.npr.org/2013/01/19/169772283/how-urban-violence-fits-into-gun-control-policy.

67. "How Urban Violence Fits into Gun-Control Policy."

68. Jeffrey Jones, "Americans Still Perceive Crime as on the Rise," *Gallup*, November 18, 2010, http://www.gallup.com/poll/144827/americans-perceive-crime-rise.aspx. Also, Lydia Saad, "Most Americans Believe Crime in U.S. Is Worsening," *Gallup*, October 31, 2011, http://www.gallup.com/poll/150464/americans-believe-crime-worsening.aspx.

69. John Pierce, "Why Would an Average Citizen Need to Carry a Gun?" *OpenCarry.org*, January 18, 2013, http://www.opencarry.org/?p=788.

70. Pierce, "Why Would an Average Citizen Need to Carry a Gun?"

71. Lisa Frazier, "Report Links Baltimore Crime Fears, TV News; Polling Group Says Researcher Overstates Impact of Media, Ignores Other Factors," *Washington Post*, June 26, 1998, http://www.washingtonpost.com/wp-srv/WPlate/1998-06/26/099l-062698-idx.html.

72. Valerie Callanan, "Media Consumption, Perceptions of Crime Risk and Fear of Crime: Examining Race/Ethnic Differences," *Sociological Perspectives* 55, no. 1 (2012): 105. Emphasis added.

73. *ABC2News: The Latest at 11:00 PM*, WMAR-TV, May 15, 2013, http://www.abc2news.com/dpp/news/crime_checker/howard_county_crime/expert-says-there-are-almost-always-warning-signs-when-children-kill-their-parents.

74. Callanan, "Media Consumption, Perceptions of Crime Risk," 105.

75. Seokhee Yoon and Nancy Wilson, "Crime, Perception and Politics: Follow-up Report 4," *John Jay College of Criminal Justice, Center on Media, Crime and Justice*, 2008, http://www.jjay.cuny.edu/centers/media_crime_justice/report4_crime_perception_politics.pdf.

76. "Dateline," accessed May 8, 2013, http://www.nbcnews.com/id/3032600/.

77. Callanan, "Media Consumption, Perceptions of Crime Risk," 105.

78. Gloria Goodale, "Why It's Always Crime Time on TV," *Christian Science Monitor*, May 26, 2010, http://www.csmonitor.com/The-Culture/TV/2010 /0526/Why-it-s-always-crime-time-on-TV.

79. Goodale, "Why It's Always Crime Time on TV."

80. Bureau of Justice Statistics, *Homicide Trends in the United States*, by James Alan Fox and Marianne W. Zawitz, 2007, http://www.bjs.gov/index.cfm?ty=pbdetail&iid=966.

81. United States Conference of Mayors, *80th Annual Meeting, Resolution Adopted June 2012: Reducing Violent Deaths Among African American Men and Boys*, June 13–16, 2012, http://usmayors.org/resolutions/80th_Conference/csj07.asp.

82. Bara Reynolds, "Trayvon Martin, One Year Later: When Will Black-on-Black Murders Get the Attention They Deserve?" *Washington Post*, February 26, 2013, http://www.washingtonpost.com/blogs/therootdc/post/trayvon-martin-one-year-later-when-will-black-on-black-murders-get-the-attention-they-deserve/2013/02/26/f3c1fa4a-7fa1-11e2-b99e-6baf4ebe42df_blog.html.

83. Krissah Thompson and Hamil R. Harris, "Residents of Violence-Plagued D.C. Neighborhood Feel Largely Ignored in Gun Control Debate," *Washington Post*, March 12, 2013, http://articles.washingtonpost.com/2013-03-12/lifestyle/37652989_1_gun-violence-gun-control-debate-gun-crimes.

84. Thompson and Harris, "Residents of Violence-Plagued D.C. Neighborhood Feel Largely Ignored."

85. Thompson and Harris, "Residents of Violence-Plagued D.C. Neighborhood Feel Largely Ignored."

86. Dennis Cauchon and Martha Moore, "Desperation Forced a Horrific Decision," *USA Today*, September 2, 2002, http://usatoday30.usatoday.com/news/sept11/2002-09-02-jumper_x.htm.

87. Tom Leonard, "The 9/11 Victims America Wants to Forget," *Daily Mail*, September 11, 2011, http://www.dailymail.co.uk/news/article-2035720/9-11-jumpers-America-wants-forget-victims-fell-Twin-Towers.html.

88. Mikita Brottman, "The Fascination of the Abomination: The Censored Images of 9/11" in *Film and Television after 9/11*, ed. Wheeler W. Dixon (Carbondale: Southern Illinois University Press, 2004), 105.

89. Brottman, "The Fascination of the Abomination," 105.

90. Leonard, "The 9/11 Victims America Wants to Forget."

91. Steven Prince, *Firestorm: American Film in the Age of Terrorism* (New York: Columbia University Press, 2009), 136.

92. A. O. Scott, "Blood Bath and Beyond," review of *Kill Bill: Vol. 1*, dir. Quentin Tarantino, *New York Times*, October 10, 2003, http://movies.nytimes.com/2003/10/10/movies/10KILL.html.

93. Slavoj Žižek, *Violence* (New York: Picador, 2008), 44.

94. "The United States Spends More on Defense Than the Next Eight Countries combined," Peter G. Peterson Foundation, April 13, 2014, http://pgpf.org/Chart-Archive/0053_defense-comparison.

95. "Operation Enduring Freedom U.S. Casualty Status," accessed May 15, 2013, http://www.defense.gov/news/casualty.pdf.

96. Congressional Research Service, *Afghanistan Casualties: Military Forces and Civilians*, by Susan G. Chesser, CRS Report R41084 (Washington, D.C.: Office of Congressional Information and Publishing, December 6, 2012), http://www.fas.org/sgp/crs/natsec/R41084.pdf.

97. "Operation Iraqi Freedom U.S. Casualty Status," accessed May 15, 2013, http://www.defense.gov/news/casualty.pdf.

98. "The Toll of War in Iraq: U.S. Casualties and Civilian Deaths," http://www.npr.org/news/specials/tollofwar/tollofwarmain.html.

99. Elisabeth Bumiller, "A Day Job Waiting for a Kill Shot a World Away," *New York Times*, July 29, 2012, http://www.nytimes.com/2012/07/30/us/drone-pilots-waiting-for-a-kill-shot-7000-miles-away.html.

100. Tabassum Zakaria, "Nominee for CIA Chief Says Casualties from Drone Strikes Should Be Public," *Reuters*, February 15, 2013, http://www.reuters.com/article/2013/02/15/us-obama-nominations-brennan-drones-idUSBRE91E18N20130215.

101. Natasha Lennard, "Fact-Checking Feinstein on Civilian Drone Deaths," *Salon*, February 8, 2013, http://www.salon.com/2013/02/08/fact_checking_feinstein_on_civilian_drones_deaths/.

102. Peter Finn and Aaron Blake, "John Brennan Confirmed as CIA Director, but Filibuster Brings Scrutiny of Drone Program," *Washington Post*, March 7, 2013, http://www.washingtonpost.com/politics/rand-paul-says-hes-satisfied-with-obama-administrations-response-on-drones/2013/03/07/9b20aa44–875d–11e2–98a3-b3db6b9ac586_story.html.

103. LaPierre, press conference, December 21, 2012.

104. LaPierre, press conference, December 21, 2012. Emphasis in original.

105. LaPierre, press conference, December 21, 2012.

106. Wayne LaPierre, speech at the Western Hunting and Conservation Expo, Salt Lake City, Utah, February 23, 2013, http://home.nra.org/home/document/the-real-consequences-of-universal-background-checks.

107. David French, "The Biblical and Natural Right of Self-Defense," *The Corner* (blog), *National Review Online*, January 25, 2013, http://www.nationalreview.com/corner/338845/biblical-and-natural-right-self-defense-david-french.

108. Larry Pratt, "What Does the Bible Say about Gun Control?" *Gun Owners of America*, August 1, 1999, http://gunowners.org/fs9902.htm.

109. Joel McDurmon, "'Bring Your Pieces to Church' Sunday," *American Vision*, April 23, 2010, http://americanvision.org/2342/"bring-your-pieces-to-church"-sunday/.

110. Pratt, "What Does the Bible Say about Gun Control?"

111. Pratt, "What Does the Bible Say about Gun Control?"

112. Martin Durham, *The Christian Right, the Far Right and the Boundaries of American Conservatism* (Manchester, England: Manchester University Press, 2001), 72.

113. Durham, *The Christian Right, the Far Right and the Boundaries of American Conservatism*, 70.

114. Pratt, "What Does the Bible Say about Gun Control?"

115. Pratt, "What Does the Bible Say about Gun Control?"

116. French, "The Biblical and Natural Right of Self-Defense."

117. Richard Land, interview by Robert Siegel, "Southern Baptist Leader: 'Gun-Free Zones Are a Fantasy,'" *All Things Considered*, NPR, December 19, 2012, http://www.npr.org/2012/12/19/167649305/southern-baptist-leader-gun-free-zones-are-a-fantasy.

118. Land, "'Gun-free Zones Are a Fantasy.'"

119. Land, "'Gun-free Zones Are a Fantasy.'"

120. Land, "'Gun-free Zones Are a Fantasy.'"

121. Wayne LaPierre, "Stand and Fight," *Daily Caller*, February 13, 2013, http://dailycaller.com/2013/02/13/stand-and-fight/.

122. LaPierre, "Stand and Fight." La Pierre is invoking a disputed and discredited claim here, one that stems from alarming kidnapping figures announced by Phoenix officials in 2008, and which prompted media outlets and politicians at the time to occasionally refer to the city as the "No. 2 kidnapping capital in the world." Doubt was cast on the credibility of those statistics several years later, well before LaPierre made mention of Phoenix in this vein. LaPierre conveniently qualifies his assertion about Phoenix's dubious distinction (saying that it's merely "one of the kidnapping capitals"), but his claim remains disingenuous. Security experts point out that there are many cities across the globe far more prone to kidnapping—and that such rates are difficult to pinpoint in any event. Compare "Dewhurst Says Phoenix Has More Kidnappings Than Any Other City in the World Except for Mexico City," *PolitiFact.com*, June 18, 2010, http://www.politifact.com/texas/statements/2010/jun/18/david-dewhurst/dewhurst-says-phoenix-has-more-kidnappings-any-oth/. An investigative report later determined that initial statistics cited by Phoenix officials were grossly exaggerated. Interestingly enough, the report notes that politicians happily invoked those inflated numbers for their own gain, such as increasing the flow of federal law

enforcement dollars to Arizona. Apparently many people have found reason to overstate the relative danger of Phoenix. Cf. David Biscobing and Mark LaMet, "Truth behind Phoenix Kidnapping Statistics," *ABC15 Arizona*, July 25, 2013, http://www.abc15.com/news/local-news/investigations/truth-behind-phoenix-kidnapping-statistics.

123. LaPierre, "Stand and Fight."

124. Butler, "Violence, Mourning, Politics," 34.

125. Butler, "Violence, Mourning, Politics," 33–34.

126. Butler, "Violence, Mourning, Politics," 42.

127. Judith Butler, "Indefinite Detention," in *Precarious Life: The Powers of Mourning and Violence* (London: Verso, 2004), 74.

128. Butler, "Indefinite Detention," 90.

129. Baum, *Gun Guys*, 158.

130. "22 Chinese Children Hurt in Stabbing Spree," *CBC News*, December 15, 2012, http://www.cbc.ca/news/world/story/2012/12/15/china-stabbing-school.html.

131. Charlton Heston, "Winning the Culture War," speech delivered at Harvard Law School, Cambridge, Massachusetts, February 16, 1999, http://www.americanrhetoric.com/speeches/charltonhestonculturalwar.htm.

132. LaPierre, press conference, December 21, 2012.

133. Liza Gold, "Gun Violence: Psychiatry, Risk Assessment, and Social Policy," *Journal of the American Academy of Psychiatry and the Law*, 41: 3 (September 2013): 337–343 http://www.jaapl.org/content/41/3/337.full; Linda Teplin, "Massacres and Madness," *Daily Beast*, December 14, 2013, http://www.thedailybeast.com/articles/2013/12/14/massacres-and-madness.html; Laura L. Hayes, "How to Stop Violence: Mentally Ill People Aren't Killers. Angry People Are," *Slate*, April 9, 2014, http://www.slate.com/articles/health_and_science/medical_examiner/2014/04/anger_causes_violence_treat_it_rather_than_mental_illness_to_stop_mass_murder.html.

134. Wayne LaPierre, interview by David Gregory, *Meet the Press*, NBC, December 23, 2012, http://www.nbcnews.com/id/50283245/ns/meet_the_press-transcripts/t/december-wayne-lapierre-chuck-schumer-lindsey-graham-jason-chaffetz-harold-ford-jr-andrea-mitchell-chuck-todd.

135. LaPierre, *Meet the Press*.

136. LaPierre, speech at the Western Hunting and Conservation Expo, February 23, 2013.

137. Liz Neporent, "NRA Takes Fire for Stance on Mental Illness," *ABC News*, December 24, 2012, http://abcnews.go.com/Health/nra-takes-fire-stance-mental-illness/story?id=18057336#.UZRdheDR2IQ.

138. Michael J. Fitzpatrick, National Alliance on Mental Illness, "Newtown Tragedy: NAMI Condemns NRA Position as 'Outrageous and Wrong,'" December 21, 2012, http://www.nami.org/Template.cfm?Section=Home&template=/ContentManagement/ContentDisplay.cfm&ContentID=148650.

139. Fitzpatrick, "NAMI Condemns NRA Position."

140. Fitzpatrick, "NAMI Condemns NRA Position."

141. Neporent, "NRA Takes Fire for Stance on Mental Illness."

CHAPTER 2. GUNS, GOVERNMENT, AND AUTONOMY

1. Josh Sugarman, *National Rifle Association: Money, Firepower, and Fear* (Washington, D.C.: National Press Books, 1992), 14.

2. Osha Gray Davidson, *Under Fire: The NRA and the Battle for Gun Control* (Iowa City: University of Iowa Press, 1998), 162–163.

3. Andrew Napolitano, "The Right to Shoot Tyrants, Not Deer," *Washington Times*, January 10, 2013, http://www.washingtontimes.com/news/2013/jan/10/the-right-to-shoot-tyrants-not-deer/.

4. Sugarman, *National Rifle Association*, 14.

5. Larry Schweikart, *What Would the Founders Say? A Patriot's Answers to America's Most Pressing Problems* (New York: Sentinel, 2011), 199.

6. Wayne LaPierre, *Guns, Crime, and Freedom* (Washington, D.C.: Regnery, 1994), 200.

7. Warren Richey, "Behind Supreme Court Case: Do Gun Rights Protect against Tyranny?" *Christian Science Monitor*, March 4, 2010, http://www.csmonitor.com/USA/Justice/2010/0304/Behind-Supreme-Court-case-Do-gun-rights-protect-against-tyranny.

8. Napolitano, "The Right to Shoot Tyrants, Not Deer."

9. LaPierre, *Guns, Crime, and Freedom*, 8.

10. LaPierre, *Guns, Crime, and Freedom*, 8.

11. Mark Nuckols, "Why the 'Citizen Militia' Theory Is the Worst Pro-Gun Argument Ever," *Atlantic*, January 31, 2013, http://www.theatlantic.com/national/archive/2013/01/why-the-citizen-militia-theory-is-the-worst-pro-gun-argument-ever/272734/.

12. Joyce Lee Malcolm, *To Keep and Bear Arms: The Origins of an Anglo-American Right* (Cambridge, Mass.: Harvard University Press, 1994), 162–163.

13. Malcolm, *To Keep and Bear Arms*, 163.

14. Saul Cornell, *A Well-Regulated Militia: The Founding Fathers and the Origins of Gun Control in America* (New York: Oxford University Press, 2006), 2.

15. Cornell, *A Well-Regulated Militia*, 15–16.

16. Cornell, *A Well-Regulated Militia*, 17.

17. Craig R. Whitney, *Living with Guns: A Liberal's Case for the Second Amendment* (New York: Public Affairs, 2012), 95.

18. Napolitano, "The Right to Shoot Tyrants, Not Deer."

19. Napolitano, "The Right to Shoot Tyrants, Not Deer."

20. David Kopel, "Trust the People: The Case against Gun Control," Cato Institute, Policy Analysis No. 109, July 11, 1988.

21. Napolitano, "The Right to Shoot Tyrants, Not Deer."

22. Napolitano, "The Right to Shoot Tyrants, Not Deer." Emphasis added.

23. Napolitano, "The Right to Shoot Tyrants, Not Deer."

24. Napolitano, "The Right to Shoot Tyrants, Not Deer."

25. LaPierre, *Guns, Crime, and Freedom*, 7. Emphasis in original.

26. Thomas Hobbes, *Leviathan* (New York: W. W. Norton, 1997), 70.

27. John Locke, *Two Treatises of Government* (Cambridge: Cambridge University Press, 1988), 359.

28. Charles Cooke, "The Right to Bear Arms and Popular Sovereignty: They Are Inextricably Linked," *National Review Online*, February 11, 2013, https://www.nationalreview.com/nrd/articles/338651/right-bear-arms-and-popular-sovereignty.

29. Locke, *Two Treatises of Government*, 271.

30. Locke, *Two Treatises of Government*, 272.

31. Locke, *Two Treatises of Government*, 280.

32. Locke, *Two Treatises of Government*, 280.

33. Locke, *Two Treatises of Government*, 275.

34. Locke, *Two Treatises of Government*, 408, 412.

35. Locke, *Two Treatises of Government*, 419.

36. David French, "The Biblical and Natural Right of Self-Defense," *The Corner* (blog), *National Review Online*, January 25, 2013, http://www.nationalreview.com/corner/338845/biblical-and-natural-right-self-defense-david-french.

37. French, "The Biblical and Natural Right of Self-Defense."

38. Cooke, "The Right to Bear Arms and Popular Sovereignty."

39. Locke, *Two Treatises of Government*, 275.

40. Locke, *Two Treatises of Government*, 276.

41. Locke, *Two Treatises of Government*, 282.

42. Locke, *Two Treatises of Government*, 350.

43. Paul Rosenberg, "Locke and Unload: Why the NRA Doesn't Understand Rights," *Al Jazeera*, December 27, 2012, http://www.aljazeera.com/indepth/opinion/2012/12/20121226104857715225.html.

44. Rosenberg, "Locke and Unload." Emphasis in original.

45. Locke, *Two Treatises of Government*, 415.

46. Locke, *Two Treatises of Government*, 416.

47. Locke, *Two Treatises of Government*, 416.

48. Patrik Jonsson, "Stand Your Ground Laws: Two Cases May Suggest Limits to Their Protections," Christian Science Monitor, May, 1, 2014, http://www.csmonitor.com/USA/Justice/2014/0501/Stand-your-ground-laws-Two-cases-may-suggest-limits-to-their-protections-video

49. State of Connecticut General Assembly: Office of Legislative Research Report, *The Castle Doctrine and Stand-Your-Ground Law*, by Hendrik DeBoer and Mark Randall, April 24, 2012, http://www.cga.ct.gov/2012/rpt/2012-R-0172.htm.

50. "Title XLVI Chapter 776: Justifiable Use of Force," *The 2013 Florida Statutes*, http://www.leg.state.fl.us/statutes/index.cfm?App_mode=Display_Statute&URL=0700–0799/0776/Sections/0776.013.html.

51. George Zimmerman, the shooter in this incident, ultimately declined to request pretrial immunity under his state's Stand Your Ground laws. However, as I will discuss shortly, the jury ruling on his case felt compelled to include Stand Your Ground considerations in issuing their verdict—which was "not guilty."

52. Susan Ferriss, "NRA Pushed 'Stand Your Ground' Laws across the Nation," *Center for Public Integrity*, March 26, 2012, http://www.publicintegrity.org/2012/03/26/8508/nra-pushed-stand-your-ground-laws-across-nation.

53. Wayne LaPierre, interview with *Fox News*, June 12, 2012, http://video.foxnews.com/v/1686041634001/nra-ceo-wayne-lapierre-the-public-is-being-misinformed-about-the-stand-your-ground-law-because-politicians-dont-want-americans-protecting-themselves/.

54. LaPierre, *Fox News* interview.

55. LaPierre, *Fox News* interview.

56. Patrik Jonsson, "Trayvon Martin Case Reveals Confusion over How Stand Your Ground Works," *Christian Science Monitor*, April 11, 2012, http://www.csmonitor.com/USA/Justice/2012/0411/Trayvon-Martin-case-reveals-confusion-over-how-Stand-Your-Ground-works.

57. Matt Pearce, "NRA Isn't Budging in Post-Verdict 'Stand Your Ground' Standoff," *Nation Now* (blog), *Los Angeles Times*, July 17, 2013, http://www.latimes.com/news/nation/nationnow/la-na-nn-nra-stand-your-ground-20130717,0,4722035.story.

58. "Acquitted Development," *Daily Show with Jon Stewart*, July 15, 2013, http://www.thedailyshow.com/watch/mon-july-15-2013/acquitted-development.

59. Jonsson, "Trayvon Martin Case Reveals Confusion."

60. John F. Timoney, "Florida's Disastrous Self-Defense Law," *New York Times*, March 24, 2012, http://www.nytimes.com/2012/03/24/opinion/floridas-disastrous-self-defense-law.html?_r=0.

61. Timoney, "Florida's Disastrous Self-Defense Law."

62. Timoney, "Florida's Disastrous Self-Defense Law."

63. Melanie Michael, "Popcorn Defense: Can Accused Florida Movie Shooter Use 'Stand Your Ground'?" *KSDK.com*, January 15, 2014, http://www.ksdk.com/story/news/nation/2014/01/15/popcorn-defense-can-accused-florida-movie-shooter-use-your-ground/4488939/.

64. Amel Ahmad, "Mixed Verdict in Dunn Trial Result of 'Stand Your Ground,' Experts Say," *AlJazeera.com*, February 18, 2014, http://america.aljazeera.com/articles/2014/2/17/dunn-trial-blamethelawnotthejuryexpertssay.html.

65. Ahmad, "Mixed Verdict in Dunn Trial."

66. Ahmad, "Mixed Verdict in Dunn Trial."

67. Ahmad, "Mixed Verdict in Dunn Trial."

68. Syreeta McFadden, "For Every Michael Dunn Guilty Verdict, a George Zimmerman Still Goes Free," *Guardian*, October 2, 2014, http://www.theguardian.com/commentisfree/2014/oct/02/michael-dunn-guilty-verdict-george-zimmerman-justice.

69. Whitney, *Living with Guns*, 26.

70. Paul Solotaroff, "A Most American Way to Die," *Rolling Stone*, April 25, 2013, http://www.rollingstone.com/culture/news/jordan-davis-stand-your-grounds-latest-victim-20130425.

71. Wayne LaPierre, press conference, December 21, 2012.

72. Nuckols, "Why the 'Citizen Militia' Theory Is the Worst Pro-Gun Argument Ever."

73. Napolitano, "The Right to Shoot Tyrants, Not Deer." Emphasis added.

74. Napolitano, "The Right to Shoot Tyrants, Not Deer."

75. Davidson, *Under Fire*, 156.

76. Brad Plummer, "America's Staggering Defense Budget, in Charts," *Wonkblog* (blog), *Washington Post*, January 7, 2013, http://www.washingtonpost.com/blogs/wonkblog/wp/2013/01/07/everything-chuck-hagel-needs-to-know-about-the-defense-budget-in-charts/.

77. Rosenberg, "Locke and Unload."

78. Bill Bridgewater, "Armed Revolution Possible and Not So Difficult," August 1994, posted on *Attack the System*, http://attackthesystem.com/armed-revolution-possible-and-not-so-difficult/.

79. Stanley Fish, "Is the NRA un-American?" *Opinionator* (blog), *New York Times*, May 13, 2013, http://opinionator.blogs.nytimes.com/2013/05/13/is-the-n-r-a-un-american/.

80. Baum, *Gun Guys*, 64–65.

81. Jean-Jacques Rousseau, *The Social Contract*, trans. Maurice Cranston (Middlesex, UK: Penguin, 1968), 139.

82. Alexis de Tocqueville, *Democracy in America*, ed. Richard Heffner (New York: A Mentor Book, 1984), 71.

83. Tocqueville, *Democracy in America*, 71.

84. Tocqueville, *Democracy in America*, 293.

85. Tocqueville, *Democracy in America*, 293.

86. Tocqueville, *Democracy in America*, 302–3.

87. Tocqueville, *Democracy in America*, 304.

88. See Juliet Schor, *The Overworked American* (New York: Basic Books, 1991).

89. Tocqueville, *Democracy in America*, 71.

90. Cornell, *A Well-Regulated Militia*, 214.

91. Cornell, *A Well-Regulated Militia*, 214.

92. Dan Baum, "On Gun Control and the Great American Debate over Individualism," *The Stream* (blog), *Harper's Magazine*, May 17, 2013, http://harpers.org/blog/2013/05/on-gun-control-and-the-great-american-debate-over-individualism/.

93. Cornell, *A Well-Regulated Militia*, 214.

CHAPTER 3. THE FACE OF OPPRESSION

1. Cooke, "The Right to Bear Arms and Popular Sovereignty."

2. Cooke, "The Right to Bear Arms and Popular Sovereignty."

3. J. G. A. Pocock, *The Political Works of James Harrington* (Cambridge: Cambridge University Press, 1977), 19.

4. Pocock, *Harrington*, 19.

5. J. G. A. Pocock, *The Machiavellian Moment* (Princeton, N.J.: Princeton University Press, 1974), 528.

6. Niccolo Machiavelli, *The Art of War*, Trans. Ellis Farneworth (Cambridge, Mass.: DaCapo Press, 1965), 4.

7. Machiavelli, *Art of War*, 41.

8. Machiavelli, *Art of War*, 31.

9. Machiavelli, *Art of War*, 40.

10. Machiavelli, *Art of War*, 30.

11. Niccolo Machiavelli, *The Prince*, ed. and trans. David Wooton (Indianapolis: Hackett, 1995), 53.

12. Machiavelli, *Prince*, 32.

13. Machiavelli, *Prince*, 35.

14. Machiavelli, *Prince*, 64.

15. Machiavelli, *Prince*, 63.

16. Machiavelli, *Prince*, 52.

17. Niccolo Machiavelli, *The Discourses*, trans. Leslie J. Walker, S.J. (London: Penguin Classics, 2003), 113.

18. Machiavelli, *Discourses*, 114. Pocock cites this precise chapter of *The Discourses* when he claims that Machiavelli equated arms bearing with civic activity; and yet, it is interesting to note that the principal example of civic activity here,

which deeply impressed Machiavelli—the people trooping out of Rome—appears to be largely nonviolent, as Machiavelli has described it.

19. Machiavelli, *Discourses*, 162.

20. Machiavelli, *Discourses*, 162.

21. Machiavelli, *Discourses*, 156.

22. Tocqueville, *Democracy in America*, 304.

23. Greg Sargent, "Sharron Angle Agrees with Radio Host Who Says We Have 'Domestic Enemies' within Congress," *The Plum Line* (blog), *Washington Post*, August 24, 2010, http://voices.washingtonpost.com/plum-line/2010/08/sharron_angle_agrees_we_have_d.html.

24. Sharron Angle, interview by Jonathan Karl, September 8, 2010, on *ABC News*, http://abcnews.go.com/Politics/video/nevada-2010jonathan-karl-interviews-sharron-angle-11585310.

25. Katy Steinmetz, "Over the River, Ralliers Gun for Washington's Attention," *Time*, April 20, 2010, http://content.time.com/time/nation/article/0,8599,1983214,00.html.

26. Schweikart, *What Would the Founders Say?* 198.

27. Schweikart, *What Would the Founders Say?* 198. Emphasis in original.

28. Wayne LaPierre, speech delivered at the 2012 meeting of the Conservative Political Action Conference (CPAC), February 11, 2012, http://www.nrapublications.org/index.php/12730/saving-the-future-of-freedom/.

29. Evan Perez, "Secret Court's Oversight of Surveillance Programs Scrutinized," *Wall Street Journal*, June 9, 2013, http://online.wsj.com/news/articles/SB10001424127887324904004578535670310514616.

30. Ed Pilkington, "Wyden Calls FISA Court 'Anachronistic' as Pressure Builds on Senate to Act," *Guardian*, July 28, 2013, http://www.theguardian.com/law/2013/jul/28/wyden-fisa-court-anachronistic-senate.

31. Glenn Greenwald, "The Due-Process-Free Assassination of U.S. Citizens Is Now Reality," *Salon*, September 30, 2011, http://www.salon.com/2011/09/30/awlaki_6/.

32. Matt Apuzzo, "Obama Lawyers: Citizens Targeted if at War with U.S.," *Yahoo News*, December 1, 2011, http://news.yahoo.com/obama-lawyers-citizens-targeted-war-us-154313473.html.

33. Eric Holder, speech at Northwestern University School of Law, Chicago, Illinois, March 5, 2012, http://www.justice.gov/iso/opa/ag/speeches/2012/ag-speech-1203051.html.

34. Glenn Greenwald, "Criminalizing Free Speech," *Salon*, June 1, 2011, http://www.salon.com/2011/06/01/free_speech_4/.

35. Andrew Napolitano, "Obama Continues His War on the Fourth Amendment," *Reason.com*, May 2, 2013, http://reason.com/archives/2013/05/02/obama-continues-his-war-on-the-fourth-am.

36. Timothy Lee, "Everything You Need to Know about the NSA's Phone Records Scandal," *Wonkblog* (Blog), *Washington Post*, June 6, 2013, http://www.washingtonpost.com/blogs/wonkblog/wp/2013/06/06/everything-you-need-to-know-about-the-nsa-scandal/.

37. Wayne LaPierre, speech at the 2013 NRA Members' Meeting, Houston, Texas, May 4, 2013, http://home.nra.org/home/video/2013-nra-members-meeting-wayne-lapierre/list/2013-nra-annual-meetings.

38. I realize there are some notable exceptions among the gun movement's more libertarian members, like Ron and Rand Paul, and Andrew Napolitano, who have been vocal critics of the way our government wages this war, and its threats to individual freedoms.

39. Daniel Junas, "Rise of Citizen Militias: Angry White Guys with Guns," *Covert Action Quarterly*, April 24, 1995, http://www.publiceye.org/rightist/dj_mili.html.

40. Fox Butterfield, "Terror in Oklahoma: Echoes of the NRA," *New York Times*, May 8, 1995, http://www.nytimes.com/1995/05/08/us/terror-oklahoma-echoes-nra-rifle-association-has-long-practice-railing-against.html?pagewanted=all&src=pm.

41. "Soldier of Fortune Magazine Articles at McVeigh Trial Were Just Tip of Anti-Government Iceberg," Violence Policy Center press release, June 11, 1997, http://www.vpc.org/press/9706mcve.htm.

42. "Soldier of Fortune Magazine Articles at McVeigh Trial Were Just Tip of Anti-Government Iceberg."

43. Michel Foucault, *Discipline and Punish*, trans. Alan Sheridan (New York: Vintage Books, 1977), 169.

44. Foucault, *Discipline and Punish*, 202.

45. Foucault, *Discipline and Punish*, 193.

46. "America's Surveillance Society," *ACLU. org*, available at http://www.aclu.org/files/images/asset_upload_file381_37802.pdf.

47. "America's Surveillance Society," *ACLU. org*.

48. Rick Jervis, "Cellphone Videos Will Be Key to Bombing Investigation," *USA Today*, April 17, 2013, http://www.usatoday.com/story/news/nation/2013/04/17/cell-phone-video-boston-marathon-bombings/2088899/.

49. James Bamford, "The NSA Is Building the Country's Biggest Spy Center," *Wired*, March 15, 2012, http://www.wired.com/threatlevel/2012/03/ff_nsadatacenter/.

50. Hendrik Hertzberg, "Difficult Questions about the NSA," *New Yorker*, June 24, 2013, http://www.newyorker.com/talk/comment/2013/06/24/130624taco_talk_hertzberg.

51. Hertzberg, "Difficult Questions about the NSA."

52. Barton Gellman, interviewed by Robert Siegel, "NSA Harvests Contact Lists from Email, Facebook," *All Things Considered, NPR,* October 15, 2013, http://www.npr.org/blogs/thetwo-way/2013/10/15/234776676/report-nsa-harvests-contact-lists-from-email-facebook.

53. Ben Popper, "Drones over U.S. Soil: The Calm before the Swarm," *The Verge,* March 19, 2013, http://www.theverge.com/2013/3/19/4120548/calm-before-the-swarm-domestic-drones-are-here.

54. Glenn Greenwald, "Domestic Drones and Their Unique Dangers," *Guardian,* March 29, 2013, http://www.theguardian.com/commentisfree/2013/mar/29/domestic-drones-unique-dangers.

55. Greenwald, "Domestic Drones and Their Unique Dangers."

56. Glenn Greenwald, "How America's Surveillance State Breeds Conformity and Fear," speech delivered at the Socialism 2012 conference, Chicago, July 4, 2012, http://www.alternet.org/story/156170/glenn_greenwald%3A_how_america%27s_surveillance_state_breeds_conformity_and_fear.

57. Greenwald, "How America's Surveillance State Breeds Conformity and Fear."

58. Gary Shteyngart, "Confessions of a Google Glass Explorer," *New Yorker,* August 5, 2013, http://www.newyorker.com/reporting/2013/08/05/130805fa_fact_shteyngart?currentPage=all.

59. Claire Cain Miller, "Addicted to Apps," *New York Times,* August 24, 2013, http://www.nytimes.com/2013/08/25/sunday-review/addicted-to-apps.html?_r=0.

60. Greenwald, "How America's Surveillance State Breeds Conformity and Fear."

61. Hertzberg, "Difficult Questions about the NSA."

62. Foucault, *Discipline and Punish,* 207.

63. Greenwald, "How America's Surveillance State Breeds Conformity and Fear."

64. Greenwald, "How America's Surveillance State Breeds Conformity and Fear."

CHAPTER 4. GUNS AND THE THREAT TO DEMOCRACY

1. David Kopel, *The Truth about Gun Control* (New York: Encounter Books, 2013) 42.

2. Kopel, *The Truth about Gun Control,* 42–43.

3. Kopel, *The Truth about Gun Control,* 2.

4. Horwitz and Anderson, *Guns, Democracy and the Insurrectionist Idea,* 23.

5. Horwitz and Anderson, *Guns, Democracy and the Insurrectionist Idea,* 23.

6. Horwitz and Anderson, *Guns, Democracy and the Insurrectionist Idea,* 24.

7. Joan Burbick, *Gun Show Nation* (New York: The New Press, 2006), 60.

8. Charlton Heston, speech delivered to the National Press Club, Washington D.C., September 11, 1997, http://www.c-spanvideo.org/program/90857-1.

9. Heston, speech to National Press Club.

10. John Fund, "The Facts about Mass Shootings," *National Review Online*, December 16, 2012, http://www.nationalreview.com/articles/335739/facts-about-mass-shootings-john-fund.

11. Maxim Lott, "Temple Massacre Has Some Sikhs Mulling Gun Ownership," *Fox News*, August 21, 2013, http://www.foxnews.com/us/2012/08/21/temple-massacre-has-some-sikhs-mulling-gun-ownership/.

12. Harlan Reynolds, "Gun-Free Zones Provide False Sense of Security," *USA Today*, December 14, 2012, http://www.usatoday.com/story/opinion/2012/12/14/connecticut-school-shooting-gun-control/1770345/.

13. Ian Ayres and John Donohue offer the following explanation to define shall issue concealed carry laws: "A law that allows a citizen to carry a concealed handgun if he or she can demonstrate a need to a government official is a discretionary, or 'may issue,' law. The shall issue laws are designed to eliminate discretion on the part of governmental officials, by requiring them to issue permit to carry concealed handguns unless specific and easily verifiable factors dictate otherwise." Cf. Ian Ayres and John Donohue, "Nondiscretionary Concealed Weapons Laws: A Case Study of Statistics, Standards of Proof, and Public Policy," *Faculty Scholarship Series*, Paper 50, 1999, http://digitalcommons.law.yale.edu/fss_papers/50.

14. John Lott, *More Guns, Less Crime*, 3rd edition (Chicago: University of Chicago Press, 2010), 164.

15. Lott, *More Guns, Less Crime*, 165.

16. Lott, *More Guns, Less Crime*, 165–166.

17. Lott, *More Guns, Less Crime*, 13.

18. Lott, *More Guns, Less Crime*, 13.

19. Ian Ayres and John Donohue, "Shooting Down the 'More Guns, Less Crime' Hypothesis," *Stanford Law Review* 55:1193 (2003): 1200.

20. David Ariosto, "All Empire State Shooting Victims Were Wounded by Officers," *CNN*, August 26, 2012, http://www.cnn.com/2012/08/25/justice/new-york-empire-state-shooting/index.html?hpt=hp_t1.

21. Ayres and Donohue, "Shooting Down the 'More Guns, Less Crime' Hypothesis," 1200.

22. Ayres and Donohue, "Shooting Down the 'More Guns, Less Crime' Hypothesis," 1201.

23. Chris Mooney, "Double Barreled Double Standards," *Mother Jones*, October 12, 2003, http://www.motherjones.com/politics/2003/10/double-barreled-double-standards.

24. Mooney, "Double Barreled Double Standards."

25. "Data on Firearms and Violence Too Weak to Settle Policy Debates; Comprehensive Research Effort Needed," National Academy of Sciences press release, December 16, 2004, http://www8.nationalacademies.org/onpinews/newsitem.aspx?RecordID=10881.

26. Mooney, "Double Barreled Double Standards."

27. David Hemenway, review of *The Bias Against Guns*, by John R. Lott, http://www.hsph.harvard.edu/wp-content/uploads/sites/247/2013/02/Hemenway-Book-Review.pdf. Lott's statistical claims, which Hemenway cites, are found in *The Bias Against Guns* (Washington, D.C.: Regnery Publishing, Inc., 2003), 216–17.

28. Mooney, "Double Barreled Double Standards."

29. Matthew Miller, Deborah Azrael, and David Hemenway, "Firearms and Violent Death in the United States," in *Reducing Gun Violence in America*, ed. Daniel Webster and Jon Vernick (Baltimore: Johns Hopkins University Press, 2013), 3–4.

30. Miller, Azrael, and Hemenway, "Firearms and Violent Death in the United States," 4.

31. Miller, Azrael, and Hemenway, "Firearms and Violent Death in the United States," 9–10.

32. Miller, Azrael, and Hemenway, "Firearms and Violent Death in the United States," 10.

33. Antonio Rangel Bandeira, "Brazil: Gun Control and Homicide Reduction," in *Reducing Gun Violence in America*, ed. Daniel Webster and Jon Vernick (Baltimore: Johns Hopkins University Press, 2013), 216.

34. William Saletan, "Friendly Firearms: Gabrielle Giffords and the Perils of Guns: How an Armed Hero Nearly Shot the Wrong Man," *Slate.com*, January 11, 2011, http://www.slate.com/articles/health_and_science/human_nature/2011/01/friendly_firearms.html.

35. Christina Wilkie, "NRA Confirms Adam Lanza, Nancy Lanza Were Not Members, Despite Certificates," *Huffington Post*, March 28, 2013, http://www.huffingtonpost.com/2013/03/28/nra-confirms-it-has-no-re_n_2972762.html.

36. Reynolds, "Gun-free Zones Provide False Sense of Security."

37. Sarah Bosley, "High Gun Ownership Makes Countries Less Safe, U.S. Study Says," *Guardian*, September 18, 2013, http://www.theguardian.com/world/2013/sep/18/gun-ownership-gun-deaths-study.

38. Harlan Reynolds, "Reflections on Newtown: A Week after an American Tragedy, What Have We Learned?" *USA Today*, December 25, 2012, http://www.usatoday.com/story/opinion/2012/12/25/newtown-sandy-hook-reflections/1787477/.

39. James McKinley, "In Texas School, Teachers Carry Books and Guns," *New York Times*, August 28, 2008, http://www.nytimes.com/2008/08/29/us/29texas.html?pagewanted=all&_r=0.

40. Eli Saslow, "After Newtown Shootings, Pennsylvania County Hires Armed School Guards," *Washington Post*, January 10, 2013, http://www.washington post.com/national/after-newtown-shootings-pennsylvania-county-hires-armed-school-guards/2013/01/10/72ba2a6c-5b4d-11e2–9fa9–5fbdc9530eb9_story.html.

41. Sheryl Gay Stolberg, "Report Sees Guns as Path to Safety in Schools," *New York Times*, April 2, 2013, http://www.nytimes.com/2013/04/03/us/nra-details-plan-for-armed-school-guards.html?_r=0.

42. Juan Forero, "Colombian Company Exports Bulletproof Book Bags to U.S.," *Washington Post*, May 28, 2013, http://www.washingtonpost.com/world/the_americas/colombian-company-exports-bulletproof-book-bags-to-us/2013/05/27/fef7589c-c678–11e2–9cd9–3b9a22a4000a_story.html.

43. Jacob Davidson, "Maryland University Invests in Bulletproof White-boards," *Time*, August 20, 2013, http://newsfeed.time.com/2013/08/20/maryland-university-invest-in-bulletproof-whiteboards/.

44. Erik Eckholm, "With Police in Schools, More Children in Court," *New York Times*, April 12, 2013, http://www.nytimes.com/2013/04/12/education/with-police-in-schools-more-children-in-court.html.

45. Eckholm, "With Police in Schools, More Children in Court."

46. Saslow, "Pennsylvania County Hires Armed School Guards."

47. Saslow, "Pennsylvania County Hires Armed School Guards."

48. Saslow, "Pennsylvania County Hires Armed School Guards."

49. Saslow, "Pennsylvania County Hires Armed School Guards."

50. Saslow, "Pennsylvania County Hires Armed School Guards."

51. Motoko Rich, "Mixed Reaction to Call for Armed Guards in Schools," *New York Times*, December 22, 2012, http://www.nytimes.com/2012/12/23/us/mixed-reaction-to-call-for-armed-guards-in-schools.html.

52. Michael Rubinkam, "Some Pennsylvania Colleges Allow Students to Carry Guns," *USA Today*, May 11, 2013, http://www.usatoday.com/story/news/nation/2013/05/11/pennsylvania-college-students-guns/2152625/. States that allow concealed carry on public university campuses include Colorado, Mississippi, Oregon, Wisconsin, Utah, North Carolina, and as of 2014, Idaho.

53. Carson Capshaw-Mack, "UNC Student Associations Stand against Gun Proposal," *Winston-Salem Journal*, July 7, 2013, http://www.journalnow.com/news/state_region/article_c5744032-ef48–11e2-aaaf-001a4bcf6878.html.

54. Adam Winkler, "The Guns of Academe," *New York Times*, April 14, 2011, http://www.nytimes.com/2011/04/15/opinion/15winkler.html?_r=0.

55. Winkler, "The Guns of Academe."

56. Winkler, "The Guns of Academe."

57. Jason Nance, "School Security Considerations after Newtown," *Stanford Law Review*, February 11, 2013, http://www.stanfordlawreview.org/online/school-security-considerations-after-newtown.

58. Nance, "School Security Considerations."

59. Nance, "School Security Considerations."

60. Paolo Freire, *Pedagogy of the Oppressed*, trans. Myra Bergman Ramos (New York: Herder and Herder, 1970), 66.

61. Freire, *Pedagogy of the Oppressed*, 67.

62. Freire, *Pedagogy of the Oppressed*, 79.

63. Freire, *Pedagogy of the Oppressed*, 80.

64. John Dewey, "My Pedagogic Creed," in *John Dewey on Education: Selected Writings* (New York: Random House, 1964), 430.

65. Dewey, "My Pedagogic Creed," 431.

66. Dewey, "My Pedagogic Creed," 431.

67. John Dewey, *Democracy and Education* (New York: The Free Press, 1944), 87.

68. Dewey, *Democracy and Education*, 99.

69. Dewey, *Democracy and Education*, 99.

70. Victoria Cavaliere, "Three Wounded as Gunfire Erupts During Argument at Texas College," *New York Daily News*, January 22, 2013, http://www.nydailynews.com/news/national/shots-fired-campus-texas-college-article-1.12 45079.

71. Arendt, *The Human Condition*, 26.

72. Arendt, *The Human Condition*, 25.

73. Arendt, *The Human Condition*, 32.

74. Arendt, *The Human Condition*, 179.

75. Mark Thompson, "When Protesters Bear Arms Against Health-Care Reform," *Time*, August 19, 2009, http://content.time.com/time/nation/article/0,8599,1917356,00.html.

76. Thompson, "When Protesters Bear Arms."

77. Thompson, "When Protesters Bear Arms."

78. Alex Spillius, "Group Armed with Rifles Seen among Protesters at Barack Obama Speech," *Daily Mail*, August 18, 2009, http://www.telegraph.co.uk/news/worldnews/northamerica/usa/6046721/Group-armed-with-rifles-seen-among-protesters-at-Barack-Obama-speech.html.

79. Mark Tran, "Men with Guns Swell Protest Crowds outside Obama Meetings," *Guardian*, August 17, 2009, http://www.theguardian.com/world/2009/aug/18/gun-protests-obama.

80. Thompson, "When Protesters Bear Arms."

81. Joan Walsh, "Who Was that Gun-Toting Anti-Obama Protester?" *Salon.com*, August 12, 2009, http://www.salon.com/2009/08/12/william_kostric/.

82. Katy Steinmetz, "Over the River, Ralliers Gun for Washington's Attention," *Time*, April 20, 2010, http://content.time.com/time/nation/article/0,8599,1983214,00.html.

83. Steinmetz, "Over the River."

84. Steinmetz, "Over the River."

85. Walsh, "Who Was that Gun-Toting Anti-Obama Protester?"

86. Rory Cripps, "Tea Party Protesters Bring Their Big Guns to Protest Rally," *Examiner.com*, January 3, 2010, http://www.examiner.com/article/tea-party-protesters-bring-their-big-guns-to-protest-rally.

87. Cripps, "Tea Party Protesters."

88. Diana Reese, "Moms Demonstrate for Gun Control, Armed Men Stage Counter-Protest in Indiana," *Washington Post*, March 29, 2013, http://www.washingtonpost.com/blogs/she-the-people/wp/2013/03/29/moms-demonstrate-for-gun-control-armed-men-stage-counter-protest-in-indiana/.

89. Al Baker, "When the Police Go Military," *New York Times*, December 3, 2011, http://www.nytimes.com/2011/12/04/sunday-review/have-american-police-become-militarized.html.

90. Baker, "When the Police Go Military."

91. Baker, "When the Police Go Military."

92. Baker, "When the Police Go Military."

93. Radley Balko, *Rise of the Warrior Cop* (New York: Public Affairs, 2013), 254.

94. Colt Manufacturing website, http://www.coltsmfg.com/company/history.aspx, accessed January 6, 2014.

95. Colt Manufacturing website, http://www.coltsmfg.com/company/history.aspx, accessed January 6, 2014.

96. Leonard Steinhorn, "White Men and Their Guns," *Huffington Post*, December 17, 2013, http://www.huffingtonpost.com/leonard-steinhorn/white-men-and-their-guns_b_4419903.html.

97. Thomas Hobbes, *Leviathan*, ed. Richard Tuck (Cambridge: Cambridge University Press, 1991), 89.

CHAPTER 5. POWER AND DEMOCRACY

1. Jay Bookman, "'Second Amendment Remedies'? That Suggests Treason," *Jay Bookman* (blog), *Atlanta Journal Constitution*, June 16, 2010, http://blogs.ajc.com/jay-bookman-blog/2010/06/16/second-amendment-remedies-that-suggests-treason/.

2. Anjeanette Damon and David McGrath Schwartz, "Armed Revolt Part of Sharron Angle's Rhetoric," *Las Vegas Sun*, June 17, 2010, http://www.lasvegassun.com/news/2010/jun/17/senate-race-armed-revolt-angles-rhetoric-candidate/.

3. Damon and Schwartz, "Armed Revolt Part of Angle's Rhetoric."

4. Damon and Schwartz, "Armed Revolt Part of Angle's Rhetoric."

5. Damon and Schwartz, "Armed Revolt Part of Angle's Rhetoric."

6. Damon and Schwartz, "Armed Revolt Part of Angle's Rhetoric."

7. Matt Bai, "A Turning Point in the Discourse, but in Which Direction?" *New York Times*, January 8, 2011, http://www.nytimes.com/2011/01/09/us/politics/09bai.html.

8. "Greene County, Virginia GOP Group's Newsletter Calls for 'Armed Revolution' if Obama Is Reelected," *Huffington Post*, May 8, 2012, http://www.huffingtonpost.com/2012/05/08/greene-county-virginia-gop-obama-revolution_n_1501510.html.

9. Bookman, "'Second Amendment Remedies'?"

10. Bookman, "'Second Amendment Remedies'?"

11. Fish, "Is the NRA Un-American?"

12. Fish, "Is the NRA Un-American?"

13. Horwitz and Anderson, *Guns, Democracy, and the Insurrectionist Idea*, 214.

14. Horwitz and Anderson, *Guns, Democracy, and the Insurrectionist Idea*, 168.

15. Kopel, *The Truth about Gun Control*, 41.

16. Kopel, *The Truth about Gun Control*, 41.

17. Cf. Baum, *Gun Guys*, 307.

18. Fish, "Is the NRA Un-American?"

19. Horwitz and Anderson, *Guns, Democracy, and the Insurrectionist Idea*, 42.

20. Horwitz and Anderson, *Guns, Democracy, and the Insurrectionist Idea*, 42.

21. Horwitz and Anderson, *Guns, Democracy, and the Insurrectionist Idea*, 217.

22. Horwitz and Anderson, *Guns, Democracy, and the Insurrectionist Idea*, 219.

23. Sari Horwitz, "ATF, Charged with Regulating Guns, Lacks Resources and Leadership," *Washington Post*, December 17, 2012, http://www.washingtonpost.com/investigations/2012/12/17/ef280abc-4877-11e2-b6f0-e851e741d196_story.html?hpid=z2.

24. S. Horwitz, "ATF, Charged with Regulating Guns, Lacks Resources and Leadership."

25. S. Horwitz, "ATF, Charged with Regulating Guns, Lacks Resources and Leadership."

26. Alan Berlow, "How the NRA Hobbled the ATF," *Mother Jones*, February 11, 2013, http://www.motherjones.com/politics/2013/02/atf-gun-laws-nra.

27. Berlow, "How the NRA Hobbled the ATF."

28. S. Horwitz, "ATF, Charged with Regulating Guns, Lacks Resources and Leadership."

29. Berlow, "How the NRA Hobbled the ATF."

30. Berlow, "How the NRA Hobbled the ATF."

31. Berlow, "How the NRA Hobbled the ATF."

32. Berlow, "How the NRA Hobbled the ATF."

33. Berlow, "How the NRA Hobbled the ATF."

34. Berlow, "How the NRA Hobbled the ATF."

35. Berlow, "How the NRA Hobbled the ATF."

36. Berlow, "How the NRA Hobbled the ATF."

37. Horwitz and Anderson, *Guns, Democracy, and the Insurrectionist Idea*, 218.

38. Michael Oakeshott, "The Political Economy of Freedom," in *Rationalism in Politics, and Other Essays* (Indianapolis: Liberty Fund, 1991), 391.

39. Oakeshott, "The Political Economy of Freedom," 390.

40. Martin Luther King Jr., "The Social Organization of Non-violence," in *A Testament of Hope*, ed. James M. Washington (New York: Harper Collins, 1986), 33.

41. Martin Luther King Jr., "An Experiment in Love," in *A Testament of Hope*, ed. James M. Washington (New York: Harper Collins, 1986), 17.

42. Saul Alinsky, *Rules for Radicals* (New York: Vintage Books, 1971), xxii–xxiii.

43. David Graeber, *The Democracy Project* (New York: Spiegel and Grau, 2013), 60.

44. Bernard Harcourt, "Political Disobedience," in *Occupy: Three Inquiries in Disobedience* (Chicago: University of Chicago Press, 2013), 46.

45. Martin Luther King, Jr., "Letter from a Birmingham Jail," in *A Testament of Hope*, ed. James M. Washington (New York: Harper Collins, 1986), 294.

46. Martin Luther King, Jr., "My Trip to the Land of Gandhi," in *A Testament of Hope*, ed. James M. Washington (New York: Harper Collins, 1986), 26.

47. Mahatma Gandhi, "Indian Home Rule," in *The Gandhi Reader* (Bloomington: Indiana University Press, 1956), 115.

48. Graeber, *The Democracy Project*, xv.

49. One notable exception, and subject of controversy among Occupy proponents, was the presence of the Black Bloc at some Occupy encampments. The Black Bloc, an anarchist group, has used and espoused violence in protests. Cf. John Blackstone, "Is the 'Black Bloc' Hijacking Occupy Oakland?" *CBS News*, November 4, 2011, http://www.cbsnews.com/news/is-black-bloc-hijacking-occupy-oakland/.

50. Graeber, *The Democracy Project*, xv.

51. Harcourt, "Political Disobedience," 81.

52. Dahlia Lithwick and Raymond Vasvari, "You Can't Occupy This," *Slate*, March 19, 2012, http://www.slate.com/articles/news_and_politics/jurisprudence/2012/03/the_anti_protest_bill_signed_by_barack_obama_is_a_quiet_attack_on_free_speech_.html.

53. Chris Cillizza, "What Occupy Wall Street Meant (or Didn't) to Politics," *The Fix* (blog), *Washington Post*, September 17, 2013, http://www.washingtonpost.com/blogs/the-fix/wp/2013/09/17/what-occupy-wall-street-meant-or-didnt-to-politics/.

54. Arendt, *The Human Condition*, 200.

55. Arendt, *The Human Condition*, 200.

56. Arendt, *The Human Condition*, 201.

57. Hannah Arendt, *On Violence* (New York: Harcourt Brace, 1970), 44.

58. Arendt, *On Violence*, 53.

59. Arendt, *On Violence*, 53.

60. Arendt, *On Violence*, 54.

61. Joseph Stiglitz, *The Price of Inequality* (New York: W. W. Norton, 2013), xli.

62. Annie Lowrey, "The Rich Get Richer Through the Recovery," *Economix* (Blog), *New York Times*, September 10, 2013, http://economix.blogs.nytimes.com/2013/09/10/the-rich-get-richer-through-the-recovery/?_r=0.

63. Stiglitz, *The Price of Inequality*, 160.

64. "2012 Election Spending will Reach $6 Billion, Center for Responsive Politics Predicts," *Open Secrets.org*, October 31, 2012, http://www.opensecrets.org/news/2012/10/2012-election-spending-will-reach-6.html.

65. Stiglitz, *The Price of Inequality*, 167.

66. Arendt, *On Violence*, 83.

67. Ed Pilkington, "Obama Angers Midwest Voters with Guns and Religion Remark," *Guardian*, April 13, 2008, http://www.theguardian.com/world/2008/apr/14/barackobama.uselections2008.

68. Baum, *Gun Guys*, 148.

69. Baum, *Gun Guys*, 162.

70. Baum, *Gun Guys*, 163.

71. Leonard Steinhorn, "White Men and Their Guns," *Huffington Post*, December 17, 2013, http://www.huffingtonpost.com/leonard-steinhorn/white-men-and-their-guns_b_4419903.html.

72. Steinhorn, "White Men and Their Guns."

73. Paul Waldman, "Not Man Enough? Buy a Gun," *CNN.com*, December 21, 2012, http://www.cnn.com/2012/12/20/opinion/waldman-guns-manhood/.

74. Binyamin Appelbaum and Robert Gebeloff, "Even Critics of the Safety Net Increasingly Depend on It," *New York Times*, February 11, 2012, http://www.nytimes.com/2012/02/12/us/even-critics-of-safety-net-increasingly-depend-on-it.html.

75. Appelbaum and Gebeloff, "Even Critics of the Safety Net Depend on It."

76. Appelbaum and Gebeloff, "Even Critics of the Safety Net Depend on It."

77. Appelbaum and Gebeloff, "Even Critics of the Safety Net Depend on It."

78. Appelbaum and Gebeloff, "Even Critics of the Safety Net Depend on It."

79. Appelbaum and Gebeloff, "Even Critics of the Safety Net Depend on It."

80. Cornell, *A Well-Regulated Militia*.

81. Cornell, *A Well-Regulated Militia*, 20.

82. Hannah Arendt, *On Revolution* (New York: Penguin Classics, 2006), 225.

83. Arendt, *On Revolution*, 225.

84. Arendt, *On Revolution*, 226.

85. Thomas Jefferson, "Letter to Samuel Kercheval, July 12, 1816," accessed at *Online Library of Liberty, LibertyFund.org*, http://oll.libertyfund.org/title/808/88342.

86. Jefferson, "Letter to Kercheval."

87. Arendt, *On Revolution*, 245.

88. Thomas Jefferson, "Letter to Thomas Cartwright, June 5, 1824," accessed at *Electronic Text Center*, University of Virginia Library, http://etext.lib.virginia.edu/etcbin/toccer-new2?id=JefLett.sgm&images=images/modeng&data=/texts/english/modeng/parsed&tag=public&part=276&division=div1.

89. Arendt, *On Revolution*, 270.

90. Jefferson, "Letter to Kercheval."

91. Jefferson, "Letter to Kercheval."

92. Jefferson, "Letter to Kercheval."

Index

gun rights movement, viii–xv, 9–10,
14–16, 61–62, 96–104, 115–18,
140–88, 189, 199–202, 231; cynicism
of, 166–67; extremism of, 50, 125–26,
143, 169–70, 173, 196, 233–34; fear
incitement by, xiv, 4, 24–27, 32–35,
40–41, 43–46, 119; goal of, xiv, 18,
144, 145–50, 157–58, 164–65; "guns
save lives" slogan, 12, 157–58; hostile
rhetoric of, xv, 25, 50, 196–98, 201–2;
intrusiveness of, 173–74; Jefferson as
hero of, 59, 64, 177, 227, 228–29;
lobbying power of, 103 (*see also*
National Rifle Association); Locke's
philosophy and, 38, 65–66, 72–73,
88–89; Manichean worldview of,
32–35; property rights and, 73;
psychology of, 43–47, 214, 215;
Rousseau's philosophy and, 93–94;
Second Amendment sanctity to (*see*
Second Amendment); theological
arguments of, 36–40; War on Terror
and, 41–42, 43, 46, 123–24
gun sales, ix, 6–8, 45, 118–19; dealer
definition, 207; larger weapons,
11–12; licensed dealers, 208;
loopholes, viii, 6, 103, 204; private,
6; secondary buyers, 207–8; waiting
period, 7

Hanks, Tom, 28
Harcourt, Bernard, 212, 216
Hardwire L. I. C., 161
Hasselbeck, Elisabeth, 3–4
healthcare reform, 100, 101; protests
against, 117, 118, 176, 177, 179, 181,
194, 195–96
Hebrews *13:8*, 38
Hemenway, David, 152
Hertzberg, Hendrik, 131, 136
Heston, Charlton, 46, 52, 143, 223
Hitler, Adolf, 56
Hobbes, Thomas, 63, 64, 66, 67, 71,
74, 187
Hochsprung, Dawn, vii
Holder, Eric, 122
Hollywood. *See* movie violence
Holmes, James, 144, 155

Holocaust, 55–56, 89
Homeland Security Department, 182
homicide. *See* murder
homosexuality, 223–24
Hopson, Chuck, 13
Horwitz, Joshua, xiii, 142, 198, 201,
204, 208
Household Gun Ownership, 8–9
hunting, ix, 53, 59, 89, 142, 189
Hupp, Suzanna, 150

inalienable rights, 65–66
income disparity, 149, 216, 219–22
individual sovereignty, 60–64, 72,
95–101, 110–15, 142; community vs.,
78–79, 100–101; gun rights
precedence, 4, 49; Stand Your
Ground and, 77; symbols of, 110;
threats to, xiii, xiv, 118–24,
127–31
insurrection. *See* rebellion
intelligence collecting. *See* surveillance
society
Internet, 129
Iraq War, 27, 29, 42, 92

Jacksonville (Fla.), 83
Japan, 5, 45
Jefferson, Thomas, 59, 64, 227–33;
change in outlook of, 228–30;
"water tree of liberty" quote, 177,
190, 228
Jesus, 37–38
Jews, 55–56, 89
Jews for the Preservation of Firearms,
55
Jones, Corinne, 6
Jones, Donald, 84
Junas, Daniel, 125
juries, 79–80, 83, 84, 85, 120
justice system, 66, 67, 70–72, 79;
War on Terror compromise of,
120–21

Kenik, David, 14–15
Kennedy, David, 19